www.triggerpublishing.com

Thank you for purchasing this book.
You are making an incredible difference.

Proceeds from all Trigger books go directly to
The Shaw Mind Foundation, a global charity that focuses
entirely on mental health. To find out more about
The Shaw Mind Foundation visit, **www.shawmindfoundation.org**

MISSION STATEMENT

Our goal is to make help and support available for every
single person in society, from all walks of life.
We will never stop offering hope. These are our promises.
Trigger and The Shaw Mind Foundation

Creating hope for children,
adults and families

This book is for you, Sammy.

*Thank you for putting my heart and my mind back together again.
I am so lucky to have you in my life.*

Disclaimer: Some names and identifying details have been changed to protect the privacy of individuals.

The views, thoughts, and opinions expressed in the book are the author's own and are not representative of **Breast Cancer Now**.

CHAPTER 1

You-know-what

Benidorm was booked for July 2009 and we had everything: tickets, accommodation, outfits, ego, and tan. One week of pure indulgence and prowling to find Mr Right. I was 25 years old and sick of being single. It had been three years and there wasn't a single sausage in sight. God knows how many frogs I'd kissed, how many princes hadn't rescued me. When I was growing up, fairy tales had never mentioned that the prince would never text back. They never said I'd be left in a state of constant anxiety just waiting for something.

Apparently, when you're a 30-year-old woman, the presumption is that you should be married and have kids hanging off you. I was 25 so, with five years to go, I was over the hill and an ugly stepsister.

But surely this was going to be my year. Right?

None of that mattered right now, though, because all I cared about was getting out of my bloody office and on an easyJet flight!

'Your tan looks amazing,' Lauren said on the way to the airport. Lauren was a close friend of mine. We'd met at secondary school and bonded over similar tastes in materialist possessions and aspirations.

We'd been inseparable since and helped each other through life. I had signed up for one of those course things I'd seen advertised around: one week of intensive "get me sun-kissed" sunbed sessions, UV rays, and eye goggles. I had been treating myself to sunbed sessions ever since I was 18, when I'd crossed the legal threshold for being allowed to be fried in a booth. I practically lived in there.

It had become an essential part of my life. It was just so easy and accessible, like buying a pint of milk. I would nip out on a Sunday morning, lunch break or Friday night and go and get baked. Fake tan had never been enough for me; I needed a massive colour boost to try to bring some life to my skin. I would pay 30 quid and get as many minutes as I could cram into my lunch hour.

I worked as an IT Recruitment officer in North London, smack bang in the middle of it all, which meant that it was fairly easy to pop out, lie on the sunbed, soak up all the high-voltage UV rays, and forget about the rest of the world. I returned to work one shade of mahogany deeper every time. And I loved it. I loved all of it; my job, my family, my friends, my pokey little overpriced rented flat in East London. I also absolutely adored my social life. No, it was more than just adoration; I was dependent on it. I relied on it to get through each day at work. No matter how bad things got, whatever went wrong, I just knew that by 7pm that night, nothing would matter. I would have vodka, cigarettes, and my friends.

Benidorm was mine and Lauren's own heaven. We loved the sun, the clubs, and the men. Our mission was to capture our dream men, to reel them in and bring them home, but we arrogantly expected them to find us first. We had our pick of men and were super popular at the resort – young, obnoxious, and up for anything.

We ran out of money twice while we were away and had to make the pleading phone call for my dad to send more money over. We drank our weights in vodka, slept all day and partied all night. We met stag parties, married couples, divorcees, teenagers on first holidays, and terrified locals. We were only interested in the men, of course – all of the other women were completely irrelevant.

After our fourth night on the town, we parked ourselves in a greasy spoon café for some heavy food to soak up all the damage the binge-drinking had caused. We ordered fried breakfasts by pointing to a cartoon drawing of a fry-up. As a frying egg spat out fat on the grill across the table from us, I could see the chef mopping his brow while pouring more oil into the pan. 'How are you feeling about next Friday?' Lauren asked me half-arsedly, her voice tinged with the pain of a good night.

For a moment, I had no idea what she was talking about. But then I remembered: that poky thing in my right breast.

A cyst. A bloody huge cyst. A week ago, I'd come out of a sunbed booth, got in the shower, and saw it underneath the glowing UV light. I don't think I would have noticed it under normal lighting. It had started off big enough, but it got bigger and bigger with each passing day. By now it was larger than a golf ball, but not quite as big as a tennis ball.

'JESUS, that is huge!' Lauren had exclaimed when I suggested she inspect it. I didn't think that it could be anything too sinister. I was too young for anything major and had no other symptoms of illness, I told myself.

I had been to see my doctor a week after I'd found it. I just needed to be reassured about it. After a lot of poking and prodding and questions about my family health history, my doctor suggested that the big lump need testing, because of the "sheer, alarming size of it". He told me that, in relation to my age, the lump was not common. Finally, after a lot of to-ing and fro-ing, he decided assertively that I needed an urgent referral. There would be a two-week wait, which was fine because it actually coincided with my pre-booked holiday. I did feel it was a bit over the top at the time. We weren't on a first-name basis, but I saw this doctor regularly. I liked him.

There was trust there, built through our constant meetings. He even threw a statistic at me as I was leaving: 'There's a 70 per cent chance of it not being too serious.' That was enough to reassure me, to let me enjoy my holiday without having it hang over me.

I had been through something like this before. Years ago, I'd had a cyst on my thyroid and I had needed an operation. I'd had two weeks off work and only four days to recover. I assumed it was something like this again. Maybe I was carrying another lump around with me but in my breast this time.

I was 100 per cent not in any way worried about it, not after what I had been through already. But I did want it to go because the lump was just there. Frequently – on the plane, off the plane, in the hotel, in a bar, in a restaurant, on the beach – I would find myself checking the cyst. Even when waking up, I would check it was still there, as though it might have magically disappeared in the night.

The fried egg had now been sizzling in what looked like six inches of animal fat for 15 minutes. The egg white was now entirely black, and the yolk completely disintegrated. 'I'm not worried about Friday,' I replied to Lauren's question. I was completely convinced that it was nothing more than what had happened last time. It had to be. My breakfast plate was thrown down in front of me, the egg now unrecognisable after its torture in the heat. It was burnt to a crisp and a quarter of the original size. I didn't eat it. Our holiday came to an end, like all must. The holiday blues kicked in as we dragged our suitcases and exhausted bodies home. Home was my flat in Walthamstow, East London, which I shared with my friend Gudrun – who, at this point, I had barely seen in weeks, due to the frantic nature of our work and social lives.

Our home was just how I'd left it: cosmetics and chaos, products piled everywhere, hangers, empty cigarette packets, and a massive pile of washing-up. I sent a message to Mum to say we were back safe and that we'd had a good time. No other details were needed. Dragging myself to bed, I fell asleep straight away. After trying to snooze off a week's hangover in eight hours, my alarm went off just after 10am. It was my appointment for the cyst in my breast. I was irritated by this. I couldn't be bothered with all the messing about that would happen during the course of the investigation into this bloody lump. For a second, I contemplated not showing up, and then quickly changed my mind. Before I went on my well-deserved holiday, I had been for a mammogram followed by a long and bloody painful biopsy. Imagine having a shooting needle the size of a rolling pin firing into your breast. It had also been both physically and mentally draining, especially considering I had done it on my own. I hadn't told anyone I was going apart from Lauren, not even my mum.

As I walked into the hospital, a tiny bit of me thought about the statistic the doctor had thrown at me: '70 per cent / 30 per cent'. I had no doubt that I would, of course, land in the 70 per cent.

I walked quickly through the corridors, trying to find the right department. I finally found it and sat in the first chair I could see. The waiting room was grey and black – dreary colours. I waited and waited and waited. I watched lots of different people come in and out, out and in. Some were armed with another person, some with groups of people. Their faces were filled with looks of desperation and terror as they went into one of the rooms and came out again.But I had more important things on my mind. Why had John (my latest chase) not replied to my text again? It was infuriating. I texted him to ask …

'Annabel Walsh?'

That was me.

'Follow me, please.'

I needed this ordeal to be over with as quickly as possible. I was told I couldn't have my phone on me. I was so impatient, desperate for this to be over, desperate for this guy to reply. Was he going to even text me back? I wondered what he'd been up to, or if he had wondered about me. Contact with a man I had known for barely half

11

a month felt so much more important than this cyst, which I knew was going to be nothing anyway.

A nurse sat down next to me as I waited. She introduced herself as Helen and informed me that my consultant would be through shortly. I could see the mammogram x-ray on the desk, a typed, formal-looking letter attached to it. I presumed they were my biopsy results. There was a folder, with lots and lots of leaflets inside.

I tried to make conversation with Helen, but she didn't give much back. I gave up and started to search inside my bag for my phone. At least while I was waiting here, I could see whether or not John had got back to me.

And then, it happened. The most significant moment of my life, at just 25 years old.

The consultant walked in, looked at me compassionately, took his glasses off, and sat down.

And then he told me I had cancer.

CHAPTER 2

BUT YOU'RE ONLY 25

'I'm afraid it's not good news. You have breast cancer.'

I wondered what this might look like from an outside perspective. I wondered what it was like for Helen the nurse sitting here with me in this hell, discussing death. He looked at me, I looked at him, she looked at him, he looked at her, and I looked at my breast.

The clock stopped ticking, my heart stopped beating, and the world stopped spinning.

Staring blankly into the doctor's eyes, hearing an echo of his words telling me I had cancer, I felt numb and glued on to the plastic chair. They were watching me carefully. On the desk directly in front of me was a box of tissues, placed there strategically for situations exactly like this. But they weren't going to be needed this time.

Realising it was my turn to speak, I said very quietly, 'Well, what do I need to do to sort this out?' I had no idea, understanding or concept of this diagnosis. The consultant spoke and spoke, and I didn't listen. I switched off after he rather abruptly and forcefully pushed the point: 'Annabel, I don't think you realise just how serious this is.' I hated him for saying this to me. It felt like a double blow. Not only had he told me that I definitely had cancer, he was now telling me I wasn't taking it seriously. He was judging me. I couldn't listen. *I have to get out of here.*

I just needed to agree to everything that was said to me and leave. I could feel (another) lump in my throat and tears in my eyes. I was determined not to take a tissue, not even one.

Helen the nurse told me she was going to be my assigned and dedicated breast nurse. She said she would be like a midwife seeing the journey of a pregnancy from conception to birth. I wondered how many journeys Helen had seen, how many people she'd helped get through this with their lives still intact.

She handed me a pink booklet. I hated that colour. On the front of the book was a smiling – perhaps reluctantly – woman, looking into a river. *And she had no hair.* There was a long silence. The consultant and Helen were still looking at me. They were looking at the tissues I hadn't taken, trying to understand my lack of emotion. They wanted to know what I was thinking, and I wanted to know what they thought, but neither party was willing to ask first.

Helen stood up. I immediately shot up with her. Everything became blurry. I followed her through endless corridors, clutching on to the official bibliography of the disease – the information booklet on breast cancer.

As the hospital corridor narrowed towards the exit, the view became lighter. The sunlight became brighter and my mind became even more blocked.

I started to sweat, my heart racing, and panic rose inside me. We walked outside of the building and into the car park. I stood next to the NO SMOKING sign and spoke up aggressively, informing Helen the nurse that I planned to smoke. Surprisingly, she just nodded and said that I would need something to get me through it all.

Helen started questioning me about who was going to help me.

Husband? Mother? Father? Friend? Colleague? *No one,* I thought. *I'm not bringing anyone into this nightmare!*

But I knew that I really did need someone, so I told her my mum would do for now, taking my phone out of my pocket. I rang her mobile and got no answer, so I called her office, waiting and waiting for someone to speak. I guessed that Mum was probably thinking I needed to borrow money, or that I'd met a man. That I had a new ...

'Hello?' Standing there smoking, clutching the booklet, I couldn't remember anything that had been said other than that I had breast cancer and my life was fucked.

I didn't wait around. 'Mum, I have breast cancer and I need you to come to the hospital ... now.' Silence.

And then, 'I'm coming. Right now.'

The phone went dead. Helen waited with me in the car park, still staring at me. I stood and shook, freezing in the cold. I felt like a small child again. Once, when I was seven, I was queuing for the toilet before a Christmas party. I trapped my fingernail in the toilet door. It was so painful. Mum came and picked me up, took me home, and put me on the magic shelf between the bread bin and the fruit bowl in the kitchen. It always made everything better somehow.

I needed that now. I was in pain. But I was going to cause Mum heartbreak and there was no magic shelf for this. I just needed her. Where was she? Finally, after what seemed like an eternity, I saw Mum and her friend Glenda walking towards me.

'There's Mum,' I said to Helen, glad that I wasn't alone in this any more.

My heart physically started hurting as I watched her approach me. Why was I going through this? Why was I putting my poor mum through this? She came closer and closer, eyes watering. She was crying loudly. I was crying. Glenda was crying. Everyone was crying.

She was still far away, but I could feel her pain. I could see Glenda's blonde hair getting brighter and brighter as they drew closer.

Glenda was Mum's close friend and she also used to teach me writing when I was younger. She let me babysit her daughter. We were lifelong friends, all of us.

I could feel the devastation hanging in the air. Mum and I hugged one another, wiping away our endless tears. We both just kept saying that we loved each other. Helen ushered us into a room where we were greeted by two dolls' heads with wiry wigs on. There was yet another box of tissues. Mum sat there holding my hand and Glenda sat alongside us, our constant support – just like she had been all my life.

Helen then told me exactly what was going on and what needed to happen. Some words stood out: 'Cancer ... chemotherapy ... sick ... hair loss ... give up work.'

And then, 'Do you have a partner?'

No, I don't have a fucking partner, and this is going to rapidly decrease my chances of finding one! I didn't need this. My poor mum should not have been listening to this. This was a disaster, a catastrophe, a hindrance to our lives. How was I supposed to go on dates with no hair? How could I marry someone if there was a chance I'd become infertile? This was an utter nightmare, something out of the darkest depths of my mind.

'I don't understand how this can happen. I'm 25.' I was confused, and for some reason, I felt intense shame as well, as though I had done something wrong.

No woman "fits the bill" for having cancer, but surely the national screening age is 50 for a reason. Five-zero, 50, *fifty*. The NHS recognises that these people are "more likely" to have signs of breast cancer, so therefore they need screening. I was *half* that age. If there was any chance of me getting it, then why hadn't I been screened? Why hadn't I been given a heads-up? Why is this the screening age? Why wasn't this detected sooner?

And then my mind started racing. I started to wonder how I got this. Was it the smoking? Was it the sunbeds? Was this my punishment for sleeping around? Or was it just bad luck?

I didn't know. There were too many possible causes, not enough solid answers. And I didn't want to ask anyone, because I couldn't bear them telling me that there was no reason for this, that it had just happened. That this just *was.*

'We are only going to call it *you-know-what,*' I barked at the three women in front of me. The c-word was never to be spoken in front of me again. I couldn't take it. All three of them looked at me blankly and then nodded, accepting my demand.

Over and over again, Mum and Glenda and even Helen kept saying, 'But you're 25! You're 25, how can this be?' And it didn't help me. Nothing they said did, no matter how good their intentions were. Helen began to reel off endless appointments at me. Everything in my life was now over, cancelled. You-know-what was calling, and I had to respond. I relied on Mum to absorb this information – times, dates, places. I would play along, do whatever they wanted. Who knew how much time I had left?

'So? What's the cure for this?' I demanded, staring at Helen.

She waited a second before replying. 'Well, there is no guaranteed cure yet, but some treatments can really help your chances,' she replied very quietly.

Chances? There was an endless scream inside my head. 'Well, they should pull their finger out and find a cure!' I cried.

'They're trying,' Helen said, but it wasn't enough.

I kept asking myself the same question, like a bad song on repeat, like a disc skipping. Was I going to die? Was I going to live to see 26, 56, 96? I couldn't help but think about all the things that I was going to miss out on, all the things that I was never going to be able to do.

Amidst all these dark thoughts, I couldn't help but wonder – if all women were over 50 when they were screened for you-know-what, then why the hell did all the dolls around me in the hospital look like they were under 29 with a full set of make-up on? I wanted to knock the wigs off their plastic heads, wipe the lipstick from their lips, smack the rouge from their cheeks.

I needed a target. I needed a plan, a schedule, a guarantee. I couldn't just leave the hospital without knowing exactly what my next steps were. I wanted to know everything. I needed to know everything.

As though she knew what I was thinking, Helen went on.

'Annabel, you need to wait five years, once there is no evidence of the disease any more. You are then in remission. So, you need to go into remission for you to be in a relatively safer "zone".' Helen spoke confidently and calmly, as though she wasn't just offering me a five-year prison sentence. But, after hearing this, I did feel marginally calmer. It became a goal for me, a target, a destination, the end of the tunnel.

But five years was such a long time. In five years, another general election would take place. In five years, you could complete a whole period of school. In five years, you could go through a pregnancy, give birth, and ship your kids off to school.

'Five years, remission, safer zone.' That became my mantra. I needed to go into remission and everything would be safe. Everything would be fine.

We went home after that and sat in silence. It felt like someone had died. My heart had just turned off. I needed something to lift me, something to make me feel again.

'Okay, so I suppose we need to tell everyone now,' I said to Mum.

We started compiling a list of names. We called it The List – capital T, capital L. It was like we were wedding planning, going through the guest list. People were added and people were crossed off. But here's the thing: this was not a positive list. It was not enjoyable to create. And it was definitely not going to be fun to act on it.

I am a sister, a daughter, a granddaughter, an auntie, a best friend, a friend, a colleague. And now, I was a cancer patient.

Much like everyone, I guess, I never thought that I would be saying 'I've got you-know-what' over the phone to someone. I wondered how it would go. First there might be small talk, where they talk about their lives and everything that's happening with them. I would have to listen, smile, say the right things. And then I might say 'I have to tell you something.' They'd go silent, waiting for this thing, and then I'd say it: 'I've got you-know-what.'

I had to tell my dad, my sister, my friends, Granny and Grandpa. All these people. *This is so awful. I can't do this.* I started to phone people, starting with the most important. The words stuck in my throat. Just like I had expected, people started talking about themselves first. And then I had to interrupt them and say it.

Then it would all come: the shock, the surprise, the sadness, the anger, the hatred, the bitterness, the pity, the sympathy.

I phoned once, and then I phoned again. And again. By the fifth time, I had no more tears left. It was getting harder and harder to say the words. I was tired of it, as though I was reading from a script like someone at a call centre.

When anyone asked, 'How are you?' I wanted to shout at them, *I have breast you-know-what, that's how I am!*

After the seventh phone call, I couldn't do it any more. I couldn't.

So I stepped back. I stopped making phone calls. I started sending text messages instead, so that I didn't have to hear the horror and shock and anger in their voices. It got easier. I was saying less to them, hearing less from them. My family and friends were brave about it all, but they were upset as well. Everyone wanted to help, but no one knew how to. This was foreign territory, a place we had never been to before. When I spoke to my dad, he was very quiet. He was concerned, and rightly so. He didn't know if it would be okay, which didn't stop him from telling me it would be.

Apparently getting you-know-what at this age was better than if I was older, because it could be detected earlier But then, on the other hand, having you-know what when you're younger is dangerous because it could spread far faster in younger people. I felt like I was in a lose–lose situation.

Later I sat in Mum's house, looking at all the photos she had on the fridge. They were lovely, happy memories of my sister and her baby Poppy, family celebrations, me at a wedding. Everyone was smiling, and no one was ill. And there I was, looking confident with my beautiful hair and cleavage on show.

I felt sicker and sicker looking at those photos. They just reminded me of everything that I was going to lose. My appearance, my health, maybe my life.

I started to cry. And then I remembered Karen.

Karen was my absolute best friend who I'd met in a nightclub years ago in London. We were the same age, personality, and shoe size. She was insanely beautiful, inside and out. We have the sort of friendship where we don't speak for a year but the second we do, it's like we're next to one another. It's something of great pride in our relationship, something that I feel people rarely have. But we did. We also write to each other, not on Facebook or Twitter, or even text messages. We sit down with a pen and paper and write actual letters. In the last letter Karen had sent to me, she told me that she was loved up, engaged, and living in Brighton with her man. I was so happy for her, but there was a small part of me that was envious. I wanted that.

But it's never going to happen, not now.

I can't ring her and hear how happy she is when I'm going to have no boobs and no man. I don't know if I can. She's my best friend and she wants to know, she needs to know, and I need her, right? Maybe we can go on a night out together? No, we can't now that I'm ill. But I don't feel ill. Oh god, I need to just get on with this!

I can't text her, that'll turn into a phone call. Can I MSN her? Is that acceptable? Hang on, I'm 25. I will live like a 25-year-old and communicate like a 25-year-old.

I logged on and saw that she was online; there was a green dot next to her name. I opened the chat and my fingers hovered over the keys. There were a lot of doubts in my head.

And then I just said it: *Hi Karen. I've got you-know-what and I'm only 25.*

That's it. I've told her. She wanted to talk about it, but I wanted to know about her instead. She told me that her life was over too, as her fiancé had left her. What an utter bastard. I told her that I would help her get a new, better, man, that it sounded like we had shit to get through together. She immediately made plans to visit me. I suddenly felt guilty for being jealous of her life.

But oh my god, something amazing was going to come from this: Karen and I were going to be reunited! Brilliant. This excitement and joy lasted for all of five seconds, and then an overwhelming feeling of confusion, terror, and anger hit me in the face as my brain remembered my reality. As weird as it seemed, my only way of coping with this nightmare was to keep living my life as normal. I kept thinking that I felt perfectly well, energised, and full of life. I didn't feel like I had a life-threatening condition.

Everyone told me to stop, take my time, and make careful decisions. But there was nothing to decide. I would do what the medical specialists wanted me to, but I couldn't stop going to work. I would not surrender my day-to-day life. I would beat this bastard and carry on working. Over the next few days, I explained to work what had happened and what was possibly going to happen. We agreed that until I knew more about my treatment, I would just sit at my desk at work like normal. Like normal. Everything would be normal.

I had worked in recruitment all my life. Thankfully, I found the job enthralling, attracting candidates all day long, week in and out. I'd interview people, asking them whatever I wanted. I had complete control over the situation. You either get a job or you don't. It was so simple but so rewarding.

While that bastard had control over my body, I at least still had this. I had another hospital appointment coming up, but until then I had work to get me through the gruelling wait.

Pretty soon after I had dropped my bombshell on the people at work, someone announced my situation to my team on a conference call. I can't imagine that they had an outline or an agenda for that type of subject matter, but that wasn't my problem. I just let them deal with the awkwardness of it all.

I suppose they could have just sent an email around, maybe cc'd me in, but then maybe that would have been worse? I don't know. But I wish they hadn't bloody told anyone. I wanted to get through it and get over it without anyone ever finding out.

But I knew that in reality that couldn't happen. This wasn't always an invisible disease. And besides, I needed people. Paradoxically, I didn't want anyone to know what was happening, but I also craved the chance to tell people – to talk to them about everything. I wanted people to support me. I relied on people to cure me.

After word got out, I noticed how my interaction with others changed, either for the better or worse. Some people started talking to me more often. Some stopped completely.

People who'd had to deal with appalling situations such as illness, heartache, and loss understood how to speak to me and how to act around me. From budgies dying to other people having had this terrible disease, there were all manners of heartache around my workplace. But those who hadn't had that kind of tragedy strike their lives just didn't know how to deal with me at all.

There were people that would give me the sideways "I know what you're going through" (*you definitely don't*) empathy stare. There were the people I thought were my friends – the ones I would have a chat with in the pub – who suddenly disappeared, didn't text, and certainly didn't talk to me. And then there was Aunt Fanny and her fucking husband, who would knock walls down just to tell you their parents had died at 90 with a brain tumour. I mean, objectively that was sad, but a nightmare for me, especially when I hadn't even received my prognosis yet.

'What is a prognosis?' I had asked Mum the day we'd first heard the news.

'A medical professional's opinion about how and if someone will recover from an illness,' Mum had replied without looking at me. We didn't have any tissues left that evening.

Toilet roll was the substitute.

CHAPTER 3

Maybe it Won't Kill You, But it Might Try

Lance Armstrong, Dad

Mum had already formed a long running list of people who had survived cancer. I sat down one day and started writing them down in my work diary, and then Dad got involved and started texting me names. I added Lance Armstrong to the list. A new name was included every day and the list grew longer and longer. It was good motivation, and good information about something that I didn't know much about.

All too soon I was sitting back in the hospital waiting room and counting down the seconds with Mum. We both felt terrified and desperate. We watched the clock, smiling at other patients, just waiting and waiting. I was there for mammogram confirmations, my biopsy, and lymph node test results. I still didn't feel ill. I felt well – great, even. That made it all even more of a head-fuck.

Apparently at this appointment, I was going to find out my destiny and the plan of action that would go with it. I hadn't warmed to the surgeon who originally diagnosed me. He was very bolshie and patronising. I didn't feel like I could work with him. I also wasn't happy that the second thing he'd done after telling me the bad news was point out my immaturity in reacting to the situation. He had to go.

I needed someone with better bloody bedside manners, for starters.

I explained the situation to my GP, who said that it wasn't a problem and that he would request an alternative surgeon. And, as if by magic, I was immediately transferred to the lovely Dr P who specialised in breast cancer. He was a nice, polite, well-mannered, quiet, and incredibly gentle man. I instantly liked him when he came to the door and called out 'Miss Walsh?'

During our time together, he didn't ever get anyone else to do anything for him, so Helen the nurse became redundant. She still sat there in the room for support, like a Christmas tree stand.

At our first meeting we sat down opposite Dr P, who was sitting casually behind his desk, smiling. He asked me about my life, my background, my job, and what I did with my spare time. It felt like he was trying to understand me as a person beyond my illness, and I appreciated it. But while answering all his questions, I felt like I was going to burst. I just wanted to know what was going on, what was going to happen next. After what seemed like an eternity of small talk, he got down to business: my breasts.

I felt oddly relaxed around him. But even though he had a calming presence about him, I knew that the information he was about to deliver might be something that would destroy me. But I liked him, no matter what he was about to say. After all, if I was going to get through this shit, I needed to work with someone I could get on with.

Dr P talked *with me,* not at me. He was direct, honest, and extremely knowledgeable. The perfect candidate. He was hired, as far as I was concerned.

He went over and over and over the initial diagnosis. Then he moved on.

'Okay, so here is your mammogram,' Dr P said, while pointing a pen at a wall.

Despite being desperate to know what was happening, I still seemed to zone out during the important words. It was almost like my brain chose not to hear them.

'What the mammogram says is that you have a tumour the size of ... , the grade the size of ... , and at the stage ...'

There was a huge pause.

He went on. 'So, it's pretty bad.'

Another pause.

The clock ticked. One second, two seconds, three seconds. No one took a breath.

He broke the silence. 'So, this is what we need to do ...'

And then I started to pay attention to the procedures, the numbers. 'The tumour is five centimetres in diameter ... like a tennis ball ... mastectomy ...'

(I didn't know what that was, but after Dr P drew a picture of my breasts with big cut marks all around them, I figured it out.)

And then he told me we had two plans:

Plan A – if the you-know-what has not spread.

Plan B – if the you-know-what has spread.

God, help me now. I really, really wanted to ask what Plan B was. But I didn't. Plan B was B for a reason. It was B because it was number two, the second choice, the backup. In my mind, there was no question that the illness hadn't spread. I refused to think there was any other option but Plan A.

Dr P talked about potential chemotherapy, discussing timelines without being overly specific. He mentioned potential radiotherapy, claiming that "it's a walk in the park". He told me that because I was 25, I could get Herceptin. I had no idea what this was, but the second Dr P said it the two nurses and Mum all got extremely excited and uplifted. I later learnt that Herceptin was called the "wonder drug" for you-know-what.

Dr P recommended a full course of fertility treatment, just in case my treatment exhausted my ovaries. And then he asked if I had a partner.

This enraged me. Why did the medical staff keep asking me this? It wasn't as though I had "single" written across my chest or tattooed on my forehead. 'I don't want fertility treatment. I don't have a partner and will not be getting one anytime soon.' I became rather loud, direct, and impatient. I just wanted this sorted out now, but I really didn't understand all of my options or the treatment. And that specific question had pissed me off. It wasn't enough that this had happened to me, now I was being made to feel inferior!

I started to ask a few questions about my treatment. All of the information I was given related to my future. I could "potentially" have chemotherapy, "potentially" have radiotherapy, "potentially" take Herceptin. But actually, none of this was a certainty – my treatment was not signed, sealed or delivered. Not until they performed the mastectomy.

The entire thing was like rowing a boat. We moved forward when talking about the mastectomy, and backwards about the future. Forward and back, forward and back. I just needed to know, most importantly, how quickly he could fit me in. I stopped him in his tracks. My eyes filled up. Helen the breast nurse looked away. Mum peered at the calendar on the wall. Dr P stared at me for what seemed like hours.

Seeing the desperation in my face, Dr P looked away from me and spoke. What he said amounted to a small miracle. 'I am supposed to be at another hospital next week. But it's not as urgent as your case. I am happy to cancel to do your surgery.'

It took me about five seconds to feel guilty, pause, and then accept it. This man was doing his best to help me. I felt bad for being selfish, but not bad about fighting for my own life.

'However, these are all things that you need to think about first, as it's a lot of information to digest.'

'There really is nothing to think about,' I said, speaking quickly in case he changed his mind. 'I have you-know-what and it needs to be gone. Please, please just book me in.' I was desperate.

I could see Mum silently agreeing with me, although surprisingly she wasn't very vocal, which only served to egg me on. I went on and on and on. I would do anything to make sure that this was gone for good.

Dr P's mind was made up: he was going to hack the infected breast and disease out of me, like the rind off bacon and the thorns off a rose.This is my kind of man, I told myself. A doer, a decision maker. He was going to fight this fucker and get it out of me.

My mastectomy was booked, my chemotherapy "potentially" lined up, and my mind was focused. I had to go for an MRI and a bone scan a week before my operation "just in case it had spread". I could barely think about this notion without feeling like I was in pain all over. Days went by and letter upon letter fell onto Mum's doormat. Night after night she would text me. I'm sure she had one saved as a template. 'You've got an NHS letter. Shall I open it?'

I felt such dread, anxiety, and fear at each new appointment. I was constantly in and out of that hospital. It was costing me a fortune in time off work for appointments and travel. But ultimately it was to speed up my recovery, so it had to be done. Saying that, it did slow down my social life. I didn't have time to meet with friends. I didn't have time to gossip on the phone. I didn't have time for anything. I just had to get to my next appointment, and that was all that mattered.

Certain people in my life – those who would move double-decker buses aside to tell me bad experiences about you-know-what – had already fully prepped me for how terrifying an MRI scan is. It made you feel secluded and claustrophobic. They said that if I'd never had fears of small spaces then, my god, I would after this.

Brilliant.

I walked into the MRI room.

'ALONE, PLEASE. NO GUESTS!' shouted Sonia, the extremely loud, no-nonsense radiographer who didn't even look at me.

I did wonder why she called family and friends of a patient going through the tunnel of doom "guests", but I didn't question her. I followed her instructions, shooing Mum back into the waiting room.

'Clothes off, gown on. Go with Gurpreet!' Sonia directed.

What gown? Who is bloody Gurpreet? As if by magic, Gurpreet (Sonia's assistant) suddenly appeared. She was tiny, like a small child. She squeaked, ushering me into a brown gown. She then walked me up to the tunnel of doom. All I could hear was those people's voices telling me that I was entering hell. I pulled myself back into reality and realised that life actually couldn't get worse than the last three weeks. So really, lying down for half an hour would be bearable.The lights went off, the room went silent and nothing happened.

'ARE YOU READY TO ROCK, GURPREET?'

This was Sonia shouting over the top of the screen in the room next door. Gurpreet squeaked and the MRI scanner turned on. There were lights and spotlights, like on a stage. Ironically, Robbie Williams' 'Angels' bellowed through the hospital scanning room. It was actually quite funny, if you forgot about the life-and-death scenario. Gurpreet generously explained to me that because I was moving "all over the place", the images might come out as blurry.

'We can just repeat it again in a few weeks if we need to.' Brilliant. Sonia thought that I had "weeks" to play with. These people were just not the full ticket, I decided. The bone scan wasn't much better. Another form, another medical history.

So, what do I put? I wondered. *Tonsils out, broken ankle, or you-know-what?* But the c-word was my present, not my past – so I just ignored the question and went along to my next scan. The woman conducting the scan didn't even speak to me this time, she just grunted. Oh, except for when she asked, almost as an afterthought, 'How many kids you got?' Just what I needed. She warmed up halfway through the scan to let me know that *EastEnders* was on half an hour later that night, that she lived in Chingford and "should make it home just in time".

It did feel like people were in this situation with me, though – my breast nurse Helen who let me smoke, squeaking Gurpreet, and Dr P. Even Robbie Williams' song about death all made this experience slightly easier.

I spent the next two days doing everything I could to distract myself from thinking about whether my illness had spread. I asked anyone, everyone, and their sister: 'Do you think it's spread? Do you think I will be okay?' I asked it obsessively, over and over again, a habit of mine that seemingly couldn't be cured.

CHAPTER 4

SPREADABLE

Another day, another appointment.

We parked up and walked down the long hospital corridors to the right department. Mum felt sick. I knew she did because I could feel it, like Reiki energy. I couldn't actually see it, but I could feel it radiating out of her.

My own sickness increased the closer I got to the right room. Our appointment was to take place in Corridor 5. The walk seemed to take forever. Corridor 1, sickness in my stomach. Corridor 2, sickness in my chest. Corridor 3, sickness in my throat. A pair of familiar and friendly faces suddenly appeared before us. Dr P and Gurpreet were standing in front of us. Why were they here? *It must be bad news.* They had come to find us instead of waiting for us to come to them. They clearly wanted to put us out of our misery and tell us that I was dying.

'We have an appointment in 20 minutes,' I said to them.

'See you there,' Gurpreet squeaked back. Then they disappeared.

I waited until they had walked away, and then I let it out.

'I'm dying, aren't I? There's nothing they can do about it!'

Distraught with worry and desperation, we carried on walking. I could feel my eyes filling up. It was bad news. Dr P wouldn't fuck about. If it was bad news, he would tell me. I should have been grateful that I had it in my breast and not my lungs or anywhere even more dangerous. I always hear that it's most easily curable in your breast – if it's caught early. But how the hell did I know if it had been caught early or not? I didn't catch it in a net, like a fish! I found it by accident and then pretended it wasn't there for eight weeks!

One day, it hadn't been there, and then seemingly the next, it was the size of a golf ball! *How could something so big and deadly not have spread?* I wondered. I was worried and desolate. Mum was a quivering wreck, not speaking at all.

We reached the room, the doors still open. We could see scan results reflected all over the wall, like repeated patterns on wallpaper. It was a room full of black, white, and grey. 50 shades of scans in our faces.

'Shall I shut the door?' Mum said. I gave her a terse nod, and she closed it. We both sat down and waited for Dr P to announce my demise.

'The scans have come back fine.'

The scans have come back fine.

The scans have come back fine.

The scans have come back fine.

'The scans have come back fine. I'm okay!' I shouted to Mum. The air was clear and we could all breathe. *It hasn't spread.* I really hadn't expected to hear this. I had been feeling so negative, and these three words literally changed my life in seconds. I felt happy, elated, and emotional.

I was going to have a mastectomy. Things were going to be okay.

Now I just needed an exciting distraction. So all that was left for me to do was to set up my online dating profile.

CHAPTER 5

PLENTY OF FISH IN THE SEA

Mum was convinced that my dog knew exactly what was going on. Dorothy, a Shih Tzu, was an integral part of the family. She was my dog, but she lived at Mum's, because I couldn't cope with an untrainable puppy while I was at university.

'She's definitely off colour,' Mum said, staring at Dorothy. Dorothy was a snooty bitch. She never ate anything unless you pretended you weren't looking and refused to walk further than five minutes down the road.

And yet, when my sister Polly was pregnant with Poppy, my now three-year-old niece, Dorothy would lie down and rest her head on Polly's bump, like she'd known what Polly was going through. Maybe Mum did have a point.

Project Love was on my mind. I had found an online dating website called Plenty of Fish. It was really a blanket website for anyone with "an open mind" who was seeking a partner, and quick. It was perfect for me.

I wrote a blurb and headline – "Where art thou, frog?" – and found some accurate but flattering pictures. *Cleavage or no cleavage?*

Let's not set them up for failure. No cleavage.

What the hell was I going to say?

I typed, deleted, typed, deleted, pondered, and stared, trying to get the words out. Fun loving. Carefree. Positive.

Bullshit. All these words were typical and generic. They did not in any way describe me. Usually it was so easy to talk about myself, so why was it so hard now?

I needed to put my cards on the table and my breasts behind the curtain, to try to portray a 25-year-old "normal" single girl who would stand out from the crowd. *Someone out there must have had a similar experience to me?* I thought. *Hmm, there should really be a dating website for young people with illnesses, for young women with one or no breasts, for young men with only one testicle (maybe a multi-million-dollar idea there!).*

My profile was turning into a load of generic stereotypical bullshit. But that felt easier than talking about my desperation, my horrendous ill-health, and the rollercoaster lifestyle that was approaching me.

I started uploading photos.

Me with Karen in a nightclub dive in Brighton.jpg – uploaded

Me posing in the bathroom mirror.jpg – uploaded

Me, after losing half a stone, head and neck.jpg – uploaded

Picture of me in a bikini in Benidorm.jpg – uploaded – deleted – uploaded – deleted

'Make sure you use the words "fun", "beer", and "football",' one of my friends had suggested. *My perfect Sunday would be having a few beers and watching the football,* I typed into my profile. I felt embarrassed as I read this back to myself. *Men surely will read and believe anything,* I thought. But I decided to keep it in.

Done. Laptop shut.

Dorothy looked at me, and then got up and walked out of the room, her bottom with tail swaying left to right as she left. So judgemental. I turned the laptop back on a little while later. No replies. Why had no one replied?!

Oh my god, it's not going to work. No one's going to want me. They all know my profile is fake. They all know I'm going to be a boobless, hairless misery in a matter of weeks.

It might sound odd, but you-know-what clouded my every thought. In the morning, my first instinct was to check that the lump was still there. I didn't bother looking because I couldn't see anything, but I could absolutely feel it there. Yep, large as life – round as an apple and evil as anything. I'd check it when I was on the phone, in the shower, at work, on the Tube. I'd check it at any opportunity, even sometimes getting my friends to check.

It had to go.

And I was reminded of it everywhere. I met my friend Theresa for coffee in Walthamstow Village one day, where we drank tea and ate cake. 'One lump or two?' Theresa said loudly, before immediately regretting her terrible choice of words.

'Just the one, I hope.'

My operation was on the Friday the following week and I had 12 days to go – 12 days of agonising waiting. On the Monday I went to work and behaved normally, gossiping with the cleaner. Did I know Sally from *Coronation Street* had the same thing I had? Yes, I did. The wait for my surgery felt even harder because no work was coming in. I wondered why. Did no one want a job in the recession? Or had my workload been redistributed elsewhere because of this damn lump?

On the Tuesday there was still no work. I spent the entire day on Facebook looking at all my events that were coming up, that I was supposed to be attending. *I can't do that … definitely won't be able to do that … and certainly can't go to V festival with one boob and a wig.*

My boss, Carl, had wanted a meeting with me for some time, but I hadn't been able to fit one in yet, what with all my medical appointments. Eventually we decided to meet on the Wednesday at King's Cross Tube station. While I was waiting for him, one of my friends rang me. We had a really nice chat where she listened and gave me welcome advice. 'You know what? You'll laugh through some of this, and you will cry through some of this. But you will be okay in the end,' she said.

This really empowered me. I stuck my lumpy chest out, pulled my fake Mulberry over my arm, and power-walked into Costa. I was liberated. I was positive and happy.

I walked in and saw Carl. He looked over at me as I walked towards him. He put his BlackBerry down and gave me an empathetic look.

'Annabel!' he exclaimed. 'How are you?'

It was time to talk about how I really felt. Everything just came out. It was good for me. Carl listened a bit, but I didn't expect him to be a friend, to have all the answers about my illness and my quest to find the man of my dreams. He had a job to do too and ultimately, we needed to discuss my health and where work fitted in with all of this. I put my case to him, explaining that I wanted to work as much as I could.

'You want to work through chemotherapy?!' Carl obviously hadn't been briefed on this option by HR. But I was determined to carry on working. I needed it to get away. I needed it to not just be the woman with you-know-what. So Carl agreed that I would let him know if it all got "too much". I would work when I could, but I would take time off for the chemotherapy. Fine. The conversation finished when Carl tried to reach out to me by telling me about someone he knew who'd gone through "exactly the same thing". (Actually, hers was in the brain and genetic, and she was a lot older than me.)

I left our meeting feeling pleased about my work arrangements, but as the days went on, I found that I had less and less contact with other people. I started to feel ignored and isolated. I wasn't getting my usual invites on Facebook, I wasn't getting any texts from blokes, and I was facing the reality that I was about to be carved up.

As I walked to work, I passed some roadworks. There was a big cement mixer whirring around and vibrating. I imagined this being the insides of my body, throwing the disease around. I likened the bad bits being cut out of my breast to the pneumatic drills cutting off old rubble. I shuddered.

Again, I needed a distraction. My automatic routine on the way to work would be to check Facebook, Twitter, and the Mail Online. Every single day, wherever I looked, I would see a screaming headline, from cancer charity slogans to mothers fighting for a cure. I couldn't bear it, so I stopped looking at the internet completely. Well, not completely. There was one place that was relatively safe from bad news, and that was Plenty of Fish. I checked my dating profile again. Three messages waited for me.

Tuesday

Message from Plenty of Fish

WELCOME TO PLENTY OF FISH! DID YOU KNOW OVER 20,000 PEOPLE MET ONLINE IN 2009?

Delete.

Wednesday

Message from Johnny Boy

[A picture of him, grinning and standing next to a face that had been blurred out.] How embarrassing. Delete.

Message from Phil

Hi there gorgeous, pass me your number and we can text, it's quicker.

Fantastic! I had attention. I'd reeled one in. *Hi Phil, sure it's 07737383 ...*

How exciting. I guess I wasn't written off completely yet.

My phone beeped.

UNKNOWN NUMBER

Oh, it's Phil, I thought. That was quick. Okay, maybe he thinks I'm gorgeous and single and ready to marry. I texted him back. *Hi, how you doing?*

Phil: *Look, I don't like messing around on these things, wanna meet?*

Oh, god. I didn't want this. In my mind, he immediately became "Unwanted Phil".

CHAPTER 6

THE BIG CHOP

It was the night before the mastectomy. I started to feel a huge spurt of anxiety, which induced a panic attack. Trying to calm down, I phoned Karen, asking her repetitive questions about my health. 'Will I be okay? Why are they not taking both my breasts off?' I had so many questions and just wished that I had asked Dr P more beforehand. I needed to grow up and face reality. I felt like an ignorant little girl, not listening to the rules. Mum, my sister Polly, and Poppy were all dressed smartly. They laid out food for me like a royal banquet. It was a bit like going to your parents' house for Christmas Day after not seeing them for months. Everything was prepared. It was so nice and so comforting.

I cried at dinner, but made sure to hide it from Poppy. She didn't need to know about this nightmare. She was a little girl who loved Peppa Pig. In her head, she had an auntie who was a bit mad and bought her loads of naughty treats. She didn't want to hear about this problem that was impacting the entire family.

We had an adult conversation. Who was going with me to the hospital tomorrow? What did I need to take with me? Did I have my button-up PJs? Who had change for the car-parking meter? It was all very organised and weird. It needed to be, though, as I couldn't think straight.

I asked Polly if she'd come with me. I knew she would be brilliant in the situation and absorb everything for me. I couldn't face putting Mum through anything close to the original diagnosis day. I just wanted her to have a break from this big mind game full of "what ifs".

We got up the next morning and drove to the hospital car park, fumbling about with change for the meter. We found the ward and I put on the brown gown.

The ward was very quiet. There was an eerie atmosphere. It was full of older women in their forties, fifties, and sixties. They were with their husbands and (adult) children. What the hell was I doing here? What were any of us doing here? Again, I had to reel myself back in with that line of thought. It wasn't helping me to think like that.

'Your bed's here. Your gown needs to be tied and you need to put your hair net on,' the nurse instructed.

I looked around the ward. All the beds had whiteboards above them, the reasons for our surgeries plastered on them in huge letters.

"MASTECTOMY SINGLE" hung above my bed, "MASTECTOMY DOUBLE" above another's.

They were unwelcome reminders of our ordeals. We couldn't get away from the horror of it all.

One woman was sobbing into her gown. Her husband was by her side, stroking her head and holding her hand. But I was not going to cry. I was meant to be happy. This was a good day. I was embracing my life by doing this.

We waited to be seen by Dr P and his nurses. We waited for what seemed like hours, but it was only around 40 minutes. When the doctors did their rounds, it was literally like Simon Cowell and Louis Walsh walking onto the stage for *X-Factor*. This was the biggest day of my life, and the people who held my destiny in their hands were walking down the corridor, armed with white coats, clipboards, and serious faces.

Dr P was like my saviour and the five nurses around him were his angels. Heaven. They were going to take this problem away from me. They were going to save my life. Dr P was not at all serious. He was smiling. He was in control, ready for my audition, and he was going to make me a star.

'Can you remind me which breast?' Trick question, it's got to be.

'It's the right one,' I said.

It's not right! It's wrong!

The pen came out. Dr P leant forward. AND DROPPED THE BASTARD PEN.

Polly and I shrieked. Dr P quickly picked it up, scribbled an arrow on me, and left. *No, don't go!* I thought. *I just want you next to me. I want you to cut me open and take this bitch out of me. Come back!*

Polly walked over to the window as it was all getting a little bit excitable. It wouldn't open. We both took our anger out on the window for a few minutes, trying to yank it open. A nurse hurried towards us. 'It won't open. We don't open it in case you try to throw yourself out of it,' she said matter-of-factly. This was incredibly alarming. I wondered if this had happened many times before.

Dr P returned for me. I kissed Polly goodbye and was led into theatre. There was no dramatic, *Casualty*-like scene for me. A team of nurses didn't push me, on a bed, down the tunnel of doom towards the operating theatre.

'It's a good day for it,' said Dr P as we walked down the corridor.

'A good day for what?' I asked, curiously.

'For the cricket. I'd rather be watching that than doing this!'

I laughed at him. These were my last few seconds of having a normal chest – of being a fully formed person – and he made me laugh. This had to be good sign for my road to remission.

Goodbye, you-know-what.

I love the feeling of going under anaesthetic. All the anxiety and hurt just leaves your body and mind. You are at peace.

After waking up slowly, I saw the angels and my sister standing around me. It was a really nice and safe feeling. And then I remembered.

I didn't speak. I just waited to be told what was happening, what was going on, and what was next. I quickly realised that this was the process of going through something as major as a mastectomy. You go to a new room, you wait and wait and then someone tells you what is going to happen next. Every step was hell, despite my being morphined up to my eyeballs. I was still conscious. I still knew what was going on.

After a few hours of recovery and seeing my dear mum, I actually felt okay. I couldn't look down at the hole in my body just yet, though. My chest was bandaged up and mummified, so it just looked normal. Dr P and his angels appeared again.

'We got it *all* out,' he said simply.

'Okay. So that means it's all gone?' I said, my eyes filling up.

'It's all out. We got all of it out,' he said again, beaming.

'Thank god. Thank you so much,' I said. Mum and I were so happy. We couldn't be too relieved, because we knew we still had a nightmare ahead. But it was just nice to have one good piece of news that didn't have a "but" after it.

I relaxed into the wiry hospital bed. After a month of emotional agony, I felt less troubled. I closed my eyes and Enya's 'Anywhere Is' started playing in my head. I imagined myself walking down an aisle, with white flowers being thrown at me. White for peace, calm, and health. In my head, I was floating. I was on air.

Liberated by my news, I oddly felt normal. I wasn't in pain, I was just keen to see what was left after my surgery. I wanted to see what it looked like not to have this horrible disease any more.

Some time passed and Helen, my breast nurse, said that it was time to show me my chest. I started to feel a bit sick as I imagined what I would look like. Would there just be a hole? Would there have been a cover-up job? I hadn't Googled images of "mastectomy surgery" just yet. It felt wrong to see other women like that. Helen drew the curtain around the metal curtain pole. It made a horrible screeching noise. Then everything went silent.

My body was numb with morphine, but my mind was completely awake. I started to cry quietly, mainly because I felt scared – scared of the remains of the old me. Helen gave me a mirror and started unwinding the bandages, which felt like it took forever. She held the mirror in front of me and said, 'You can look when you're ready.'

I looked down slowly. On one side, there was a breast ... and on the other, there was none. Actually, surprisingly, it didn't look that bad. It was a line, like this:

XXXXXXXX

That's all it was. It was like "X marks the spot". I had the c-word and now I didn't. And this is where my new breast would be.But despite knowing what that line meant – and the good news that came with it – it was still upsetting to see my gorgeous boob gone. And don't even get me started on what I was going to do about outfits on nights out!

But it was gone, and that was that. I had the X-Factor. I was a fresh, new, untarnished star, ready for reconstruction. Ready to be moulded into something great. And for now, that was all I wanted.

*

Over the next few days, I was surrounded by friendly faces and love. All my friends, family, relatives, and anyone who could book a slot (three at a bed only) came to see me.

I enjoyed it a bit. I had always craved attention and people were finally giving it to me. Good. This was something I deserved, after everything I'd been through.

Surprisingly, Lauren (my Benidorm buddy) hadn't been in touch since the night before my operation. She said she'd been really busy with work and "stuff", and I understood. Not all of us could take a few days off to lie in a hospital bed. But I was really keen to see her and hear her news, to hear about what was happening in her life. It would be a great distraction. I knew she'd make me feel better and we could start planning what fun we were going to have next. *Maybe we could plan another Benidorm trip?* I wondered.

When Lauren did arrive, she flounced into the ward like Cheryl Cole: tanned, thin, full hair, and, to my horror, tits completely out. She plonked herself down in the armchair next to my bed. She gave me the sideways empathy look, the one I'd become used to.

What had happened to her? Why was she dressed like she was on a night out?

Has she been on a night out? And where are my fucking Ferrero Rocher? I thought.

'How are you?' she asked, eyeing up a box of Dairy Milk chocolates next to me.

'I feel okay. They got it all out,' I said.

'That's amazing news!' To my relief, she seemed genuinely happy for me. She hadn't moved on. She had simply come in and showed me what we were missing out on. She was showing me that we were going to be single and gorgeous together.

One of Dr P's angels came in and said that she was going to change my dressings. 'Okay, I'll be on my way then,' Lauren said, jumping at the opportunity to leave, already halfway out.

'No, stay!' I wanted her to be in my life, stroking my head and holding my hand, telling me it was all going to be okay. Not bolting out the door at the first opportunity!

She sat back down. I sat up.

As the nurse attended to my dressings, Lauren leant back into the chair and yawned. YAWNED. I glanced at her. Was she bored? Tired? No, maybe she was hungover? It was hard to tell, and she was giving me nothing.

The angel started to commentate on what she was doing around my chest. 'I'm going to take the bandage off now, which may feel a bit uncomfortable.'

Lauren started going through her bag and pulled out her phone.

'Okay, the bandage is off now. Do you want to have a look?' the angel suggested.

Lauren, who was now texting on her phone, peered over. 'They've done a good job,' she said. And then she went right back to her phone, as though nothing had happened.

At this point, I was starting to get angry.

Lauren's phone suddenly went off, a cacophony of noises. Her second massive fail on this visit. Not only did she have her phone switched on in a hospital ward, but she was also bloody answering it. I didn't know who she was talking to, but she definitely didn't sound like the normal Lauren. She spoke in a weird, high-pitched, excitable voice.

And there was laughter. Lots and lots of laughter. *Fake* laughter.

My blood was *boiling*. I felt like I was going to explode. I wanted to get her horrible old Nokia and bash her over the head with it. But she interrupted my thoughts with the straw that broke the camel's back. She mumbled something about "going out tonight with Jake" as her excuse to leave.

To leave! Leave me! To go and put on a dress, pull a man, and drink her weight in vodka!

Make-up? Yawning? Phone? Texting? Night out? JAKE?

I exploded.

'WHAT THE ACTUAL FUCK IS GOING ON HERE?' I shouted. I'm sure they must have heard me from all the way down the ward.

I completely broke down. 'I've just had my breast removed. I woke up from my operation less than 24 hours ago. And all you're doing is sitting there on your phone, talking about a night out after you've come in to see me. What are you going to do next? Take a selfie of you and the mastectomy?'

She stuttered a bit. She made another excuse – or at least tried to. But I didn't want to hear it. I kicked her out.

Out of my sight, out of the ward, and out of my life.

The nurse added to the drama by swishing the curtain back around me, loudly.

The cheek. The cruelty. The attitude!

She looked beautiful and stunning and gorgeous, and I was ill and vile. Lauren needed to go. She was blacklisted. We were done.

And there was definitely no selfie to take.

CHAPTER 7

A NEW CHAPTER

It was two weeks after my operation. I was now back in my overpriced, shabby East London flat.

And I felt okay. Physically, at least. The lump was out, and my health was in some sort of order. For now, anyway. My chest healed quite quickly after the operation, but there was excess fluid that was in my armpit and areas of my chest. This had to be drained regularly, which wasn't a fun task for the drainer or the drainee.

I was also waiting for my chemotherapy, which was starting in a few weeks, and psyching myself up for the transformation that would come with it. I was going to get rid of the nastiness and be cleansed from inside and out.

My friends tried to distract me as I waited. We went to the pub, but I didn't drink. We attempted meals out, but I didn't eat much. And if I did, it was only the healthy stuff. We stayed in and chatted.

At one point, my good friend Matt – who I'd met at college – and I ventured out into East London. We got the bus and I felt 14 again. Matt had never been the talkative one, but he had a brain on him and was a brilliant friend. I was always the talker and he was always the silent observer. And it worked.

He told me about how he had met a girl called Nicola and they'd been on a few dates. Good, I thought. I was pleased for him. He had always been the same as me: never entirely lucky in love. And so I was happy to hear something good.

I did wish that I'd driven, as we sat there on the bus. And we had nearly risked it, but in the end I couldn't do it. I had already been faced with my own mortality once. I refused go out in an accident on the A406, the busiest A-road in London. It wasn't that I doubted my own abilities. I was a pretty good driver, having driven since I was 17 years old. Admittedly, I had written off two cars already, but I wasn't responsible for either of those incidents. But suddenly, after the surgery, I started avoiding driving. And soon it developed into a fear, which grew into a phobia. I physically couldn't drive. I didn't even really like getting into other people's cars any more. So here we were, standing up on a packed-out bus. There were horrible screaming kids, loud men, and women all on their devices. I had to hold my swollen arm up, supporting it with my other arm. This was a dangerous situation. I really should have tried to barter for a seat, but there are no official exceptions on public transport for cancer patients. It wasn't like I was pregnant. But at least the journey and the chat with my friend made me feel like a normal member of society again, even despite the swollen arm.

Days later I was back at the hospital, having the excess fluid drained again.

'That okay?' Gurpreet asked me, with a blank expression.

It was fucking agony. 'It's VERY sore,' I said.

She didn't reply.

The silence and the lack of acknowledgement just made the pain so much worse. But that stuff had to come out. It made my arm twice the size of the other one. It also developed a small, horrendous, saggy flap of skin like a dog's ear.

As I was leaving the hospital, Gurpreet gave me a leaflet about post-surgery bras. The hospital had given me a prosthesis, which I would be able to start wearing in the upcoming weeks. But I needed a post-surgery and mastectomy bra to support it. The "breast" itself felt nice to touch, like a massage ball, but it was incredibly heavy to carry.

After dismissing the retailer's budget mastectomy bras, I found a boutique which specialised in these kinds of bras and took Mum with me. Mum and I had always shopped together, taking big trips to Oxford Street and Bluewater in Kent. 'Have anything you like!' Mum would say to me as we approached December, the month that celebrated Christmas and my birthday. We would spend all day shopping, help each other make choices, retire at lunch for a moment's relief, and then hit the shops some more. I loved those days.

This was a similar experience and, though it was for a less positive reason, it felt like old times. It felt like fun. We found an underwear shop that was "appointment only". I liked that term. I couldn't handle the thought of being around other people for something like this, so a private appointment was great! I had the VIP (Very Important Patient) treatment.

The shop was in London and set up like a Chanel couture house. It was really quite impressive. It had 20 racks of the best quality material, catered for a big range of sizes, body shapes, and provided accessories to match. They had something for everyone.

Most of what was on display was made from the most exquisite fabric, satins, and silks, as we quickly found out by brushing our hands over everything. It was the right kind of luxury for the kind of wounded body I had.

'*How much?!*' Mum screamed with gritted teeth when we saw the price tags. I couldn't afford these prices. I was going to have to ask her to pay. We agreed to buy some of the underwear.

I knew it would do so much for my confidence, wearing such specialised underwear. 'Feeling good is priceless,' the assistant told me helpfully. I went to try on some of the bras before buying. The changing rooms were just as royal as the shopping experience. Each cubicle was the size of a small room, with velvet backed chairs for your audience. These were behind a rich red velvet curtain, tied back with bright, gold-coloured tassels. The mirrors were ancient and grand and covered in lights. It made me feel so special, like a princess.

I tried on so many different bras, which all fitted me well. The shop assistant slipped my "new breast" into my bras. As I looked into the reflection of the mirror, I saw a slim body with a beautiful emerald green satin bra on. Two breasts, not one. I looked nice. I looked my age. I felt like me again.

I wondered, while gazing happily into the mirror, if I would ever be standing in a bridal shop like this, with a big velvet curtain and an assistant placing a veil over my face. I wondered if Mum would choose my dress, if I'd have bridesmaids around me.

The shop assistant had an expert level of knowledge about mastectomies, so they knew what would work and what wouldn't. I could tell that they were surprised about my age, but they were too professional to comment on it. I left that shop over £100 lighter and three bras heavier. And I had never felt so happy.

*

Soon it was time for my prognosis consultation. We'd find out what treatment I was going to have, and how long for. Oh, and of course, we'd find out the extent of the damage that had been caused inside me.

Mum, Polly, and I crammed ourselves into the consultation room. I spent at least 20 minutes deleting endless and badly written text messages from Unwanted Phil, who hadn't given up on me. Deleting the texts was a welcome distraction from the situation at hand.

I was also trying to keep the names of all the c-word survivors in my head. Dad had now started to text me them every other day. My consultant's assistant arrived. It was Gurpreet. She was clutching *that* pink booklet again. How many times was my diagnosis going to be rubbed in my face?

Technically, I didn't even have you-know-what any more. Dr P had got it all out, and there Gurpreet was, holding up the memento of the day that ruined my life. I realised why the woman on the cover of that booklet was watching her reflection in a river. She was thinking about throwing herself into it. Gurpreet shouldn't have been holding that leaflet. She should have been holding my V Festival timetable. (V Festival, I should add, wouldn't give me my £200 refund. I was determined to fight that one later.)

I felt hopeless again. The fear kicked in once more. I was full of despair, and a real brat about everything. I was very angry. I couldn't stop myself from thinking, *What have I done to deserve this? Why is the woman on the front of that booklet smiling? She has no hair. That's nothing to smile about.*

I'd known this was coming, but now it all felt so real. The negativity weighed down on me like a ton of bricks. The door opened and a short, emotionless, camp man walked in. This was the oncologist, Dr Caster, who I would come to name The Judge. He wasn't pleasant. There were no niceties, and all he was concerned about was getting down to hard facts. The atmosphere in the room changed immediately, and we were all under his spell. He started to talk about my prognosis. He used the same words and statements we had heard a thousand times at this point. He reeled them off, like he was reading from a script. I didn't like this. He had an entirely different approach to Dr P. He was cold and clinical about what was going to happen and how. He spoke like he was narrating an audiobook. Occasionally, he would say something that I would take note of.

I didn't really want to listen, but I had to.

'I'd never seen such severe growth in a 25-year-old before. But the breast cancer has been removed. However, it did go into 48 of your 50 lymph nodes,' he said with a big enough pause to allow me to digest it.

I thought quickly about this – 48 out of 50.

Christ, that was bad. I didn't even know I had lymph nodes, and 48 of them could have killed me! I started to analyse it in my head.

48 out of 50. That was life-threatening.

48 out of 50. *I guess I'm fucked then, aren't I?*

So this disease had not only poisoned my breast, nipple, and everything around that area, but now it had gone into my lymph nodes. And into 48 of the bastards. It was like the Thames Barrier being opened during a storm, the definite worst-case scenario. I became more and more aggravated and worried.

'Hello?' The Judge stared at me.

'Sorry, go on,' I said, as though I hadn't just been given the worst news I'd heard since this thing had made its way into my life.

'It's standard procedure to check if the cancer has spread into your lymph nodes. And it has, as I've mentioned. Therefore, we removed all of them.'

We were frozen still. We didn't know if this was good or bad. I started to question him. 'This news isn't good, is it?' I asked, tears in my eyes, a lump in my throat, a croak in my voice.

'It wasn't good news at first,' The Judge replied. 'But they are out now, and it's gone from there. So it's unlikely that the cancer could have spread from that point … Now, chemotherapy is vital for your protection in the future …'

He went on, explaining what type I'd need and over what time frame it would be administered to my poor, weeping body. 'Can give you the intense treatment that you need … purely for insurance purposes … preventative … '

I focused on the numbers and specifics.

'There will be six sessions, every three weeks, over six months. In addition to this, we will put you on a course of Herceptin that'll continue for 18 months.'

'18 months?' I echoed. Too many numbers flew around in my head, and I could sense that my mum and sister were confused as well.

'Yes, but there won't be any side effects with Herceptin,' he said in a matter-of-fact tone that made me want to believe him. This would later be revealed as a lie.

I'd researched Herceptin before this meeting and actually, I'm glad that I had, despite everyone telling me not to Google anything. I'd found out that Herceptin was a complete and utter life-saver, and that I was lucky to be prescribed it. I had Googled and memorised: *Herceptin can be used to help control the growth of cancerous cells that contain high amounts of HER2. It works by blocking the effects of the protein and encourages the immune system (the body's natural defence system) to attack the abnormal cells.*

'You will, of course, need to have a scan of your heart to make sure that it can cope,' The Judge said, adding to the devastation sandwich he was currently serving us.

He took a breath. He was finished, phew!

But then he went on.

'I would highly recommend a course of fertility treatment!' he said, and my heart froze. 'At your age, we're unsure of how your treatment will affect your menstrual cycle. Therefore, egg preservation and other options are freely available. We really would suggest you take them. Now, I know that at your age, you're not in the position to make a decision easily, especially when you don't currently have a partner.'

Don't even get me started.

I was fuming. He knew that I had made my mind up before and it was a big fat no. And yet here he was, saying it again.

'As for freezing your eggs, I would strongly recommend that too, as it might secure your chances of having children in the future.' He was firm on this, I could tell from the way that he spoke.

But all I could hear in my mind was "48 out of 50 lymph nodes ... 18 rounds of Herceptin ... and six whole months of chemotherapy."

The Judge didn't want to mess around with endless chat. This guy aimed to put a plan in place and just get on with it. He moved on to the inevitable: the hair loss. Finally, my emotions defeated me. I don't know why this hurt me so much, because I always knew this was going to happen. From the day Mum and Glenda sat with me in that horrible room with the wigs, I knew it was a definite reality for me. But I had never believed it, not really, and to hear the words from The Judge was terrifying.

As he finished telling me that my hair would definitely fall out, I shouted 'Noooo!' in anguish. It was like something from an *EastEnders* scene, right before the theme tune kicks in. I was terrified of my £200 European Remy pre-bonded keratin hair extensions being pulled out by this devil of an illness. *It wasn't fair.* I had never been a perfect size 12. I was a 14 (sometimes 16). I needed my hair. It's a woman's prerogative, for god's sake! But I had no choice. I would have to have the treatment and the hair was going to fall out.

I could tell my sister and Mum were just as upset as I was, but they said all the right things on the way out. Defeated and beaten, we left the hospital feeling traumatised.

> Gail Porter,
> Dad

> She had alopecia?
> Annabel

> SAME EMOTIONAL BATTLE,
> Dad

*

I had to get a good wig. I idolised Jordan (the glamour model) and saw that she was in a new, exciting, happy relationship with her latest beau – a gorgeous alpha male who was going to sort her life out. But she didn't even need him. She had her health, big breasts, and her beautiful black, wavy, curly hair. 'And her children!' Polly chipped in purposefully.

I wanted Jordan's life. I wanted her beau and I wanted her hair. I was going to try to copy it. I was going to be the you-know-what victim in disguise who looked exactly like Jordan! But I would need an aid to help me make this transformation. My best friend Karen!

'Lashes,' Karen said instantly when I told her my idea. 'You need MAC ones, they're the best. Flash Bash do them, but they're shit. You need big eyes, a wig, and good eyebrows. Tattoo them! We can go to Liverpool. I've been Googling and they do a deal for £50. If there's two of us maybe we can get it cheaper?'

This was perfect. Karen knew how to sort me out, and she did it properly. For days following my hair crisis, she flooded with me emails at work. No, I had not realised that Jordan wore wigs all the time – even in the bath! Okay, so Karen was exaggerating slightly, but I let it go. Her messages of support flooded in. Ideas, idols, hair type, colour, make-up, tone, shape, style. They kept coming. And I loved every second of it.

I was still working every day, but was gradually losing the will to do any proper work. My growing anger at my situation was taken out on every applicant at work who wanted a job. No, they are not eligible. Why? Because they're already successful; they have a family, they have a career, they have their health and their freedom. I didn't have any of that. As the applications kept coming in for jobs, so I kept rejecting them. 'We regret to inform you that you have not been successful on this occasion.'

HA! Fuck it, fuck you, you fucker. Your destiny is in my hands and I'm fucking it up for you. Just like someone is doing for me.

I knew I was being very mean and nasty, but I couldn't help it. I became angrier and angrier. Anything could trigger me – at the slightest comment I was done, jumping over the fence with an axe.

Karen had realised this and made the decision that I needed to get on with the dating thing as a distraction.

Recruitment was very similar to dating, so it doesn't take too much to do them at the same time. You read about people's lives, you make a choice, you interview them. You hire them or you don't. It was a simple, black-and-white process that I was extremely good at. 'Sort out your image, be confident with that. And then sort out your man,' Karen had said over MSN. Fine.

Hang on a minute! I thought as I shut my laptop down. *If I'm going down into this dark and crazy world of internet dating, she can come with me!* I couldn't do it alone. I needed her to be with me. But Karen lived in Brighton. She had decided to get away from London after working her way up within the retail industry. She wanted to get away from the pollution in London. At the time I had thought she was mad. How could she leave London?!

She worked as a buyer in a little boutique and lived a small distance away from the pier. The sea and the hustle and bustle of the gorgeous town was very familiar to me. Mum used to bring me and Polly to the seaside for special days out. I would always wear my yellow polka-dot dress and Polly would wear her rainbow dress. We would get in the car, play games, and be given stacks of pennies to blow on the arcades. We would choose any place we wanted for lunch and shop around the ancient lanes. But Brighton was more important than just childhood trips. Mum and Dad had met while doing their degrees in Brighton.

Mum was always quiet, kind, and perfectly presented. She had hard-working parents who often worked abroad in places like Kenya, Australia, and America. My dad was born in Surrey. Extroverted and eccentric, he grew up as an excited and creative child. He loved wildlife, parrots, colour, wireless radios, and adored Abba and Slade.

He also believed in Father Christmas until he was eight. He passed this trait onto me – father to daughter.

His appearance always grabbed attention, wherever he went. He looked like a wise old hippy; tall, with very curly grey hair. And he always wore a pair of Converse trainers.

My parents both studied in Brighton. They met, socialised, partied, and went to festivals. As different as they were, their relationship worked. They married in the 70s and moved to East London. This was where the work was at the time. Mum became a teacher, Dad a social worker. Mum gave birth to two girls, my sister Polly in 1980 and me in 1983. Their different personalities collided again as my dad argued strongly for calling us Mercedes and Porsha. I'm sure he's where I get my eccentricity from, because when I heard about this, I thought that the name Porsha was great.

Both Polly and I were a handful. When we were babies, my mum would happily hand us over to dad the second he walked through the door. Eventually, they moved from a flat to a house, and as Polly and I started to grow up, the contrast of their personalities eventually got the better of their relationship.

My parents split when Polly and I were quite young. I know it's good that it happened this way, because it meant that we never experienced a row or any tension between them. As soon as things started to turn sour, they nipped it in the bud.

As a single parent, Mum managed childcare really well. But at times she struggled financially. She worked her fingers to the bone to provide us with the best clothes, after-school activities like horse riding and ballet, and the food we needed. Everything we wanted, we got ... within reason, of course! And we would go on day trips – to Brighton, for example, which became a favourite pastime for the three of us.

Polly and her partner Tim also moved to Brighton a few years after they left Manchester (where they'd met while Polly was studying her degree). They chose a pretty flat on the seafront, renting it at an extortionate price. But though Brighton held so many great memories for me, my current trip there wasn't for such positive reasons. I was a complete mess. As I drove down alone in my car, I missed Mum and Polly and our game of "who can spot the sea first". I missed trawling around The Lanes looking at weird and wonderful jewels in the windows of antique shops and choosing which restaurant to recover in.

But I was equally as excited to be there. I wasn't wearing my sunshine dress and I definitely wasn't going to be wandering around The Lanes, but it was still Brighton.

We had a nice weekend, Karen and me. By this stage, my chest had fully healed, although my mind had a long way to go. We talked through every minute of each day. Karen was still struggling due to her fiancé leaving her, and she felt that she had been left with a big hole in her life, just like the one in my chest.

Both of us were clearly dealing with very heavy mental health issues and it was therapeutic just being together, eating pasta and cheese and playing dress-up. I loved it. I felt good again, like a normal 25-year-old. She encouraged me to try sexy underwear on and use my new padded prosthesis breast. I started to feel alive again, like maybe there was some hope at the end of all of this.

We even took a trip to Ikea as we'd decided that my dive of a flat needed a little bit of TLC. It would make me feel comfortable while I was dealing with the side effects from chemotherapy. 'Lamps … lighting … mirrors … fur … cushions … plants … what about fake flowers?' Karen was filled with ideas on the trip down to Ikea. And we chose all of them, not thinking about money as we bought them and threw them into the back of my car.

After buying half of Ikea and coming back to London together, we started to tackle my room. We transformed it with loads of pillows and cushions and light pastel colours, nothing garish at all. We wanted to make it cosy and warm. It took us a while, but when I was done, I liked it. It felt good, a good place to be ill. I was proud of where I was, in my own flat, in London, just like Bridget Jones.

I felt happy and relaxed as we stood in my room, absorbing our hard work. But this was short-lived as we were rudely interrupted by my phone ringing.

Oh my god, it's Unwanted Phil. He'd notched it up a gear and he was calling me. This was an invasion, harassment. A lump clinging on to me that I couldn't shift. 'Karen! This guy is a psycho!' I shouted at her accusingly, as though somehow it was her fault. The phone stopped ringing and then started up again.

'No, you're the psycho! You gave the first man that messaged you your number! He could be bloody anyone!' I went to argue back, and as I did, the phone rang again. We were now up to five missed calls and it was freaking me out. 'JESUS! BLOCK HIM, BAR THE NUMBER, CUT IT OUT, JUST GET RID OF THIS!' Karen screamed at me.

I looked down at my phone and I knew she was right. But I didn't know why it had taken me this long to figure it out.

*

The next hurdle for me would be the wig. I just didn't know how this would work out.I was sitting with Matt in a local pub drinking a soft drink. It was easy to just be with Matt. When I'm with him, we just become comfortable like the furniture, sitting there for hours, not talking any sense. It's good for me. I'm usually so talkative, speaking so much I worry I might take his ears off at times. But this time, we both knew it was different. Our roles had changed completely. He was the one who was talking all the time. He didn't mention the bad, the ugly, or worst-case scenarios. He just talked positively about our happy times, funny moments on nights out, and my future. It was everything that I needed. And then he started talking about a survivor of you-know-what.

'My auntie,' Matt said, smiling with pride. Scribbling down her name in my diary, I listened as he told me about everything she had gone through. He told me about a fantastic wig shop that had the best of the best wigs, called Hair to Ware. It was in Hertfordshire. It specialised in wigs for chemotherapy patients, and I imagined it would be a similar experience to bra shopping. I decided to go and check it out.

I knew this was a big step. I loved getting my hair cut, dying it, and wearing real hair extensions. I had, over the past two years, copied Jordan's latest look, sporting big, full, brown or black bouncing curls. With a lot of back-combing and hairspray!

As Mum and I arrived at the shop, I looked around at all the wigs. It seemed there was every colour and style possible. It was impressive. And yet, I couldn't help but hate every single one of the wigs on show, because I knew that my own hair was going to be gone soon.

I tried on a couple and I had to admit that they didn't look too bad. But I couldn't deal with it. The shop assistant, who was placing these cat-like wigs upon my head, kept referring to "hair loss". It made me more pent up and annoyed. I reluctantly chose a very long, straight brown wig with a side fringe. It half-resembled me. Mum paid (once again) and we left.

The second I got home, I stuffed that beautiful handmade box underneath my bed.

CHAPTER 8

DON'T JUDGE A BOOK
BY ITS COVER

Miranda from Sex and the City, Dad

How did my Dad even know this?

*

A couple of days went by before, surprise surprise, yet another appointment. This one was significant, though.

This was about my fertility, about my eggs. Or oocytes, if we were to name them correctly. I had two options: to freeze or not to freeze. Freezing eggs is for heterosexuals, homosexuals, singles, and couples who aren't able to conceive. With the magic of IVF, the miracle of children is given to those who might not have been able to have it before. But no one wants a rotten egg. The chemo would most likely *knacker* my ovaries or damage my womb. The drugs would work their way through my infected body, destroying cells, throwing my immune system out of the window. And when that was over and I would start to recover, the Herceptin would go in and change all my cells. So, by the end of all this, my body wouldn't have a bloody clue what's going on. And by the time I was done healing myself, it might well just keel over!

I kept thinking, over and over, about what all of this gruelling treatment could do to me and my helpless body. Things that had been mentioned were buzzing around in my brain.

'Periods could stop ... womb damage ... ovaries affected ...'

But worse still: I could go into early menopause. I struggled to make a decision. My mind fought against the idea of having my eggs frozen, because I didn't want to accept that this was happening. But I knew if I didn't have them frozen, I'd be destroying my chances of having a back-up plan.

I thought about all the facts I had been told, everything I'd researched, printed off, and repeated to myself over and over again. Was this all just a false sense of security? Could I really just pull them out one day and use them? "The eggs have to survive being thawed," I'd read. "Success is not guaranteed." Success was a major factor for me. I had always been successful – until about three months ago, that was. I tended to get what I wanted, and I worked very hard for it. From what I could tell, this looked like an intensive and invasive process. Funnily enough, I'd had so much of that, I didn't fancy doing it just for the sake of it, if complete and utter success wasn't guaranteed. Plus, it could delay my chemotherapy treatment.

But fertility success seemed to be down to Mr Science, Mrs Universe, the powers of medical chemistry and biology, and just pure old chance.

Through time and deliberation, my mind settled. I decided on what end of the seesaw I was content to stay on. I knew that, in the future, I might not be able to conceive regardless of storing these eggs. But it would mean that I'd have an insurance policy when (if) I met "The One" and he wanted children. Eventually I was sold on the idea.

*

Mum and I sat waiting for the appointment. The room was full of couples, mainly middle-aged heterosexual couples, and the odd woman on her own. And then there was us; me looking completely knackered and Mum looking anxious. She was given all the declaration forms, information, and next-of-kin paperwork that would later get shoved into that damn pink booklet.

'That's mine, actually,' I said, interrupting as Mum took the paperwork. She was commonly mistaken for me in everything we went to. The nurse gave an embarrassed and muffled 'Sorry' and glanced at us both, eyes dashing between one and the other. *Who's the patient?* I could tell she was thinking. *It can't be her, she's too young!* I was paranoid as I sat down and avoided eye contact with everyone. No one was talking. And I couldn't see any other pink booklets anywhere. The table in front of us was filled with all my favourite magazines – *Grazia*, *OK!*, and *Hello!*. But I didn't dare pick one up for fear of my gesture being over-analysed by everyone around me.

What am I doing here? I thought.

'You're lucky,' a friend had said to me, when they'd heard what I was doing. 'You're getting this for free.' I wondered if my situation could ever really be counted as "lucky".

Soon I was sitting in front of some poor consultant who smiled ... a lot. 'You're a cancer patient!' he said.

Hmmm – I couldn't make up my mind if I liked him or not.

'Treat this as your Plan B!'

'I am unclear of Plan A,' I wanted to say, but didn't.

'Consider how you might feel if you decline the treatment and go for fertility testing later on!'

Mum and I deliberately didn't look at each other and I shrank into my seat even further. *Right, enough of this back and forth,* I thought. I needed cold, hard facts.

'What's the success rate?' I asked.

'The success rate of implantation and conceiving through IVF is 2–12 per cent.'

'Very low,' I said.

'It's even lower if you don't go ahead!' the consultant replied, grinning.

I started to wonder about him. He was either a very peppy person, found this situation funny, or he was taking something.

I needed to test him. But how far could I go?

'What's the worst that can happen with these procedures?' I barked at him.

He stated a few facts and figures and numbers, all of which I took in. Then one statement smacked me right in the face.

'The chances of cancer developing as the result of IVF is very low and minimal. *He's just gone and said the bloody c-word! What a god damn … c-word.*

'Annabel, are you even listening?' Mum interrupted my angry thoughts, through gritted teeth.

I wanted to put my hands over my ears, to shake my head, to run out of the room. I didn't want to listen.

Mr Smiley finished: 'I would suggest that you think over this carefully. You should definitely take this opportunity. You might never even have to use it! But it's good to have.' He didn't stop smiling at me.

I needed to make a decision then and there. I didn't like going away and thinking about things. My star sign is Sagittarius, a fire sign. I have burning heat inside me. I get what I want quickly, I make decisions promptly, and I act immediately. I needed to walk out of there, knowing what the plan was. Showing me the insides of a woman's body on a huge mannequin, Smiley used his stick to remind me where the vagina was, where the fallopian tubes, ovaries, and womb were. I paid little attention, debating my choices in my head, back and forth.

After his demonstration, Smiley sat there and listened to me as I spoke at him, trying to talk myself through the decision.

'Possibly could see myself as a mother ... Would hope it'd be likely to work if I'm going through all of that ... Trendy IVFers ... May not bloody happen ...'

And then, after a few seconds of silence, I announced, 'I'm doing it.'

Everyone smiled. Smiley dug out some forms, pens, and clipboards. I talked over the silence, adding, 'I just don't want to rule out an avenue of my future just yet. At 25 years old. 'I decided there and then that actually this guy was pretty much on the money. I guess if I had, deep down, really believed that the whole idea was pointless from the start, I wouldn't have been Googling until 3am. I wouldn't have paid more attention to longing mothers and doting fathers, and I certainly wouldn't be sitting here in front of this man, who – I'd decided – I actually did quite like and trust, even if he did smile a lot. But ultimately, I wasn't going to let this thing put a stop to any hope in the future.

Mum breathed yet another, but definitely not the last, sigh of relief.

I signed the declaration form to have my eggs frozen. I was immediately assigned a fertility nurse, a woman named Joy who couldn't have been further from gleeful. She was young but somehow old-looking, frumpy, and bloody miserable, which made me resent her. I had to visit her for an afternoon of lectures, intensive medical information, and a big summary of the process. Following this, I was told I needed to go home with needles and inject myself (*in my bum!*) every day for two weeks. I panicked that I wouldn't remember to keep up with that – I had a job to do, men to meet, and you-know-what to beat! On top of that, I had to carry around a personalised IVF kit with me everywhere.I soon discovered that fertility treatment feels like a full-time job, and I had to combine this with my actual full-time job, as well as everything else that I had going on. Suffice to say, it involved a lot of interruption and inconvenience. I had to leave meetings at work and inject myself in the toilets. I had to do it during lunch at Granny and Grandpa's, during car trips to Homebase – wherever and whenever it was time. Trousers down, knickers off, bum out, injection in. I was officially a junkie. A hormone junkie.

'The most crucial part of this treatment is making sure you follow the correct course, with accuracy and detail to timing,' I had been told. This seemed impossible. Sometimes I missed injections, overslept, or forgot things at home. Whatever the reason, I just couldn't keep up with it. What was worse was that the chemicals were completely changing my hormone levels.

As the days went on, I became tetchier and more sensitive. I became full-out argumentative, which then evolved into my wanting to kill everyone around me. My meetings with Joy the fertility nurse became even more joyless.

'But is it normal to feel this insane?' I asked. She would know out of everyone, surely. This was her job, after all.

'Oh yes, quite. But only two more weeks to go!' she said, not even bothering to act sympathetically towards what I was going through.

During this time, I'd been receiving messages from friends asking me to go out for dinner, lunch, drinks. I declined all of them. I didn't think they were a good idea. I wanted to save my nights out until I felt something close to half-sane again, until I had something to celebrate.

*

Finally, the time came for my next operation. During this procedure, the doctors were going to take out some of my eggs for freezing. My dear mum took another day off work to come with me. There was little waiting around. They got me onto the bed, gave me the anaesthetic, and I went under.

Enya's 'Anywhere Is' was playing in my head. I pictured angels scattering white flowers over me. I'd started to crave that feeling of going under with the aid of drugs. It was the only time I felt relaxed. It felt like I was resting in peace ... but definitely not dead.

I woke up after the procedure feeling a bit woozy, but with no pain. Mum and Joy were sitting around me, not speaking. In the days before the operation, I'd had a minor altercation with Joy. She'd asked me to sign yet another form, and I was so tired of it all, I didn't even read what she had given me. 'What is this form for?' I asked her. I might have been too tired to read it, but I still wanted to know what I was signing.

'Well, if you don't recover from your treatment, we'd like to use your eggs,' she said quickly, skimming over the words like stones over a pond.

Pause. Silence. Tension. Tears.

Shouting.

'*IF* I DONT RECOVER?' I screamed at her. 'I AM WELL! I HAVE NOT GOT YOU-KNOW-WHAT ANY MORE AND THIS IS AN INSURANCE POLICY FOR MY FUTURE WITH THE LOVE OF MY LIFE!'

I had lost my mind. I could barely believe the audacity. How dare she?!

If I didn't recover! I began to doubt all humanity.

Had Dr P been lying to me about getting it all out? Was The Judge's comments about "insurance policies and preventative treatment" just tongue-in-cheek? Was Gurpreet's squeaking just another play on me?

Fuck it! I'm out of here. This is awful. How could they do this to me?

'Calm down! Sign the form, and then we can complain about it afterwards,' Mum instructed me. But even though she was seeing things with a clear head, she was still angry.

Hence the very long silence after the operation. 'Well!' Joy exclaimed over-enthusiastically, trying to compensate for her massive balls-up earlier. 'It was a great success and we managed to take four eggs! However, one isn't able to be used. But the overall result is very good, so we're really pleased. They'll be stored on an ongoing basis for 10 years and rolling ...'

She announced it like I had just won the health lottery.

Joy needs to go.

'Great, I can potentially have kids.'

Now jog on, Joy, I'm going home. Afterwards, something of an apology was sent to me on Joy's behalf, for the "distorted and inaccurate comments which may have had an effect on the emotional well-being of Miss Walsh ..."

Brilliant.

CHAPTER 9

The Twelve Months of Cancer

It was two weeks into September 2009. It was a couple of months after my initial diagnosis, one month after my mastectomy, and 14 days after my fertility treatment. Today was the day of my first chemotherapy session. Things had moved so fast, but it was good. I wanted it that way.

With my focus on the upcoming chemotherapy, I forgot to tell people about the small operation I was having to have a port inserted into my chest, as evidenced by the following email chain with Carl, my boss:

Can I have Tuesday off please? – Annabel

Yes. Is this for another appointment? – Carl

No, just a minor operation, but I've only just remembered! – Annabel

??? – Carl

The port was a small disc made out of plastic about the size of a 10p. It was going to be inserted under the skin in the centre of my chest.

A catheter-like tube would be connected to the port to allow the chemotherapy to be administered during treatment. I'd been recommended this option after being told that an intravenous one in my hand would bruise and be very painful after the full 18-month treatment.

Things like this are huge to some people in normal circumstances, but for me an operation like this was genuinely like a drop in the ocean.

I took slightly longer to recover from the port operation than the few hours I'd predicted, but that didn't matter, because now it meant that the time had come. My first chemotherapy session was around the corner.

In preparation, I'd begrudgingly had my hair cut into a bob and lost a bit of weight. I'd cut out bad food completely from my diet. No fat, no sugar, and definitely no alcohol. Just salad, fish, and vegetables. I didn't consciously decide to do this, or at least, not with the same self-awareness I'd had when starting other diets. My head and heart had just changed the way I thought about things. I was ill, this was all real now, and a healthy diet could contribute to my survival. My body was in combat mode, and this was just one of the survival techniques I was employing.

As I'd sat for my haircut, I had to make some very awkward small talk with the hairdresser, who didn't know me.

'Night out, is it?' she had asked, as she aggressively pulled out my beautiful and very expensive pre-bonded hair extensions. I couldn't look at the pile of long, brown hair on the floor. I felt guilty. I knew this hair had come from someone who genuinely needed the money, so much so that they had literally sold the hair off their head. Perhaps to feed a child?

I had to stop this line of thinking. I didn't want to feel bad or drive myself towards misery or suicidal tendencies. So instead I found myself going into a full-blown lie about my amazing night out, how it had been planned for ages, blah, blah, blah. I just wasn't in the mood to go through my usual 'I have the c-word …' conversation with someone I didn't know.

Mum took a photo of me a few days later and put it on the fridge. I looked thinner, with new clothes and a new haircut. I was smiling. The smile was real, so maybe that's why she liked it. I was smiling because I felt good and happy.

But there was something off about the photo. It made me feel uneasy, for some reason. I stared at it for a while until I realised why. The photo was right next to a picture of some daffodils – which featured on the Marie Curie charity logo! *Oh my god, I'm going to be the next advert for this thing.* The thought sent shivers down my spine.

I tore the photograph down, shouting at my mum across the kitchen, raging about charities. 'Annabel, I think you really have to reassess your anger towards charities. Well, towards everything really,' Mum said to me.

She was right. Charities are the ultimate gift, the reason that I'm here right now, writing this book. But I was struggling with some of their campaign ideas at the time. Whenever I walked down the high street, I would dread seeing the swarm of pink costumes, there to raise money. I couldn't help getting angry when I saw someone in a green wig, prancing around or offering cupcakes in the shape of breasts topped with marzipan nipples.

From my personal perspective, it just seemed like they were highlighting what we were all losing: the hair and the breasts. Somehow I couldn't imagine a charity for men selling bollock-shaped cookies, strapping on a Willy Wonka to do a fun run round Hyde Park. But then, they were raising money to help me stay alive. I needed to stop being so ignorant and start seeing the positives. I had to give something back to the charities at some point. I couldn't continue with this unjustified anger. And who on earth gets angry at a flower, anyway?

*

Chemotherapy was going to be intensive and exhausting. I had been told that many times. But being told something is different from actually living it.

The morning of my first session arrived. I had to be up at 6am – a killer. Mum and I urged Dorothy to hurry up and finish her morning wee, but she took her time. We locked up and took the journey on the train from Walthamstow, through to Farringdon. As I sat on the train, I spent the entire time wishing I was on the way to work, to the cinema, to a date. Anything but on the way to the hospital. The Royal Hospital of St Bartholomew is a beautiful, historic, and, quite frankly, wonderful piece of London. Its widespread grounds, set in Farringdon, are a sight to behold. It's one of the most prestigious oncology hospitals.

But that didn't make it any better.

The train journey was quiet and full of pissed-off commuters and miserable Brits on the way to their jobs, tapping away on devices, not speaking to each other. I knew they'd become inevitably more miserable if their journey was delayed. No wonder London is such a difficult place to meet anyone. The only time you ever get the chance is on a Friday night at 10pm after five Jäger bombs, when everyone has finally got over the stress of real life. I joined in with the device squad and spent the entire journey receiving and replying to text messages, my phone continuously shooting in and out of signal. Good luck messages and well wishes flooded my phone, but I couldn't appreciate them. I could only get angry. It was always my defence mechanism for the next bloody battle I was about to face.

I didn't like the words "good luck". Why, could something go wrong? I didn't like the words "thinking of you". Those words always made me think of death. Did they think I was going to die?

But most pressingly, I took note of the people that said nothing, the people that didn't think to even send something.

We arrived at the hospital and walked through long, dark, impressive corridors. This way, that way – we didn't know where we were going. Somehow, Mum and I ended up on the right ward, greeted by a team of angels mainly from Vietnam. I loved their voices. They always sounded happy, even if they were delivering a difficult message, which definitely came with the job description.

The ward completely shot down the stereotypical scene I'd made in my head. It was diverse, with men and women, both young and old. It felt like an airport departure lounge: you checked in, you dumped your bags, and you went to your seat. It was hot, stuffy, and eerily quiet.

We waited in complete silence for a while, and then the double doors to the room opened. The sound of squeaky, metallic trolley wheels came in from the distance. Some people brought in the dream machine, the one that was filled full of bright purple chemicals that looked exactly like Ribena. The chemotherapy medication was called Fec, so you can imagine many a joke went around the ward to the name: 'Fec this and Fec that.' The Ribena-looking substance was presented to me like a lobster in a posh restaurant – with flourish and extravagance.

Four angels surrounded us and spoke at exactly the same time. 'Confirm your name, confirm your date of birth, which session will this be, which hand for the needle?'

It was impossible to answer them in any logical order, so I mirrored their style.

'Annabel Walsh, 20/12/83, first of six treatments. I have a port in my chest,' I said.

They didn't ask me to repeat anything. They just disappeared. Good. They were in control. This was normal. I'd been there for two hours and no one had even mentioned you-know-what. *This is all about insurance and prevention.* I knew I should remember that in case I freaked out. I was anxious and eager to just know what chemotherapy was going to feel like, how I was going to react to it. I just wanted to get this first session over and done with.

And then the needle went in. The machine was on, the insurance striking its first blow. Mum sat next to me, clearly wanting to ask loads of questions about how it felt. Was I okay? Did it feel alright? Could I feel my hair falling out yet? I just kept telling her that I was *fine,* a word I've grown to detest, because it doesn't mean a single thing. What is fine? What does fine feel like? I sat back, feeling very tense. I tried to hear Enya's 'Anywhere Is' in my head, but I couldn't. I could just hear a lot of medical terminology and chatter. I didn't want to listen to that. I didn't want to listen to anything anyone was saying. I was scared of hearing anything that might be wrong with me. What if they knew something I didn't? I gave in and just watched what was going on around me. The people sitting around me were mixed ages, ethnicities, and marital statuses. I quickly realised there was a community that had developed in this room; the people were talking to one another instead of just their plus ones. So I eavesdropped on the nearest conversation from the patient next to me.

'Where's Wig Man, he here yet?'

'Nah, he comes in at three.'

Oh my god. Who was Wig Man? Were they taking the piss? Would they be calling me Wig Woman when my hair fell out? I couldn't bear to see him, whoever he was. I bet his wig was really awful. I couldn't stop thinking about my own hair, wondering when it was going to start falling out.

An elderly man suddenly came in through the double doors with an assistant. The two of them slowly walked round to see each patient. The routine seemed to be to hand the patient a wig brochure, ask a few questions, wait for a simple "yes" or "not needed", and then they moved on. *Oh! That kind of a wig man!* That's Wig Man, the man that deals with the NHS wigs! *Okay, this is fine, I can deal with this,* I thought, feeling relieved.

Mum and I started talking about how there was no need for me to have a wig appointment because I'd already purchased my beautiful, very real-looking human hair wig the week before. It was actually just like my extensions, but rather than a few small ones, it was just one big one and probably easier to deal with. I was even looking forward to wearing it … maybe.

'Hi, Ms Walsh?' I heard a voice.

The assistant was looking at me. I looked back at her. It was Jackie Gregory from college.

Bloody hell. It was the 25-year-old East London bike, who had more notches on her bedpost than a playboy bunny. But it was okay … she didn't recognise me. She was either being very professional (highly unlikely) or was just too stupid to remember (likely). Mum and I continued to earwig as we sat there. Conversations about wigs flew about, debates occurred about mouth ulcers. And then the subject of our common interest, if you could call it that, reared its head: *what type of disease did you have and will you be okay?* The reality was that I was sitting next to people, both old and young, who had you-know-what. Some of them might have survived it, some of them might not. The patients with the more serious cases seemed to be the most vocal. Why shouldn't they be, after all? Their anger was warranted, given that this disease was taking over their entire lives.

The double doors opened again. Bizarrely, a tea lady came in, with trays piled high full of sandwiches. *Ugh, they look vile,* I thought, but every single person asked for one or two. Someone even asked for three.

This entire thing was so fascinating to me. It suddenly occurred to me that just two weeks ago, I had been wondering how I was going to recruit someone with a full driving licence, who had five years' work experience, who could start one of my vacancies in a month. Now, I was wondering who was going to have tuna sandwiches and which person's chemotherapy was going to clock off first.

There was a loud beep after a while and my machine went off. It was over, my first session completed. I felt totally normal. I could walk, breathe, and think clearly. But my brain was anticipating sickness, pain in my head and aching in the legs – all the things I had been told were associated with chemotherapy.

I didn't feel any of those symptoms as we walked out. We got a black cab and I insisted on going back to my own flat. Mum urged me to come home to be with her and Dorothy. But I had already decided that I wanted to protect her from all the side effects Google had told me I'd get straight away. Mum already knew what emotional pain we were both in – she didn't need to witness any more. Reluctantly, Mum went back to her house with her mobile switched to loud. And I imagine it didn't leave her side. I kept my mobile close by too, just in case. It was best to be cautious here, to play it safe.

I was still feeling as normal as ever. I had maybe a slight headache coming on, but nothing I couldn't cope with so far.

A couple of hours went by and I wondered what to do. Watch *EastEnders*? Make something to eat? Probably not a good idea ... My laptop stared at me. *OPEN ME NOW*, it screamed out, neglected for all of 12 hours. I turned it on, and I noticed there was something wrong with it straight away. The screen was very bright, with yellows and greens everywhere. It was broken. Or wait, was it? Or was it my eyesight? Was I starting to feel ill?

I heard Gudrun – my flatmate, my oldest school friend, and a very nice person inside and out – turning the key in the lock. It was so loud and when the door closed, it felt like a prison cell door slamming, shutting, and locking. She walked up the stairs. THUD, THUD, THUD. I could hear her coming up the stairs. She dropped something down the stairs, and it crashed all the way down. 'ANNNNNNNNNNABEL?' she shouted out.

'Yes. Here,' I replied, trying to sound as normal as possible. But every sound I heard was somehow amplified.

Gudrun appeared at the door like a frightened little mouse. 'Are you okay?' she asked. It felt like she was saying it in slow motion and it was so loud.

'Yes, I'm fine. I really am. Thank you.'

'You know where I am if you need me,' she said. Gudrun and I had met in 1995 when we were little girls. We were both 11 and went to an all-girls school in East London. We became aware of each other because we both liked grunge music and bands like Nirvana and Green Day. We had dyed hair (which was definitely against the rules) and we had matching revolting plastic rings. We spent most of our teens hanging around Walthamstow market. We spent a few years of falling in and out of friendship over absolutely nothing. Books, boys, banter – there was always a problem. When there was booze involved, it was even worse.

However, I like to think it was inevitable that Gudrun and I would someday live together. We fell in love with our flat as soon as we saw it. There was one large kitchen as well as two huge bedrooms and two double beds. Everything was pink. The flat was perfect for recovering from hangovers. Never did I imagine that one day, my bed would turn into my sickbed.

When I found out I was ill, Gudrun was high up on my list of people to tell. But she had been away for two weeks when all this had dumped itself at my door. So the planned, rehearsed version didn't work out so well.

'My flight was delayed!' she said when she got home from her family holiday.

And I'd replied with the bad news.

My god. I always had to steal her thunder. Her big brown eyes filled up, and I knew that she wanted to cry. I'd never seen Gudrun cry, not once in all our time together. I wanted her to let it out, to cry and scream and shout about it. But she wouldn't. She held it in and was the loyal, brave, and kind friend that she always had been. Today, she was totally on the spot. She just ranted at me, but it was a good kind of ranting. Instead of how "I" was going to beat this, it was now "we" who were going to show this bastard what's what. I really appreciated it.

I sat on my bed with my laptop, checking my emails on Plenty of Fish. I had 13 emails waiting for me. One of them said, *Hi babe, you look HOT!*

He said I'm hot! Actually, I did feel some sort of heat in my body. I contemplated going into Gudrun's room to tell her.

No, I wasn't just hot. I was burning, and my face and feet were stinging. What could Gudrun do? Run me a bath? Put frozen peas on me? Call an ambulance? *No, I'm fine.*

I grabbed my hair. Thank god, it was still there. I felt hotter and increasingly tired.

I gazed at nothing, staring away into the distance. And then I fell asleep on my big bed.

I woke up and the room was not dim and cosy. It was hot, wet, and a really odd colour. I could see everything in yellow with black spots. I had a huge, horrendous headache. My chest felt bruised where my port was. My hands were clammy and my head was spinning, backwards and upside down on a roundabout, whirling into hell.

Maybe I had actually died, I thought at first. But no, I couldn't have been dead. If I was dead, I wouldn't have felt so awful.

I opened my mouth to retch. The sickness was starting, the morning after the night before, as though I was three months pregnant, or I'd had a bad curry. As if I had a disease. The sickness attacked me. And it wouldn't give up after the first time, wouldn't let me off that easily. Six, seven, eight, and nine times. I brought everything up. Hours later, I was hanging over the toilet. I felt slightly more in control in my head, but my body felt crazy, like someone had taken control of it.

Every time I recovered from one sickness episode, I calmed down. And then the grumbling in my belly started again. It was horrid. Over and over again. I started to panic. I needed to call Mum, Gudrun, anyone who could help me out of this situation. I turned my phone on and the light stung my eyes. The ringtone went off and a blurry name came up. I squinted at the screen, trying to read whoever this intruder was.

Uwann …

UwanTP …

Unwanted Phil

FUCK OFF, Unwanted Phil.

I finally managed to ring Mum. I just cried down the phone at her. Gudrun heard and walked in, sitting in the sick with me. It felt so degrading, but I was beyond caring. Gudrun didn't speak. She just sat there with me, but it was all I needed. Poor Gudrun. I had no clue what was going on, what time of day it was. Had she missed work to sit with me? I didn't know. But I knew I needed to leave. This environment was making everything worse.

Everything about the flat made me want to throw up again, made me want to cry. And it was so cold. We never put any money in the meter for the heater. The stairs were really steep, there was never any food in the fridge, and, even worse, there was only one bathroom which I was going to be sick in all the time.

'So come and live with me!' Mum said down the phone. I could just imagine Mum beaming. I knew she'd clearly wanted to say this before, but was waiting for the right moment. And there was no greater moment than this.

Pause.

I quickly tried to come up with an excuse.

I didn't know what to say. I knew what the answer was, but I couldn't admit it. I had worked so hard (or borrowed so hard) to finally live the life I wanted. I had my independence and I had my individuality. I loved my flat and everything in it. Okay, so it was a dump and we needed a cleaner, but it was everything that I had ever wanted!

'Your stairs are so steep and the doors are so heavy,' Mum protested.

'But it's my own flat and my own rules!' I said haughtily.

'But you need someone to look after you,' Mum cried.

'I want to look after myself!' I said, crying.

'I can look after you,' Mum pleaded.

'My life's going backwards,' I bawled.

'But Dorothy would love you home!'

I gave in and laughed. There was nothing else to do but laugh. If I hadn't laughed, hadn't tried to find some humour in it, I might have done something drastic ... like throw myself off those very steep stairs in my flat. Yes, I was losing my independence. But what independence could I actually have while being bedridden for a week, every three weeks? Being at home would be comforting. No matter how much I tried, my overpriced pokey flat would never be my real home, no matter what I did to it.

'We couldn't really afford to live here anyway,' Gudrun added. Negative, yet so true. The decision was made.

CHAPTER 10

FEELING UNWELL

I had prepared myself for the treatment, the appointments, the endless cycle of it all, but nothing could have prepared me for the paranoia that came with having this disease.

Karen would commonly wake up to an array of text messages from me, demanding to know my destiny. *Will I be okay? Will it come back? What will happen if* ... I was tormenting myself with these questions, but I needed to throw them at someone else, to just get them out of my head. I often turned to Mum – my number one, the one who had protected me from the second I was born – for mental strength.

When, aged nine, I fell off my horse during a lesson, she was there with a hug and a lift home in a warm car. When I had my adenoids taken out at the age of 10 and was on a fasting diet, she was the one who sneaked me in a Mars bar. And now, with me at the age of 25, she was the one who was holding my hand through these dreadful and terrifying appointments. I needed her reassurance. If she told me that something would work or it would be okay, I normally believed her. But not with this. None of us knew anything, really. We constantly said: 'Of course it'll be fine,' but we didn't actually know anything. And

I didn't want to disturb Mum's day with even more negative thoughts. She probably had plenty of her own.

I was still feeling rough. 'The sickness tends to last from day one to about day four,' The Judge had said.

It did not!

The sickness lasted from the night of my first session to the second I reentered the chemotherapy building, three whole weeks later. It was always there, always. And if it wasn't in my body, then it was on my mind. I was now officially, completely, utterly, very ill. I had been given some stronger medication which would "control the sickness", but it wasn't improving things.

Sometimes I felt so bad I would just lie on the floor, because it even hurt to move my eyes. Day after day would just be spent lying in bed. It felt so surreal; I would go from one morning through to the next without any awareness of time. I learnt to be able to tell the time of day without a clock, by noticing the different tone of light coming through Mum's bright pink curtains. It was a nice colour, and it comforted me sometimes.

I felt like I was slowly losing myself in time. I spent most of my day just occasionally walking to the bathroom and back to the toilet, if I could keep water down. The illness was constant, a wave of grey mist that took over my body and my mind, using me as a host. It took me a long time to get used to the lack of showers and the lack of human interaction, and to accept these things as normal. No matter how much I wanted these things, I couldn't do it. There was barely any strength left in my body – just about enough to get through it all. Death was like a person, and I could feel her hovering over me, threatening me. Mum would sometimes come into my room and offer me tea, water, soup, bread, company, conversation, and visitors. I rejected all of them.

There was only one thing I'd have: imperial mints. The ones you'd get at the end of a night at a restaurant with the bill. The first time

I had one, I was surprised to find that I could taste it; cold, sharp, hard, and minty. *I'm going to have another one,* I thought, which was another surprise. Two, three, four, five, several dozen later and my sickness wasn't as bad as it had been. I had found my cure! Well, chemotherapy was my official cure, but this was the cure to the cure.

Imperial mints. Worth their weight in gold, if you ask me....

On about day seven, I ventured into the shower. Mum pounced on the opportunity and suggested that we go for a lovely lunch at our local pub. Walthamstow Village wasn't really a village, it was more a row of middle-class shops that, over time, have become more interested in *The Guardian* and less in *The Sun.* Over time, our hometown gradually become wealthier.

Why not go out? I thought to myself. I still had my hair and my skin was in good condition. I just felt sick ... no one would know!

We walked through the streets, and it was all very bright and loud. That was the one word that I could use to describe everything: LOUD. The birds sounded like hawks, the cars sounded like fireworks. It was hard work.

We got to the pub and sat down. I was beyond starving. I had been given a huge quantity of steroids to help keep me strong. But my god, did they give me cravings! Looking at the menu, Mum made conversation.

'Lasagne? You love that. Or maybe a burger? Or something lighter like a ham sandwich?' I looked at the menu. All I could see were attractive words with hearts round them.

CHEESE

CHINESE

CAKE

CHOCOLATE

CARBS

CALORIES

The menu was incredibly appealing. I would have all of it, I decided. This was going to be good. I ordered a portion of fish and chips. For about half an hour we chatted, but it was really hard to have a conversation. Because this process had swallowed up my life. I literally had nothing else to talk about other than chemotherapy and the gruelling after-effects that came with it, feeling so bad that, at times, I didn't see the point in carrying on. I felt so overweight, filled with negative thoughts all of the time. I didn't have any plans other than appointments and at this moment, my friends were kindly hiding all of their positive news from me. Every so often, I would feel momentarily grateful that I was hopefully going to have a few more good years. But then the negative thoughts would return.

The only other aspect of my life I could have talked about (other than our dog, Dorothy) was my internet dating. But I didn't think it was a great time to bring it up, as it would just be another worry for Mum. As we talked about me going back to work next week, I drifted off and deliberately started eavesdropping on other people's conversation. Since my diagnosis, I'd noticed that my mood depended on other people and what came out of their mouths. Were their conversations in any way, shape, or form connected to me? Did it affect me? Were they thinking of me as they sat there? It had turned into an unintentional self-obsession. I listened to a nearby conversation that sounded half-appealing. It felt like *The Archers,* but in Walthamstow ...

'What time is he meeting us?' – A date, I decided, and all fine.

'I've got an awful hangover. Hannah's the same.' – Fine, I had a sort of hangover too.

'We out Tuesday, what you wearing?' – I wondered if it was revealing, and couldn't help but be a little jealous.

'Everyone's getting the train up there and we're getting the first train back in the morning.' – This sounded fun. I was jealous, slightly bitter.

'She got engaged on holiday!' – I was *beyond* jealous.

'Who wants a shot? Slippery Nipple?'

This was the straw that broke the camel's back. Nipple! What if you didn't have nipples!? I no longer had one of my nipples, and everyone in the neighbourhood knew it. I couldn't handle it. We had to get out of there. It was one thing talking about a self-inflicted side effect of drinking. It was another for Hannah to get boozed up on "Slippery Nipples" around me.

I suddenly felt a sharp ache in my head. I felt so angry, so filled with hatred for all mankind. Self-pity, anxiety, despair, and turmoil swirled inside me. I hated my non-adventurous, non-starting, imperial mint-chewing crappy life. And I just knew that it was only going to get worse; the more chemotherapy I had, the worse I was going to look and feel. I was never ever going to find a man. Ever.

'KILL ME NOW!' I screamed out loud. Mum stood up quickly, appalled, shocked, and upset.

'We are leaving,' she said. She looked mortified. And I felt bad. I knew that she cared, she was worried, and there was me shouting "KILL ME" like some sort of mad woman.

What on earth had happened to my life?

CHAPTER 11

Piling on the Pounds

Two chemotherapy sessions along, and my hair was still on my head. My eyelashes were slowly falling out, but I could live with that. Jordan had just brought out a new range of fake eyelashes and I needed them in my life. So what better excuse than my own falling out? *I might even be able to keep them for my victory celebration night out, after all this is over.* God, I couldn't wait for my victory night out. Karen and I had planned it already – the pre-drinking, the dressing up, the pubs.

Right now, what with the chemotherapy, I definitely couldn't get drunk (I could barely keep water down!) but I was looking forward to it anyway.

I was fat at this point. Not just fat – I was extremely huge. The steroids I was taking made me balloon, even with the little I was managing to eat and not throw back up. There was no way anyone could ever look at me and say I wasn't fat, not even to be polite. And if they did, I knew they were lying.

Karen came down to visit one day and we decided to go out into London. I felt slightly paranoid about how many pounds I had piled on. I felt nervous about going out in public, especially on the Tube. I had been advised not to mix with anyone while my immune system was weakening. But being who I was, I decided to do it anyway. I was young, I told myself, and I wasn't going to let this bastard beat me on the London Underground.

But maybe Walthamstow to Oxford Circus on a Saturday morning wasn't the best time to test my newly weakened immune system. I dressed up, made an effort, and made my way out. We got on to the train and chatted about our dating profiles.

Who was nuts? Which one was a prat? This one was a potential! What female celebrities were we like? Who didn't we like? Which men were fit and which weren't? We started chatting about TV. We skipped over the fact that this year's *Coronation Street's* special was going to be all about Sally Webster getting you-know-what. 'And did you know? She actually has it in real life!' someone at work had most unhelpfully told me one morning.

Someone around us started to cough, which turned into a splutter. I winced and tried to ignore it. I prayed that I wouldn't catch their cold, that my lungs weren't filling with the germs that I knew were all around me.

My head started to itch and feel hot. I pointed at my hair. 'Is it falling out? It's itching so much!' I whispered to Karen. She just shook her head and smiled. The coughing continued, but we carried on ignoring it. We approached Finsbury Park and then Highbury and Islington. We headed towards Oxford Circus, where we could actually get out and walk.

'Mind the gap!'

This train was packed. I was the lobster, the Tube was the pot, and there was no way out. We watched the passengers rotate around the seats. People very reluctantly gave up their places for elderly, pregnant, and one very obese woman. Why didn't the London Underground make chemo patients a priority? Why didn't it think about those with conditions that you couldn't see? I was going to write to them ... I was going to write a full-blown letter ... My angry thoughts were interrupted by a very welcome announcement.

'Oxford Circus!' We walked through Oxford Street on this calm, breezy, and warm day. The high street shops' windows were full of this season's colours – pinks and yellows, blues and whites. Pink had been my favourite colour until recently. But not any more. That was the sign for you-know-what, my rubber stamp that I was part of that gang. I had started resenting it.

We walked into Boots and down the aisles. There were green Macmillan banners everywhere for the awareness month. October. A red mist descended in my eyes and belly as I angrily pointed out to Karen, 'It's not a month. It's forever.'

'Yes,' Karen said, with the patience of someone who had heard this a thousand times before. 'But it is the month for awareness, to raise money, to keep the funding going to support patients and research.' Karen pulled me right back on track. I felt less angry.

There were stalls full of loud and shouty women in fancy dress selling cupcakes, with the song 'Girls Just Wanna Have Fun!' blaring. Why was Cindy Lauper suddenly the theme tune for you-know-what? Why would 'Girls Just Wanna Have Fun' be a good song for this disease, when we feel 100 stone and permanently sick?

If anything, they should have been playing Kylie Minogue! After all, she knows what the meaning is behind everything – she had it herself.

'And survived!' Karen said, finishing my thought for me. I couldn't stand being approached by these volunteers. I felt like they had point-blank picked me out in an identity parade and knew that I was the victim, the sufferer.

We quickly found the eyelash aisle and I tried to forget about the volunteers. I was surrounded by eyelashes of every length, texture, and size. And there, on an individual pink faux fur stand, bright as stars, we found them: Jordan's lashes. Karen and I bought matching pairs and carried on shopping along Oxford Street. I really enjoyed it, but I was exhausted by the entire thing. Karen suggested that we go into a high street retail shop to look for some new clothes for me. I knew what she meant by this, but she didn't say it outright because she didn't want to make me feel bad.

I had been dreading the day I'd have to venture out and find clothes that would fit my new body. I couldn't buy anything that showed an inch of neck, chest or cleavage (the cleavage that I definitely didn't have any more). So what Karen really meant was, 'Let's get you some clobber in a much bigger size.'

'Oh, don't try anything on, we can just buy it and return it if you change your mind,' Karen had suggested when we walked into the shop, saving me from the palaver of changing-room politics. Wandering around the aisles, Karen picked up hangers and did the head-to-the-side look on herself.

Over the next hour we chose three average tops, baggy smart blouses, and an over-the-shoulder one (the right-hand side, so it hid me beautifully) for when we would eventually go out. I felt so excited, happy, and confident. This was a step forward with my new look, body, and mind.

My bubble was short-lived. As we approached the till, I noticed that the 'Fashion for Cancer' campaign was all over the counter, aisles, and in the front rows of clothes. Why had we not noticed this before? I mean, for god's sake, there was a size eight model wearing a 'Fashion for Cancer!' vest top, and with ample amounts of cleavage! Not only did they have the audacity to put a thin model up there, but with a bouncy pair of beautiful breasts and nipples clearly on show!

I looked down at my own chest, feeling empty and flat. How would I ever be blessed with wearing a vest like that ever again? Even if I ever did get a reconstruction, they could never create anything near that. I would be ugly and scarred forever. No man would ever want me. I could understand the marketing campaign. No one wants to see an empty vest, and that top needed to sell. After all, it was women's clothing and it needed to be filled, by a woman with breasts. We all know that tits and sex sell. And the psychology of it goes beyond just that. What would a calf do if its mother cow didn't have any teats? The calf would be adopted by a worthier mother, who would be able to provide what that calf needed. The first cow would be useless. That's what I was – a useless cow.

And I looked like a failed fried egg, just without the yolk. My eyes filled up and I cried silently into Karen's shoulder. I couldn't fulfil the criteria for a woman any more.

We dumped the hangers on the floor and walked out of the shop.

This shop has to go.

CHAPTER 12

MAD NIGHT OUT

It was nearing November. I'd had a chemotherapy session the previous week and I was set to go back to my day job. After intense, serious conversations with my ever-so-concerned boss, we agreed, after a lot of persuasion from me, that I would be attending work where and when I could.

My family and friends really thought it was a bad idea, and I was given every opportunity to bail out of it. But I knew I was going to do it. I would be the one who worked while having chemotherapy. And I did it.

I needed a distraction from the reality of my life, and my social life wasn't cutting it any more.

My first day back at work came quickly. No one was looking forward to me doing this. Not Karen, not Mum, not my boss. But I really thought that I was ready for it. As I walked slowly up the high street towards the office, I suddenly remembered a girl at school called Kirsty who we all used to constantly take the piss out of.

She told us she was a fairy hunter, who caught the creatures and then rehomed them in trees. We bullied her, laughing at her while smashing her fantasies into small pieces. 'You're mad!' we used to shout at her at the bottom of the playground as she danced around the daises. It was only while being ill and making myself believe in a future, in positivity, and in my new-found religion of angels that I started to connect with the way Kirsty had been thinking. She wasn't mad. We were the mad ones for not believing in something more – for not finding comfort in something beyond the real world.As I walked in the office, I was in a dream world, knowing full well I had been advised against it by all of my medical team. I was in my "fuck you, I'm back to work" suit and I was here to stay.

I flounced in 45 minutes late (because I could) without even a glance at my shocked colleagues, who clearly were not expecting me back so soon. We exchanged pleasantries – nothing about the disease – and then I cracked down to business.

The current situation in hand was that we had five companies opening in 10 weeks, and we needed to recruit 40 managers. Piece of piss. This was me all over, my forte.

I quickly found that I couldn't walk in stilettos any more, even though my dating profile stated I could "run in heels". I felt off balance wearing them, so I shuffled along to my next interview and quickly removed my tiny kitten heels while hiding my feet underneath the desk. Candidate after candidate walked in and I really started to enjoy my day. I felt like a sense of normality had returned to my life; finding out more about other people, their lives, and their talents made me feel good. I even enjoyed having a big row with my colleagues about who we wanted to recruit and why. It was exciting. It was miles away from the rest of my life.

I was also secretly checking my phone every two minutes. I had about four men on the go (well, emailing them at least), and it gave me a thrill. I had mastered the art of having my bag open just enough to not be obvious, for the phone's light to be in my eyeline when each message came through. I felt naughty. And I had to admit, before I got this, I would never have dreamt of being so cheeky at work.

The last interview of the day came around and a young, inexperienced waste of time walked in. At first glance, her CV looked like it had been written by her cat, and within seconds I discovered she had a mouth that needed washing out with saline. *This isn't going to take long,* I thought. Even so, I gave her the chance to sell herself. She had no experience, no desire for the role, and absolutely no idea which company she was being put forward for – or even what they did. But it wasn't her fault. The agency who we worked with had misled her about the role. I felt like I was pulling my hair out as I sat there talking to her.

I felt an odd, soft ball come away in my hand as I scratched my head in despair.

Oh my god, I was actually pulling my hair out!

It was coming away from my head, roots and all. Very definitely not in bits, like the websites say. It didn't come out in tufts and little clumps, and definitely not in the shower either. My hair was falling out at my fucking desk! This was a disaster.

I didn't have a clue what to do. I didn't have my wig or my mum by my side.I gave the candidate a massive congratulatory smile, said, 'Well done, we will be in touch,' and got out of there quickly as I could.

*

'YES, IN HUGE CLUMPS ... WHILE IN AN INTERVIEW! IT WAS ALL OVER THE BLOODY FLOOR, I HAD TO HIDE IT UNDER THE TABLE!'

I couldn't stop shouting at my friend Theresa over the phone. The whole thing was madness.

Theresa was laughing, and I was too by this point. We all knew it was going to happen anyway, and I felt lucky that it had taken so long. Some people had said that it would happen straight after the first chemotherapy session, but I had my third coming up the following week. I sent a text to Mum – *Hair falling out, but I'm FINE with it. Staying at my flat tonight xxx*

Mum texted me back: *Love you xxx*

I was grateful for her short text. I really didn't want to have the conversation with her and worry her even more. It was Friday night and that meant one thing for Mum: a night of curry, gossip, and wine. Every Friday, Mum and her girlfriends took it in turns to host each other at their houses. It was their form of therapy, away from the chaos of their lives.

Theresa met me back at my flat and came into the sitting room. We sat on the floor and planned what we were going to do about my hair situation.

'Okay, so look,' I said, as I casually pulled a clump of hair from the back of my head.

'Wowwwwww!' Theresa said, very loudly and slowly. 'Madness.' She looked completely shocked. But that was fine. This was a stressful situation, and she was just being honest. I'd rather she did the whole reactionary thing than simply say it was okay and do nothing. 'Okay, so we have just one option. We need to cut it all off, don't we?' I said, admitting defeat.

'Yes, but first things first. WHISKY!' Oh my god. I was actually in love with her. She came here ready to get rid of my pride and joy, and she had brought some medicine to ease the pain. This was pure friendship, right here.

I really didn't know if I could drink. I considered it for half a second, and then ran back from the kitchen with two full pint glasses. 'Okay, here we go,' Theresa said hesitantly, her voice wavering a little.

'Wait!' I said, leaping up and knocking the blunt scissors out of her hand. I tried to ignore the fact that Mum had used the same scissors to cut Dorothy's hair.

Right at that moment, our song suddenly came on the CD player: 'Bulletproof' by La Roux. This was ours, we'd decided, when I first got diagnosed. We just kept listening to it over and over again, and it made us feel empowered and liberated. We played the song.

We drank the whisky.

Snip, snip, snip.

The song went off and one of us kicked it back on, finding it increasingly funny as the pile of hair next to us grew bigger and bushier. I found it surreal to think that my hair was on the floor, sitting there next to us like a dead dog. We swigged the whisky, sang along, and carried on taking my hair off, transforming me from a full-haired woman to a bald creature.

Oddly, it was just a really lovely situation. I was in crisis and my friend was there to help me through it. Devastating as it was to cut off all my hair, Theresa made it all so much fun. We just laughed all the way through it. Two hours later, half a bottle of whisky down, and with 'East London Beatz' FM on the stereo, Gudrun came in and shouted up the stairs with her usual public transport update: 'NO SERVICE FROM VICTORIA TO BRIXTON! I MEAN, WHAT AM I SUPPOSED ...'

She saw the living room, the mess, and then realised what we were doing. 'Oh, you did it!' she exclaimed.

'Yes, we did. And now we're going to get the wig and go on a night out!' Theresa said decisively.

'Are we? What if it looks fake?' I worried. 'What if it falls off?' Gudrun started petting me, attempting to comb the tiny stubble on my hairless head.

And then the wig went on. It was long, lustrous, pretty, and definitely not polyester. I loved it. It was like a permanent perfect hairstyle. All I needed to do was mess it up a little to make it seem more realistic. We spent the next hour admiring it. 'It's just like Jordan's!' we concluded.

Then it was decided that I was going to put on that dress. Karen and I had bought it, then discarded it, then repurchased it online: an orange, one-sided dress. I looked into our cracked full-length mirror to admire how I looked, with my well-fitted underwear and my concealed breasts that looked completely real. And there it was, right on the top like a star on a Christmas tree – my wig. It was shiny but not unnatural, long and black, and everything I'd wanted. I had a huge smile on my face – not the kind that I'd had when I was dying inside, but a genuine one. I felt like the old me and I felt ready to go out, to face the world with my new-found armour. Eyelashes on and whisky drained, we stumbled up the road laughing, shouting, and generally being excitable on a night out.

On the way, we passed Mum's house and made the instant, drunken decision to ring the bell and shout 'SURPRISE!' when she opened the door.

Mum's friends Glenda, Marie, and Sherry were all in the house. We walked into the kitchen where they had clearly been talking about me and my hair. They were looking straight at the top of my head, without even trying to hide their stares and gaping jaws. But the feeling in the room was pure happiness. Mum's eyes filled with tears as she looked at me, relief on her face. Maybe it was because this reminded her of my nights out before you-know-what, or perhaps it was because I seemed genuinely happy. Or maybe it was both.

We woke up the next morning, the three of us, all happy and relaxed. My new Jordan wig had lasted the entire night, but I certainly had not. We'd stumbled in a drunken state into a bar called Shots in Kentish Town, our favourite haunt. We'd danced and talked to randoms, and I'd made endless trips to the toilets to check my hair ... I still felt very self-conscious, even though I felt so good in my wig. I was also mindful that it could potentially fall off at any point, exposing my secret to everyone around me.

We kept an eye on it, and on every man who walked through the doors. I was waiting for my Mr Right to walk in and, though he never did, it felt just like old times.

In fact, everything felt normal. I had normal drinks, I did some normal dancing, and I had normal conversations with other people we met. I didn't talk about breasts or eggs or fertility or death. There was no mention of doctors or hospitals, and there were certainly no mental health problems. I spoke only of normal things, of TV and film and music and everything else but you-know-what.

And so the following morning, I felt utterly exhausted from a build-up of nervous tension and excitement. That, and from the chemo side effects.

We gossiped for what seemed like hours in bed, until we were interrupted by the doorbell. Oh god, who was it? Was my wig on? Was it straight?

A concerned voice shouted through the door.

'ANNABEL?'

It was Mum with Dorothy, of course. I opened the door and she stood on the doorstep, asking me questions.

'Yes, and then we got the night bus home ...' I said, answering Mum's millionth question.

'THE NIGHTBUS!? Jesus, you've just had bloody chemotherapy and you're on night buses in North London!' she said hysterically.

'Fun, though!' Theresa piped up.

'Fun? Don't you mean terrifying?' Mum shouted as Dorothy started to do a wee, right up the side of my car. 'You just can't be doing this while you're in recovery,' Mum scolded.

I began to feel a little frustrated. 'This is *my* life. And I'm trying to get on with it, living every day to whatever maximum I can. You know I'm trying to find a man, and don't need you to be putting your foot down on my fun!' At that moment I was struck with a terrible cramping in my stomach. I definitely couldn't reveal it, otherwise my argument would fall flat on its face.

'Annabel, you've had fun all your life. You just need to rest so that you can enjoy the rest of it,' she continued. 'Also, what's wrong with your stomach? Why are you crouching over like that?' Of course, she had spotted it immediately.

'All my life? I'm only a quarter of the way through it, remember,' I mumbled. I pretended not to hear the comment about the stomach pain, agreed with everything she said, and quickly said goodbye.

Dorothy stared at me straight in the eyes as she and Mum tottered off down the road. Dorothy had a swagger that made her look so in control, so know-it-all and obnoxious. It definitely felt like she was telling me off.

We went back inside and my phone bleeped. Seventeen Facebook alerts. *What?*

I had been tagged, my face named and shamed in every bastard picture, like in magazines when they put a red circle around a double chin. But this was worse. It was like a red arrow and cross, announcing my wig to the world! I couldn't believe my friends would do this to me. Yes, the wig looked fantastic in real life, but why oh why did they advertise it all over Facebook? For everyone to see?

I'd always hated and distrusted the intrusion of social media into our lives. It made stalking so acceptable. It was too easy to just go onto someone's profile and have a look to see what they're doing. And now I was a poor girl with a deadly disease, being body shamed

Facebook has to go. I deleted my profile that evening.

CHAPTER 13

SWOLLEN

'I'm feeling really awful, very bad. I get hot and cold at the same time,' I said, choosing to be entirely honest this time.

It was nearing December and this was my appointment with The Judge after my third chemotherapy session. I was finding things hard, and that was an understatement.

As The Judge continued to write down what I was saying, condemning me for all I knew, I carried on with my moaning, listing my problems and symptoms.

'Cold sores. Pain in chest. Heartburn. Aching bones. Stomach cramps. Headaches. Extreme sickness. Like five, six, seven, eight times a day unless I take my medication, and even then we're talking up to four times a day!'

'Which you should be doing,' The Judge replied without looking up.

'Yes, I know. I'm just telling you what's happening to me because I don't understand it.'

I hated The Judge. Every single time I was in there with him, he acted like he was superior to me. He never looked at me when he was talking, and he definitely didn't listen to me. 'Carry on,' he said.

'Cold sores ...'

'You've already said that,' he said without looking up again.

'And there's BLEEDING IN MY BUM!' I shouted at him.

His pen dropped.

We then had a long, detailed, and very frank conversation about the bleeding in the bum situation. Mum sat there very seriously, listening to everything.There was a pause.

'So where does the blood come out from?' The Judge asked.

Silence.

This conversation was officially now more painful than chemo.

At the end of this excruciating check-up, we established there was nothing wrong with my bowels. We also established that I had put on another nine pounds and that I had three more chemotherapy sessions to go. No one warned me that I was going to have a weigh-in club at the end of each chemo session. 'You have been rewarded for getting through hell by putting on another seven pounds!'

I was on steroids, and I was getting fatter each day. And here was a chart to prove it all. The only way forward was to get bigger and bigger.

We then waited to see my breast nurse about my acute paranoia, which was telling me that the strong aching pain in my surgery arm was something to worry about.

'My arm is really swollen and sore, and not just that, but it's double the size of the other one. Like there's something in there, something infectious, something lumpy and contagious and screaming to get out and kill me and—' I said to the nurse, only stopping when Mum gave me a look.

Apparently it was because I hadn't done my exercises. I'd ignored the advice offered to me previously and the pink booklet had inevitably been used as toilet training for the dog. We waited again to see another nurse who could answer all my questions.

I felt really stupid and lazy; how could I have not done my exercises? As a result of all of my lymph nodes being taken out, I had nerve damage, meaning the muscle needed to be rebuilt.

The longer I sat there, the more intensive the paranoia became. I started interrogating my mum. 'Is it really because of the exercises? Is it actually the you-know-what again? Is it in the blood? Is it in the BONES?'

'ANNABEL WALSH?' came the call.

Noreen, a beautiful Irish oncology nurse, as delightful as a flower and equally as graceful, called my name. And I was glad it was her. She had the power to turn a really difficult conversation into a happy one and just made everything really easy. I looked forward to my appointments with her more than anyone else I had met along this journey. She had a perfect face and manner. I wanted to be her. The first thing I noticed about Noreen was the lack of a wedding ring on her finger. Immediately, I started to question it. Surely, she had a partner, someone as lovely and pretty as her. *Maybe she's married but doesn't wear the ring to work.* I didn't know, but it seemed very important for me to know. 'You have lymphedema, which is caused by the removal of lymph nodes during your treatment. It's basically fluid retention, and it isn't really curable.'

'Phew, I knew it!' I said, smiling at Mum.

I felt bad for Mum. I tried as best I could to make her feel better about everything that was happening. Her normal life had basically ended when I was diagnosed, and I knew it was all because I didn't have a partner, someone to lean on for this. Part of my drive to find someone was to take the strain, pressure, and stress away from her. I wanted to take her pain away. But it was too late now; I could hardly expect someone to offer to come to my chemotherapy after the second date. Imagine! ...

I hated my appointments. It felt like there was a new problem every single time. If there was nothing wrong physically, it was something that felt very real in my head. This is why I needed a distraction, something which made me feel productive, worthwhile, wanted. And that thing was work.

After three months of my new routine, I was starting to get into the swing of things with my job. I was really enjoying doing something that I was actually very good at. Everyone was nice to me (well, at least those who dared speak to me), there was no pressure, and I felt like I was back in control. I consistently met all my targets, even with the absences in my diary, which everything had to be planned around.

'I can do the 10th, 11th, and 12th but unfortunately not the 13th, 14th, and 15th,' I'd say down the phone, and then wait as the person tried to fit themselves in around my hectic lifestyle. I wondered what I must have seemed like to them. Some kind of busy woman whose calendar was always filled with glorious things, perhaps?

People in the office often flung bemusement / amazement / bewilderedness at me. *This was what it must feel like to be a serial sickie at work,* I guessed. As the chemo went in, I started to feel like the bad things needed to come out, to disappear. It all had to go: all the anger, fear, negativity, disloyalty from people like Lauren, my hair, the retail shop that pissed me off. All of them had to go. I needed to get them out of my life.

My way of handling this was to deal with each aspect individually. If something just wasn't performing – be that a friend, a colleague, or just an aspect of my life I didn't like – I would get rid of it. Delete it completely, blacklist it. This really helped the way that I started thinking about everything: chemo in, bad stuff out. And the result? A nicer person with a healthier mind. Helen, my breast nurse – the original angel – had told me that this illness "changes you" and had pointed to her head. *Changes the mind?* I thought.

Well, that was my interpretation of it, anyway. And yes, my mind was changing. So were my decisions.

The winter months had started to come around and it was getting colder, the nights longer, and the mornings shorter. I was struggling with the side effects of chemo and had now fully moved back with Mum and Dorothy. I loved being at home in the winter; it was so cosy and warm and there was always food in the fridge, no matter what happened. I knew that I could come home after work, eat all the food I wanted, and spend all evening on my laptop, searching, searching, and searching for a man. To ease the pain from the chemo, I was taking up to six doses of co-codamol to try to numb the pain. It rarely worked for me after one dose, but it did after five. It became my routine.

Living at home also meant that after a chemo session, I would return to a warm, house and go to bed for a week, with Dorothy's head on my lap. Then I could work from home, searching for great candidates. Karen had also offered to come to my next three chemotherapy sessions with me. I'd almost bitten her hand off. At one point, I had considered going alone, but that was too ambitious and probably (definitely) not safe. It was decided; Karen would come with me.

There is a god after all, I thought. Now I had someone to take the pain away from my dear mum. She didn't think that at all, of course. She wanted to be there, to see it for herself, to be Mum. But I wanted her to have a break from this ghastly ward. I didn't want her to watch me become ill with every treatment. She had found out that her daughter had a deadly disease, cancelled her luxury holiday with her family, and had had to attend every single horrific, brutal appointment with me. I hated it on her behalf. I knew I could handle it, but I just wanted her to have some protection from it. Just for a while, at least. I dreamt of taking her to an appointment where it was good news.

'Annabel Walsh, we have your results and it's never coming back.'

God, if only.

*

December. Christmas preparations were well underway. London is truly beautiful at Christmas, whether you're in King's Cross or Knightsbridge. Every tree is lit, every pub is open, and everyone and anyone is out and about. It's the season of fun, love, health, and happiness to all men ... Wait, why is it just for all men? *That sentiment has to go.* I had endured a two-hour emergency meeting at work regarding our Christmas party. Where would it be? When would it be? Would wine be included on the table? Were husbands and wives invited?

'Er, hello,' I said. 'Some of us are under 30 and not there yet. Can it please just be colleagues?' There was a ruffle of papers, and some frustrated and unhappily marrieds shot me grateful looks. The decision was made. No partners. Thank god. I wouldn't have gone otherwise. And it wouldn't have been a party without me there, surely.

I made my you-know-what excuse and left because of a "persistent headache". As my dose was becoming more regular and habitual, the co-codamol wasn't working as well. I should have noticed it, but I'd been too busy. Actually, I should never have said I needed to go because of a headache. I should have said it was because they had been talking utter bullshit for the past two hours and I was starving. I wanted to go home because my niece was arriving that evening, and I couldn't think of anything better than just hanging out with her.

I got home and Polly and Poppy were in the kitchen with Mum and Dorothy. I was happy to be home. Poppy told me all her news, and luckily she didn't notice my wig. I had been anxious that it would affect her, but it was clear she couldn't tell, so that was a relief. I told them all about my awful meeting, the partners debate, and the excitement of Christmas and the party. They'd fallen on dates when I wouldn't be ill, so I'd be able to glam up and be there. Mum and Polly were excited about it for me. They agreed I'd have a great time. After dinner, I ran upstairs; I wanted to check my dating profile emails. Were there any potential dates to take? (Surely the no-partners rule at my work Christmas do could be changed at the last minute.)

I was interrupted by a knock at the door and Polly walked in. I felt that she had some sort of news, because she looked at me nervously and sat down on my bed. I instantly started to panic, thinking she was going to tell me she had something wrong with her. I was hit with dread, fear, and anxiety.

'Annabel, I'm pregnant again,' she said, in an excited but tearful way. She genuinely looked apologetic. I felt mixed emotions of delight and joy, but also extreme jealousy, anger, rage, and bitterness.

'I'm so happy for you! This is wonderful!' I said, and hugged her. I meant it. The creation of life, another child, a brother or sister to Poppy ... it was just wonderful news. And then I cried.

I was being so incredibly selfish. My sister was young and beautiful. She had a little girl and a partner and a house in Hastings. She was going to be a mother again. I realised my tears were about resentment. I wanted a life like hers. But maybe it could still happen.

I quickly hugged her and apologised for my extreme selfishness. I told her I was truly happy for her, but also felt so grateful that she had talked me into attending my initial IVF meeting.

We hugged and talked for a bit, and debated about the possible sex of the baby. Then we went back downstairs.

That's it, now I have to find my man.

CHAPTER 14

Empowerment

'I just need to find someone who lives in London, but not too far away from Walthamstow. Because on chemotherapy days, I can't really walk or travel. And I need someone who's a real man's man, you know? The type that holds the door open for you but then slaps your bum on the way out! I love Simon Cowell's arrogance, his attitude, but I also love David Walliams and his camp, feminine side act. I need a mix of the two. Maybe older. Yes, I think older. And someone who likes animals, because they need to accept Dorothy as part of the deal. I need a man who doesn't think Jordan's a dickhead. A man who wants to party, but also likes to have a takeaway every now and again.' I poured out my requirements to Karen like I was ordering food, like I was ticking boxes on a website before clicking "order".

'He's got to be tall. You're 5'8, so you can't wear heels and date a midget,' Karen pointed out very loudly on the train. It was my third chemotherapy session and we were on the way to Bart's. For some reason, when we looked around at that point, every single man around us appeared tiny. We got off the carriage and started to walk, before we offended anyone with our comments about small man syndrome.

We walked through the empty fish market, up the cobbled streets, talking about nights out we'd had where we'd struggled in heels on the pavements. We reached Bart's and I felt absolutely knackered. I was breathing deeply and Karen was looking slightly concerned. Declining her asthma pump and an offer of a seat on the bench, I carried on walking. My legs were now like jelly, wobbling, shaking, and hurting. The pain was so bad. I knew that we just needed to get in the lift and sit in that chair.

We were nearly there. I could see the silver doors of the lifts in front of us, and I imagined them with a huge bow around them, waiting to be unwrapped. We arrived at the lift. There was a sign on it:

OUT OF ORDER

'THIS IS SO OUT OF ORDER!' I shouted at Karen. 'THERE ISN'T EVEN AN APOLOGY!'

At this point, I felt like crying. This was definitely the worst-case scenario. Ward G3 was at the top of the building, with at least two flights of stairs. The walk to the top was an unbearable, relentless, forced, torturous exercise. But the lift was out of order and we had to walk, so we did, and I leant on Karen so much on the way up, I was surprised she wasn't broken herself by the time we got up there.

I felt so exhausted and sick that I was too angry to be angry vocally, which was probably a good thing. But this was not a good start. Karen looked equally as exhausted as we finally got to my designated chair.

The angels asked me their usual questions. I answered them all. The needle went in, the machine was turned on. I relaxed.

I sat back and closed my eyes. The ward was so bright that it didn't make any difference with my eyelids open or shut. It was painful. I tried to get to that place that relaxed my mind. But there was no Enya's 'Anywhere Is' to be found. It was so hard to settle in the ward. It was the hub and honeypot of this disease, and everyone in there knew it. The room smelt of it, sounded like it, felt like it. I've heard people say that their relatives have genuinely felt unwell after spending a couple of hours by the side of a patient. Headaches, nausea, dry mouth ...

I was also starting to recognise other patients by this point. I knew their names and their backgrounds. Who was with them this week? Who wasn't with them this week?

I also sometimes had discussions with other patients who told me they were going to die imminently. I never knew what to say whenever this came up, and I hated myself for being so useless.

I would chat with patients like myself who were going to continue their painful journey a bit longer. I never really knew what to say here either, because what else was there to say to that?

There were two groups – those who were going to die and those who believed they wouldn't die. I didn't know which one I belonged to.

It was so sad and unfair. It was hard to even believe it was happening. Sometimes I could meet someone here and instantly know their destiny. I'd get a sunken feeling in my stomach when I heard the words 'No, it's terminal'. The only terminal I had ever been faced with was that in an airport. But sometimes the poor person opposite me would tell me that their life was being taken away. When I first met a terminal patient, I instantly felt like I was dying with them. There were no words to be said, because the end was here. It had arrived, without really giving us much time to prepare for it, and now it wanted the world.

I respected, admired, and kind of loved every single one of these individuals. But I also pitied them, empathised with them, despaired for them. And I know they must have thought the same about me. There was a sense of community on the ward, to care for one another, to want for one another what we wanted for ourselves.

There were also conversations had between "insurance patients". These were patients like myself, who'd had the you-know-what removed from their bodies, but also had to have months of treatment to destroy any additional cells in the blood which could have been infected. Some of these people were also given Herceptin.

Herceptin was the ultimate insurance policy. It changed the cells so they were less receptive to cancer. It was there to make sure that we never got it ever again. I felt so grateful to be given it ...

Three sessions into my chemotherapy, I met a lovely woman called Audrey. She was a middle-aged Caribbean woman from East London who had been through this horror twice in her breasts. Outspoken and loud, she knew what she wanted and was very positive in life.

We were sitting next to Audrey and she smiled at me, showing a full row of gold teeth. She was also always writing. I really admired that. It was so therapeutic.

'What are you writing?' Karen asked Audrey.

'I'm writing some research about the cold cap,' Audrey said.

So "the cold cap" is the cap that's cold. Actually, it's fucking freezing. So much so that not many people want to endure an added layer of hell. There has been medical research to show that it prevents the hair follicles falling out during chemotherapy. But with that comes extreme and intense cold. I wasn't offered it and if I had been, I would have refused. My head had enough to deal with inside and out without that, thank you very much, and I couldn't bear the thought of any more pain and worry.

We didn't pass judgement on what she was doing; we just respected her wishes. She went on to say that she had been writing about the cold cap and that she, if asked, would encourage people to use it.

'What made you do this?' I asked.

'The first time I had cancer, I didn't use the cap. My hair fell out and I felt ugly, and I didn't feel like a woman any more.'

'Awful,' I said, trying not to think about the stubble on my own head.

'But now, I have used the cap and less hair has fallen out,' she said. 'My own husband doesn't even know I got cancer again!'

Karen and I were shocked. 'Audrey, how on earth?!'

'What he don't know don't affect him,' she said, as though it was as easy as that.

What an incredible woman. She had a husband, and protecting him was more important than relying on him for support. That is love. I adored this woman, every single part of her. *Maybe I don't need a man,* I thought as I sat there by her. *This woman has one and is looking after him, not the other way around.*

'I DONT WANT A FUCKING BANANA!' came a shout, interrupting my thoughts.

That was Ernie, a moody cow who always had something to say to someone. Admittedly, the tea lady was impossible to communicate with, and was always the centre of attention on G3 ward. There was some sort of altercation happening.

A clever patient only worsened the situation. 'Ernie will only have a straight banana.'

'FUCK OFF, CAROLE!' Ernie shouted back.

'NO, YOU FUCK OFF, YA COW!'

The word "fuck" was shouted out over and over again. It was so undignified in this situation. It was like a dog in a restaurant – completely unwanted. I wished they would stop. But it only got louder and louder.

Oh Christ, there was actually going to be a punch-up on the chemo ward. How odd. What if one of them killed the other?!

Whatever happened, we never made eye contact with Ernie. Never, ever. It made her feel on edge if you happened to glance in her direction. And if Ernie felt uncomfortable, my god, she would let you know.

I had forgotten to tell Karen about Ernie, who was now staring at Karen.

'AND WHAT DO YOU WANT, DARLIN'? LOOKIN AT ME ALL FUNNY!' Ernie hissed over at Karen.

I had to step in. 'It's alright, Ernie, this is my friend, Karen. She just wanted to read your magazine.'

"ERE, 'AVE IT THEN!' Ernie shouted and suddenly a copy of *Grazia* flew across the ward right into Karen's lap. Maybe Ernie should have tried her hand at basketball.

'Never stare at her again!' I hissed. Ernie was harmless really, but an absolute liability.

Karen flipped through the pages of the magazine and then ripped out a picture of Gareth Gates. 'This ward needs livening up a bit!' she said mischievously. Oh god, what was she going to do?

She then shoved the topless model on the wall chart for the whole of the ward to view. Funny, but highly inappropriate. The clock was on, time was ticking, Ribena lowing right into me. And all I could see was Gareth Gates's abs staring back at us all. The more I squinted at him, the smaller he looked, his abs poking out. *That's a symbol of fitness, to have a six pack? But why having your ribs on show make you fit?* I realised I didn't fancy Gareth Gates, which was a good thing.

'And who's that older woman over there?' Karen asked, trying to be discreet and failing. The elderly, five-stone, wasting away patient smiled at us.

'Bernice, meet Karen.'

'Hi Karen, what do you have?'

Karen looked confused.

'Oh, no, no, no!' I said quickly trying to rescue the situation, as patients always welcomed newbies. I could see how this situation might develop and possibly offend someone. 'She's come with me, for support.'

'Oh, like my daughter,' Bernice said, smiling back proudly. 'There she is now.'

A young, small, frail, double vision of Bernice shuffled in, wearing slippers and a gown. She walked up to her mum, kissed her on her forehead, and sat down on a treatment chair. 'She can't sit there, she's going to get moved,' I panicked to Karen through gritted teeth. The double doors opened and the four high-pitched angels ushered themselves in, along with their trolley and laptop.

'What's your age? What are you being treated for? Which treatment is this?' the angels said to the young girl.

Bernice's daughter replied, 'I'm 19. I have terminal lung cancer ...'

CHAPTER 15

SICK LEAVE

This horrible illness happened through all seasons. It didn't know or care which holiday it was ruining. Because it was December, the big double doors to the ward had been partly decorated with red and green tinsel, just to keep everything festive. I didn't know if this was appropriate or not. But my god, there must have been some health and safety risks.

We had to divert our attention away from my illness and talk about safe topics, as we were all getting seriously depressed. This was making me (and Karen apparently) feel more ill.

'So, do you think I can find a man like the one I described?' I asked, changing the conversation.

'No, probably not. But I need to tell you about Kieron. He's been messaging me for two months, asking to meet up. He's tall, good-looking and keen to meet. Not just up for a one-nighter either,' she said very loudly. Her voice was booming through the room.

I cringed and hunched down in my seat, finding comfort in the hard, cold packet of co-codamol stuffed in my jogging bottoms. It was like a security blanket. The room was so quiet and really, this conversation just shouldn't have been happening – especially on this ward. But we continued, a little bit quiet this time. 'Go on,' I said, apprehensively.

'So yes, Kieron texts and asks to come over ...' she says, drawing the sentence out.

'Okay.'

'So he arrives at 8.00pm on the dot, dressed up really nice. He's wearing a smart shirt and a pair of pressed trousers and looks so handsome!' She paused, maybe for some dramatic purpose. 'He has a bag with him, which I didn't really pay any attention to. We flirt, I cook, and we have some wine ...'

(I started to feel sick at this point, imagining the red wine. It reminded me of the Ribena-like medicine in my chemo machine ...)

'So then he says he wants to ask me to do something really special with him!'

'Oh my god, what?' I asked, knowing I was about to hear something good.

'He opens the bag and points to a BUCKET AND A TUB OF CUSTARD. And HE WANTS TO POUR CUSTARD OVER MY HEAD WHILE I MASSAGE HIS FEET!'

I was silent for a second, as I took in what she had said. And then I burst out laughing. We were both in uncontrollable hysterics. This was a true story, and she was talking about it at the top of her voice in a bloody chemotherapy ward. How could this situation be real?!

We spent the next two hours – while I was being given my insurance policy (Herceptin) – going through my Plenty of Fish profile. I emailed, deleted, replied. Thank god this ward had free Wi-Fi. They really had thought of everything. We spent the next hour after that trying to convince the tea lady that we really needed another sandwich. And then, when we admitted defeat because she was never going to give in to our demands, we started researching Farringdon to see where the nearest Maccys was.

We got told off for being too loud and were moved to another bed for the second half of the treatment. My eyes started to hurt and I couldn't look at the phone screens or the lights any more. It was so bad. Karen lay on the bed next to me and put her iPod on.

After a little while my sense of humour started to come back, and the pain started to leave. We danced in the bed, laughing and planning a night for New Year's Eve. We felt like we were naughty girls at school, having been sent to the headteacher's office for doing something bad.

Finally, we left. I stumbled out of the ward and we hailed a cab. We tried to stay silent throughout the journey, but the cabbie kept making irrelevant conversation. He talked about London, traffic, football. I didn't care.I felt so sick. And to make matters worse, he had abandoned the main roads and now he was going through every back road, street, and country lane to get back to Walthamstow. We went over what felt like a thousand speed bumps. Every time we were raised in the air, I felt sicker.

But I tried to smile, because today had been fun. And I knew I could get through this journey, at least with Karen by my side.

We pulled up outside my house, all lit up and cosy. The walk to the door looked completely impossible. But I did my best to look at my friend, to show Karen I was grateful for her time with me, that everything was fine. Karen waved at me as she left for her journey back to Brighton.

Later on that night, I woke up in my usual daze. The aching in my bones was getting worse and the pain in my horrid, chubby, and swollen arm was terrible. But I was slowly getting used to the rest of the post-chemotherapy symptoms. I began to wonder what it would feel like to wake up pain-free, and when that would happen again. I couldn't wait for an actual hangover, something that I had done to myself. I could smell something in the air. A toilet-like smell.

Could it be poo? Oh Christ, I think I've actually shat myself. I couldn't bear to look down. How could this be? I was 25, recovering from you-know-what, and I'd just shat myself in Mum's house, on her John Lewis cotton sheets, on her iron bed frame in her Laura Ashley-style room. I couldn't believe it.

I opened my eyes, squinting. They were throbbing with pain. Dorothy was staring back at me, and there was a look in her eyes. *She'd* pooed in my room! This could not be happening! I sat bolt upright. 'DOROTHY!' I screamed.

She scuttled out with her nose and bum in the air. My phone beeped and then rang, the sound like bells in my ears. *Who on earth could that be?* I needed to vanish. I needed carpet cleaner. I was definitely going to be sick.

My friend Ciera had texted. *Hi, still on for tonight? See you for dinner at mine at 8.00pm?* I really didn't want to go. *I need an excuse,* I thought, as I headed into the bathroom and applied two sets of false eyelashes. My stomach cramps had worsened overnight, and the pain really was quite bad. I started to write out a text to Ciera, making up a reason for not going. I sat on the toilet.

Knickers down.

I weed.

I looked down.

Red spots.

BLOOD.

The cramps were period pain! Not chemotherapy pain! My period was here! I could have cried with happiness. I was well and truly poisoned with chemotherapy by this point, and my body still understood that I was a woman who would want to try to conceive one day, when all of this was over. I had never been so happy before to see my period blood in the toilet, to experience the specific type of stomach cramps that came with it.

I went downstairs and shared the news with Mum and my family, who were equally as happy. My body was normal. And that meant the world to me.

I deleted the cancellation text to Ciera and had a lovely evening with her, eating and drinking and laughing.

I got into bed late, exhausted but happy. I was quickly woken back up by my mobile.

Beep.

Message from Plenty of Fish

(I sure as hell could be bothered to read this!) *Hello, fitty!* I thought.

Andy, the six-foot-one postman from Kent, just around the corner from me, had got in contact.

A couple of days went by and I established over email that this guy had no kids, no ex-wife / girlfriend / boyfriend, he didn't own a snake (my fear) but did own a car. I wasn't sure about the posty job just yet, and how that would work with my schedule, but hey, I had an open mind. Just like Plenty of Fish had told me to. We agreed to go on a date in a few days, just before Christmas....

'THE WEIGHT WILL FALL OFF YOU AFTER YOU'VE RECOVERED!' Mum shouted at me.

I was standing in Mum's room, looking in the full-length mirror. I was three stone heavier than five months ago, my wig almost too small as my head seemed to have expanded, and I had no eyebrows or no eyelashes. I was fat, hairless, and knackered. Today was December 20th. It was my 26th birthday and my mum, my friends, and I were going for a meal to celebrate. I was dreading it. Everyone was going to look gorgeous and there I would be, bitter in the corner, eating my weight in meat and cake. But I was also really happy about my birthday, because who knew if I would even get another one?

I thought about Mum's encouragement about my weight and thought about her coming home from work, watching me eat myself alive. Sometimes I would feel so sick, I would go to Tesco Express and just buy packets of cakes and biscuits, all of them for me. I just wanted to fill the painful empty hole inside me. It genuinely made me feel better. I don't know, maybe it was the sugar rush, or maybe I felt so bad about myself I just had to fill myself up on goodness. Whatever was going on, I was getting fatter and fatter and fatter. I could barely recognise myself in the mirror.

The weight has to go. Later that evening, we all walked down to a lovely restaurant in Walthamstow Village: me, Mum, Glenda, and her daughter Alexandra. And of course, Marie, Mum's best friend, had to be there. We talked about their children, their work, food, wine, TV, anything. And you-know-what was completely forgotten about.

And to make matters even better, my date with the postman was coming up. It was going to be on a Sunday. Sundays are definitely not drinking days. Sundays are days of rest, days of Ikea shopping, and roast dinners.

I pulled on my old reliable Topshop one-shoulder dress, conditioned my wig, and put on my Jordan eyelashes. I had got this down to an art form now. And I had to admit, with the eyelashes, I even looked half-decent.

'You look GORGEOUS!' Mum said, slightly hysterically. I had told her a small lie about where I was going. I said I was meeting Dad for some food. It was believable. Food, Sunday, Dad – it had always been the same since I could remember.

I drove down the A406, one of the busiest roads in London. The road of dreams: Ikea, McDonalds (don't tempt me), Carpet World, Next, Pets at Home.

That's where we were meeting. It was his suggestion, the Pets at Home car park. Classy, romantic, and totally one of a kind.

As I parked up, I realised I wasn't nervous in the slightest. That might have something to do with looking death in the eye.

I got out of the car and saw him straight away. He was alright-looking and very tall.

'Alright, babe?' Postman asked. He was cockney, and it was like he was doing a Vinnie Jones impersonation.

'Yes, good, thanks, pleased to meet you,' I said, in a fake voice.

'Yea, I'm thinking we go down the hannnns,' he said, drawing the last word out so much that I could barely understand what he was saying.

'Okay, how about the hannnnsssss?' I said, imitating the way he was speaking, so I didn't look like an idiot. I had no idea what he even meant.

Why was I speaking like this? No, actually why was he speaking like this? It was incomprehensible! It's nothing to do with being from East London or cockney or any of that. It was just laziness, and I was far too tired for that. He had already pissed me off and we were only just leaving the car park. And also, I couldn't help but wonder if he had noticed my wig.

'You mean The Hounds?' he said, smirking at me.

You've got nothing to smirk about, you bastard, I thought. *If you had pronounced that word properly the first time I wouldn't be standing here trying to figure out your lack of articulation.*

I needed to get out of this mood. I could not be pissed off with him. He had done nothing wrong! I needed to calm down. Why was I so angry all of the time?

We walked to the pub and he talked all the way, about his car, football, and interestingly his ex-"bird". My ears pricked up at this point. I really wanted to know what she looked like. It was like a hunger inside me. Knowing what she looked like would tell me if looks were important to him, what kind of people he was into, what kind of women he was into. But he didn't give me a description of her and if he did, I probably wouldn't understand it anyway. This was turning into a long bloody walk.

'OIIIIIII ROY! OIIIII ROY!'

He shouted so loudly across two lanes of traffic, I screamed in fright and my fake Mulberry fell off my shoulder. My phone, keys, wallet, and all of those pretty important things started rolling under cars. I got on my hands and knees to search for them frantically. I couldn't lose my keys. How the hell would I get out of this dump? I couldn't not have my phone. What if I needed to do an SOS? I could live without my wallet, so I was willing to let that go. But not my phone!

'How are ya, you fackin ol' prick!' he shouted again at a man who I presumed was Roy.

I couldn't bring this "man" home to Mum, my dear grandparents and to Dorothy! What would they think? He and Roy had a brief, but loud, conversation, and then we got to the pub and sat down. I then started to talk (interview) him.

I asked about his background (he didn't get this and started talking about last night "with the boys").

I asked about his job (I got bored listening to him talk about his rounds).

Did he live at home with parents? (No. Oh, that was hopeful.)

Where did he go and what did he do in London? (He gave a list of things I didn't care about.)

What were his other interests? (They were the inevitable – beer, birds, and booze again.)

We went silent. Mute. I had run out of things to ask him. I waited for him to ask me a question, just one. I waited and waited. I could have broken this awkwardness with something, but we had been here for an hour and he was supposed to be the man. In caveman times he'd have to provide the meat and feed me. But instead he lay there while I hunted and fed him. I couldn't take this silence. What was he thinking? Could he be looking at my wig, trying to figure out what was wrong with it? Was he wondering why I was so damn fat?

He suddenly leant forward and his large hands and massive fingers went towards my hair. 'WHATYOUDOING?' I squealed. I jumped up, thanking my lucky stars he had not pulled my wig off. A few of the locals turned around to see what all the fuss was about. I bet they were hopeful that it was all going to kick off.

'Calm dahnnnnn, girl. Just gonna pull a pound out from your ear! It's me party trick!'

He has to go. And he felt the same clearly. We both made our excuses and left. We walked back to our cars in a welcomed silence and said goodbye to one another. There was no follow-up date mentioned, no talk of texting one another afterwards. We both knew what the other was thinking, but no one needed to say it.

I got into my car and turned my phone on, to be greeted with a text message from Bernice.

At 7.00am that morning, Bernice's daughter had died.

CHAPTER 16

GRATITUDE

'But it's not fair. She didn't deserve to die. She was only 19. What if it happens to me? What if it comes back and kills me? I would rather be dead than go through this again.' I was wailing at Mum, while lying wigless on her bed. It was a few days past my 26th birthday. And it was fair to say that we'd had the year from hell. However, good things had happened too. I had got rid of you-know-what. I had made friends and started to sort my life out, very slowly.

But I needed to sort out my mood. I felt sorry for my poor mum. She had woken up to Dorothy barking her head off and me trampling up the stairs, throwing myself onto her bed, like a little girl wanting the tooth fairy or Santa to come. What if it just wasn't worth it? The hours, days, and months of treatment? Years, with the Herceptin thrown in. I couldn't stand the constant references to my age, the sideways glances from other patients, the continuous relaying of yet more bad news to my poor mum.

I couldn't take much more of this. I'd had enough of Mum spending her life between working and watching her daughter deteriorate. I'd had so many emotional breakdowns in front of her. It must have been horrible. Is there anything worse than watching your child be told they might die? Watching them crumble every day? Never knowing what news might be around the corner just waiting for them?

I didn't know how she found the energy to tell me everything would be okay, to tell me that I would get well again. I couldn't believe what had happened. I was shocked. I sobbed in bed, my cheeks on fire. I needed a break. I couldn't have a break from chemotherapy; that just wasn't an option. But maybe I could just have some time off work. I spoke with my boss and decided that I would take some well-earned sick leave. I shouldn't have been working. I should have been at home resting, doing anything to make myself feel better.

'I think that's a very good idea,' was the general consensus from Mum, Dad, my sister, Karen, Theresa, and Granny.

'Makes total sense to me. You've gone through so much, all of which is just so incredible!' my boss had said. I was pleased with his response. And yes, he was right, I had done the unthinkable – I'd survived chemotherapy.

'Christmas is always dead,' Carl said. 'January … well, that shouldn't be too busy,' he said, lying through his teeth.

Everyone who works in recruitment knows that January is not pretty busy. It's gridlocked chaos. Everyone who gets fed up of their job drowns their sorrows over the Christmas period, and as the New Year countdown starts, they decide that they hate their jobs. On "TEN" they start wondering what they should do about it. By "THREE … TWO … ONE … HAPPY NEW YEAR!" they've decided to hand their notice in!

January was going to be busy, guaranteed. However, this wasn't my problem. 'The door is always open, come back when you're ready,' the whole team had said. Good. What a relief. One less stress. Work didn't normally stress me out. It wasn't usually something that I needed to escape from.

But over the next few days, I slept, recovered, slept again, and thought a lot about poor Bernice and her daughter. I sent Bernice multiple messages of support and talked with my family and my friends. Seeing Bernice and her beloved daughter really made it all hit home: the importance of the connection and the bond between mother and child. Nothing can replace it. I was alive and kind of well, and I needed Mum to know how I felt. She needed to know how grateful I was for everything that she had done for me.

Mum and I had a long, overdue chat about the small things – and also about the bigger things. Up to that point I hadn't taken stock of everything that had been happening. I sat and spoke to her and I still couldn't say everything I wanted. I just knew that it would hurt too much, and I wouldn't be able to get the words out.

So I wrote her a letter and left it for her on her bedside table. I thanked her, not just for being my mum but for everything she had done for me on a minute-by-minute basis. I knew that she hid bad news from me. For example, friends and relatives were also getting ill and then dying, and she kept that all to herself, keeping the pain close to her chest so that I didn't have to suffer through it. I thanked her for buying me special button-up pyjamas to wear after my mastectomy. I thanked her for relaying my medical news to everyone throughout my chemotherapy. I thanked her for sitting through countless appointments, absorbing the news, good and bad, and paying for the cab on the way home. I wanted her to know that I recognised every single gesture she made, putting me and my health first throughout everything. All I could do in return was protect her. I didn't tell her how lonely I felt, even with loads of people around me. And I didn't ever tell her how scared I was of dying. I shared only my happy moments with her, like my night out wearing a wig.

Mum cried when she read my letter – and that said it all to me. She had needed it, perhaps even more than I'd realised.

But I needed to change my attitude. I needed to stop the anger, the hate. I had to stop doubting everyone and everything, and just try to be happy. I didn't have you-know-what any more. I was clear. All this treatment was just a precaution. As far as the records went,

I was healthy, so I should have been happy. Life is meaningless without the relationships we form, and I wanted to embrace this. I didn't want to spend every waking minute arguing, complaining, and thinking about what could happen. I'd deleted my Facebook profile because my friends wanted to share happy pictures, including ones of me. Instead of seeing it as love, I saw it as a battle, as an attack against me. I started wondering why I was looking for love when I had so much of it around me. My friends and my family. Even Dorothy loved me ... sometimes.

Yes, people had pissed me off. But maybe my constant, selfish, negatively charged mind pissed them off too. People were there for me, with cards, letters, text messages, emails, phone calls, messages passed on full circle, and presents in the post. Mum's sister-in-law had sent me a woolly hat and scarf "to keep me warm while having my chemotherapy during the winter months". My sister's partner had sent my sister a music video with birds flying in the sky, to calm her down when she was feeling low. When *she* was sad about everything that was happening to me. I hadn't even thought about how all this was affecting her, with her second child on the way.

And then there was my wonderful granny, who'd had you-know-what and recovered at a time when the treatment wasn't available. 'I know that you'll be fine,' she'd told me as she ate another Kit Kat, her favourite. Whenever she would have a Kit Kat, she'd always would repeat a funny story about her cleaner having a special relationship with their Irish terrier, Blue. He was a red, beautiful, fierce, and loyal dog. And he loved Betty, their cleaner. 'Turns out, Betty was feeding Blue the Kit Kats on her coffee break!' she'd end the story with. Every time she told it, it made me laugh.

The note I had written Mum was cherished and carried around with her every day. It made me feel happy and sad – happy that I'd done it, that she carried it around wherever she went and that she could read it whenever.

But I was sad that I hadn't sent it sooner....

It was now the full-blown Christmas season. Everyone had the Coca-Cola advert, cinnamon-scented candles, "buy everything with a price-tag" mentality. I loved Christmas.

We had a really nice time as a family, even though I was feeling so rough and everyone knew it. We looked forward to a year of better things to come. The food was the same as always, but I ate more than usual, filling myself until I felt like I was going to burst. Everything just felt good, with the presents and the love and the company. We even had a Christmas argument about my sister talking the whole way through the *EastEnders* Christmas special and hogging the cheeseboard. We all felt really passionate about watching *EastEnders* as the Christmas episode was always brilliant, bringing together storylines from weeks and months past. To talk through it was almost a sin in our house!

New Year's Eve had always felt like a bit of an anticlimax. But I knew that this one had to be slightly different. 2009 could well and truly do one. I wanted to give birth to a 2010 that glittered and shone.

We made last-minute plans, complained about the extortionate prices. We looked forward to the crowds and the outfits. Deciding what to wear was always the biggest drama. I'd had a mastectomy. I'd had fertility treatment and a port inserted. There'd been five sessions of chemotherapy and Herceptin, and I only had one more to go. It was like the 12 days of Christmas, but the 12 stages of you-know-what instead.

I had really been suffering with pain in my bones and the swelling in my arm was getting worse, but I was absolutely determined to have a good new year. I knew that I didn't want to spend New Year's Eve in London. I wanted to spend it with Karen in Brighton, and I knew that would be far better. So I travelled up to stay with her. We literally spent two days getting ready, swapping terrible dating stories and planning our big New Year's Eve night out.

We were naughty and always had a bit of attitude when we were out, a defence mechanism to hide the fact that we were self-conscious and perhaps a little nervous. We always had our guards up. We were very similar like that. We couldn't always have our own backs, but we always had each other's. Our protective approach was simple, but men hated it and only saw it as aggression.

My own aggression was getting worse as time went on. I'd had five months of chemotherapy and I was at my limit. My sister's baby was due in a matter of months and I was so excited, but I didn't have the energy to show it. I kept writing to her and sending my niece Poppy presents, to try to show them I was always thinking of them. Having endless conversations about how I felt had started to make me feel guilty, because it was *always* so negative. I had no positive news to share, other than the countdown until my treatment would finish.

I'd gone out an awful lot as my chemotherapy sessions had continued. And not just for a few drinks either, but for many. When I could hack it, I would go out, join in with all the girls and let my (fake) hair down. It went against all the advice of doctors. But actually, if alcohol made me feel better and forget my next appointment then fine, I'd do it. But sure as anything, I didn't tell anyone other than the people I went out with exactly how much I was drinking and how often. They would have been mortified.

'Right, it's New Year's Eve and it's good luck to contact men on New Year's Eve,' Karen said. She was getting more obsessed with Plenty of Fish than I was. It was inevitable. When we liked something, we loved it, and when we loved something, we obsessed about it. It took over, became our life. And the same went for internet dating. We were now one of those "device gangs" – people who were constantly on their devices, logging in to whatever free Wi-Fi they could find and turning themselves off to the rest of the world. We now knew more local free Wi-Fi hotspots than actual names of places.

Karen and I spent the entire Saturday putting on different wigs, make-up, outfits, and, of course, high heels. Karen had suitcases full of them. She just loved buying shoes. She had pairs and pairs of six, seven, eight-inch heels that we would never have otherwise dared to wear in public. But we just had to get that "money shot" – the profile pic that would deliver us our dream.

As we slowly drank our rosé wine, I had to admit that getting dressed was becoming easier. I could lift my arms above my head now. But more than that, I could now look at myself in a mirror and not cry, not miss the person I had been before.

Now that I'd had time to grieve my old body and accept my new one, I felt more used to it. I didn't feel like a teatless cow. I felt more like a formed woman. I felt that, with very good filtering, editing, and make-up, I could look borderline sexy. So we uploaded pictures onto our profiles and refreshed our inboxes every two seconds.

'Hmm, what do you think of him?' I asked Karen. Someone I hadn't noticed before popped up. 'I think he's new on here.' Between us, we knew who was on there within five miles. We even knew who had set up new profiles under different names and photos. And on a good day, we could identify which men had contacted both of us at the same time. Then there was the odd, awkward occasions whereby we would stumble over a colleague from work or one of our friend's boyfriends. But apart from that, it was all fun!

So, this profile. I needed to have a look. I had lots of questions halfway through the first sentence of the profile so I went into recruitment and interviewing mode. *Saddler Sam – why saddler? Hi, I'm 23* (too young), *6'8* (doubtful) *and in the army* (sexy!). *I love my job and I'm looking for someone potentially for a relationship* (tick). *I love the countryside and the outdoors* (not really my thing) *and also enjoy going out and socialising* (very generic, but important). *Living in London* (tick but whereabouts?). *Non-religious* (tick). *Please message me if you're interested.*

I looked at the pictures:

1. Headshot – *good-looking, nice bright blue eyes!*
2. Standing up – *He's tall, really tall. He can't fake that, because he's next to a tree and the branches are at shoulder height. That's good.*

'Go on, open the rest!' Karen encouraged me.

Loading, loading, loading …

3. Saddler Sam on a tractor … *On a tractor? What does that mean? I thought he was a soldier? Why's he dicking around on a tractor with a serious face? He might be lying about being in the army …*

Karen did her pitch. 'Look, it's fine. You like the description, you like the profile. He's an okay age and he's tall. Just message him!'

I'm not sure.

'Hang on a minute …'

Picture 5 was loading … loading … loading … loading …

Oh. My. God.

It was him and Jordan! Him and Jordan! *It's him and JORDANNNNN. My ideal, my number-one woman, the business! We were the same!* He loved Jordan and I loved him! Well, not yet. I could barely believe it. True as you like, Saddler Sam was sitting next to Jordan who was sitting on a horse. But wait. Was that his horse? Was that *her* horse? Did he know her? In what capacity did he know her? Could I get to know her? Was she his ex?

I read the caption underneath … "Me n Jordan LOL." (Not grammatically correct, but that could definitely be excused.) "LOL" – I detested this word. It's awful.

'Shut up and stop nit-picking. Message him now. He's online,' Karen said, pushing me.

I started to type and suddenly lost all my words.

Message to Saddler Sam – *Hey, how are you? I'm Annabel. You look nice!*

Wincing at my terrible message and shutting the laptop, we left the flat, walking into the night, forgetting about it for just a few hours.

CHAPTER 17

10, 9, 8 ...

> Who is Katie Price?
> Dad

Wig on. Chest covered. Legs out. It was New Year's Eve and we were buzzing. We opened the door of Karen's flat and tottered down the steep steps. The view was just beautiful – dark skies, glistening navy-blue sea, and stars everywhere. I'd been told to thank them a lot, and so I did that night.

We waited for our cab, got in when it came, and inevitably interviewed the cab driver all about his life. Was he doing overtime for work? What about his kids? Wife? Family? What did he have for dinner? He loved it, answering all our questions like he was on a chat show. And we had fun, just being us.

We got to the heart of the town centre and went into one of the busiest, dodgiest, chaviest clubs in Brighton. But we had so many good memories there that we were fine with it all. We were hardly drinking and sat for most of the night, but had an amazing time. I had gotten through the last six months without dying, something that had seemed impossible to me, and I was likely to get through the rest. What more could I want? It got to nearly midnight and everyone was getting very excited. Then there was a big sound over the top of an anthem song. The countdown.

TEN, NINE, EIGHT ... 'Karen, I've got no signal!' I shouted at her.

THREE, TWO, ONE ... 'Can we go outside for a signal?' I shouted louder.

We went outside – he'd messaged me back! This was so exciting. My message had been short and simple, but he must have liked my pictures and my description. Maybe it was because it was New Year's Eve, but he was messaging *me*. I felt like Jordan.

We missed the stroke of midnight, but when we got back in, one of our songs was playing. So we started dancing and messing around. We danced, sang, twerked, and slut-dropped. I noticed that there was an empty space on the dance floor, and suddenly I could see a rather plump, black cat sitting in the middle.

What an odd thing to be in a club, I thought, before my brain caught up with my eyes. My £200 wig was dancing on her own on the floor of the club.

FUCK.

In slow motion, we removed our arses from the dance floor and Karen pounced on top of the wig that had left my naked head. I ducked down with one hand, trying to cover the stubble on my head before anyone else saw. Karen passed the wig back to me and slapped it onto my head like a rugby ball over the line. It went on. No one, that we were aware of, had noticed. Lucky escape.

A few hours later, we ended up in an overpriced cab trying to persuade the driver to pull over for a kebab. This was going to be my last night out for a while. But if we couldn't celebrate on New Year's Eve, then when could we? No one knew us in that club, no one knew our stories, and no one knew I was any different from them.

I didn't know any of them either, and I had no idea what was going on in their lives.

*

The start of 2010 was good. Actually, it was really exciting. I was now in a relationship. Well, a virtual relationship, but a relationship nonetheless. Saddler Sam and I were messaging back and forth, two, three, sometimes four times a day. We were having really simple but nice conversations.

Internet dating felt so crazy to me, to sit there in front of my laptop, having a virtual relationship with someone I didn't know, their identification hidden. Who was this guy? He could be a nutter, just like Unwanted Phil.

What are you doing this weekend? he asked.

Oh, going out Friday and Saturday night and then meeting up for lunch on Sunday, I wrote back. I had to think on my feet and lie my little socks off, so as to not give my game up. This guy was alright and seemed nice, but what if he worked me out for what I was (a complete and total mess)? If he found out that on Tuesday, I had spent all day in bed with aches and pains; that on Wednesday I went out shopping and was approached by a you-know-what hospice which sent me into turmoil; and that on Saturday I would be in bed, saving what little energy I had for my chemotherapy session on Monday, he'd definitely not be interested any more.

This was challenging. Lying was stressful and very hard work, because liars can forget what lies they've told. Especially when the liar, like me, doesn't lie a lot. But the person who receives them doesn't forget the lies. I didn't want to muck this up before I even met him. 'I think we should speak. I want to talk to you properly,' he had written.

Okay, this was good. But I definitely could not mess up. We agreed a time – 7.00pm – with doors closed / privacy / no interruptions. Just me (and Dorothy, of course) waiting for the phone to ring.

18.56

18.57

Waiting was an utter nightmare. What if he had cold feet? What if he had forgotten? What if he didn't call me?

18.58

18.59

It felt like I was waiting for 10 minutes for the last digit to move.

INCOMING CALL – SADDLER SAM

Do I accept? Reject? Accept? Reject? Accept?

'WOOF!' Dorothy barked, urging me to answer the bloody phone. I guess she'd become invested in the relationship.

ACCEPT (Obvs, who was I kidding?)

'Hi, this is Sam.' Very formal. Very to the point. Loud and direct. I liked it.

'Oh, hiiiiii!' I replied, acting surprised, like I hadn't just spent the last half an hour staring at the phone, waiting for him to call.

We spoke for three hours, to be precise. We talked about his job, life, and family. And, just as equally, we talked about mine. We talked about London, the countries we had been to, the places that we wanted to go. We even talked about what we had for dinner. It was nice, it was easy, and it wasn't awkward. It felt comforting talking to this man. He didn't seem like he had a game to play. He was mature, direct, and really frank about everything. There were no grey areas; he was just all black and white like a mammogram without a shadow. Eventually we said goodbye to one another. I reflected on our conversation all night. I missed talking to him already, I realised. I needed to meet this man.

CHAPTER 18

Dog Days are Over

'What's your name? Confirm your date of birth and what session you're on,' the angels said automatically.

'... and today is my last session,' I finished. Today was January 5th 2010. Six months and five chemotherapies down, today was the day. My final chemotherapy session. I felt like I was on top of the world. My Herceptin would continue for another year after this, but I was okay with that. I wanted it. All of it. Karen had done her usual six-hour round trip and come to Bart's with me. The trains were delayed, but I didn't panic. I knew she'd get here. Nothing could go wrong. It was my last treatment session, and I had the Saddler Sam conversation going around my head. It was the only thing I could think about.

Waltzing in to ward G3 with a huge grin on my face, I felt three feet taller and three stone thinner. Bernice, Audrey, Petra, Michael, and even Ernie were all there smiling at me, and I was smiling back like I had nothing to lose.

'I'm just going out for a fag before me next round,' Ernie told one of the angels, in a matter-of-fact, don't start, I've already made up my mind kind of way. *Why not? What harm is it actually going to do?*

She's already got lung you-know-what, and it seriously couldn't get any worse than that.

Karen and I didn't discuss this like we usually would. Nor did we banter about other things in our lives. In fact, we had no conversation. We just appreciated the significance of the situation that we were in, and that we would never be here again. Yes, I had to come back for the diamond Herceptin, but that was different. That wasn't going to feel like torture, and my hair would start growing back.

Karen put her iPad on and I listened to Florence and The Machine's 'Dog Days Are Over' on repeat. And before I knew it, it was done. My chemotherapy was done. It was very, very weird and emotional finishing my chemotherapy. I needed it and I knew it had worked. But I couldn't help but wonder, *what happens now?* I left. I didn't say goodbye to anyone there, because I didn't want to remind them that they still had time to go. I just thanked the angels and waved at my new-found friends. As I left, I whispered good luck to them all.

I felt really ill. There were five lots chemotherapy medicine whirling around in my poor body. But I smiled and took pride in walking out of that ward. We hailed a cab. The journey back wasn't so bad. The lights of London were beautiful. It was a freezing evening, but I wanted to feel cold, so I wound the window down. It was a beautiful, heavenly feeling. Better than going under had been. Better than Enya's 'Anywhere Is'. Better than anything.

We pulled up outside of my house. I couldn't even look up at Karen as she got out of the cab for the station at Walthamstow. All I did was go straight into the house and hug Mum. Chemotherapy, and the five months of hell that went with it, was over.

*

The morning after that was my date with Saddler Sam. We'd had a little trouble setting the date. Well, not trouble exactly. Saddler Sam had stated the dates he could do, and I had immediately jumped on the first one, not really thinking about it. It was only afterwards that

I'd realised when it was.

'The day after your chemotherapy? Good god,' Mum had said, without even looking up from the paper. She was so used to these mad-cap ideas that she barely even reacted to them now.

I woke up, and though I had never felt so excited in my head, I had also never felt so bad physically. I could hear a Radio 4 presenter arguing loudly with some victim and Mum tutting her disapproval. Through the curtains I could see very thick, white, beautiful snow swirling everywhere.

SHIT. I had overslept massively and it was already noon. I was supposed to be meeting Saddler Sam at two o'clock, and at this rate I'd be turning up at five.

'There are two exits at Knightsbridge Tube station: Harrods and Sloane Street. I will meet you at the Harrods one,' Sam had said, directing me over the phone the night before. God, this guy had sophistication. A first date and we were meeting in Knightsbridge, not only one of the wealthiest and most glamourous places in London, but at Harrods – the shop for the rich, the famous, the tourists, and the locals. The only shop in London which allowed itself to be festive all year round! Fairy lights weren't only for Christmas in Harrods; they were there to light up the heart of London. The only time I'd been to Harrods was to see Father Christmas, and even he'd had a gold tooth in his huge smile.

Thankfully, I now had the getting-ready process down to a fine art. I'd put on my foundation, always going for a dark tone that would team up with the fake tan. Fantastic. It worked well because I was always so hot and flustered. (Was this the start of my menopause? Oh god, I just didn't have time to think about it.) I needed to straighten my wig and get out of the house.

I'm so sorry. Can we make it 3.00pm? I panic-texted Saddler Sam.

There was no reply for what seemed like a very long time.

'Why's he not replying?' I asked Dorothy, who was sitting on the end of my bed supporting me, for once, like a friend advising me on what to wear.

His reply came in a little later than I wanted: *Yeah, we can do. But if you have changed your mind then that's fine.*

Bollocks, this guy's getting cold feet.

I re-read the text message.

Yeah, we can do. But if you have changed your mind ... No. I was wrong, he thought I was the one getting cold feet. I just replied and left. Half an hour later, Dorothy and I were sitting on the Victoria line counting down the stops. We'd arranged to meet on a Saturday, when we were both available. He didn't know I was on sick leave, so this was believable.

My god did I feel sick after the chemo. My skin was really hot, which gave me an overwhelming feeling of dehydration. The more water I drank, the sicker I became. So I had to stop drinking. As the Tube stops raced by, I was getting more and more nervous. A group of French tourists got on the carriage and stared at us. They started pointing. I just avoided eye contact with them. They started to snigger, which then turned into laughter. I looked at Dorothy and she appeared totally miserable. They were pissing themselves laughing. Oh god, they were bullying Dorothy and I couldn't take it! Was Saddler Sam going to bully me when he found out I had one boob and no hair? *Maybe I should go back,* I thought. But then we pulled into Knightsbridge.

I'm here. I fired off a quick text to Saddler Sam. I was angry, I was freezing, lost, and cold. And it was coming out in my text messages. There were absolutely no kisses on the end.

He hadn't arrived and it was snowing. No, it wasn't just snowing, it was bloody throwing it down. I was freezing and Dorothy was shaking. But then a man walked towards me. 'Annabel?' It was him, and he was very tall and totally handsome. He was wearing a smart black jacket, dark jeans, and smart shoes. 'Hi, I'm Sam.' He held out his hand to shake mine.

'Hi, nice to meet you. Sorry, I went to the wrong exit and—'

'Shall we walk?' he said, politely interrupting me. This guy was confident, strong, and decisive. He wasn't wasting any time. We walked for a few minutes, but it was filled with an uneasy silence. Normally, I'm full of chatter and always have something to say, but my mind was blank and nothing was coming out of my mouth. Someone needed to talk, quickly, or this was going to be very, very awkward. 'Nearly there,' he said. I realised I didn't actually know where we were going, but it was exhausting. We walked past Harrods and Burberry. In the distance was Hyde Park. I could see the trees, their branches completely covered in white. We walked up to a building with huge brick walls, barbed wire, and CCTV everywhere. Okay, we were at his barracks. I remembered now that he'd mentioned this plan.

Saddler Sam was in the Household Cavalry Mounted Regiment, the most iconic regiment in the world, serving queen and country, the only escort service for all royalty. 'There will always be a need for a ceremonial regiment, as long as there is a monarchy,' Sam said proudly as we walked up to the big iron gates. He showed me around the barracks, which were very impressive but also completely terrifying. Soldiers walked about in complete silence, and all I could hear were commands being given in the background, which seemed to echo forever.

He then took me into a small, office-type door, which looked like a huge horse tack room. 'So, this is it,' he said. 'The saddlers' shop.' I kind of knew what Sam being a saddler meant. I knew that it had to do with horses and their clothes and equipment and stuff. Which was great for me, because I loved the smell of horse manure and leather. I found it comforting, as it reminded me of my childhood riding lessons, where it would cost something close to a million pounds to trot round a field for half an hour.

Sam looked at me, almost reading what I was thinking, and said, 'It's a bonus working with horses, because we can ride whenever we like.' I was so jealous of that. 'Would you like a cup of tea?' Since I'd started chemotherapy, I had lost a lot of my taste buds. So I didn't drink tea or even coffee, and a lot of people found that weird. But I couldn't think of a decent response to say if he asked why I didn't want tea.

'Yes please, with sugar,' I replied.

'One lump or two?' he asked, looking straight at me. I winced inwardly.

'Just the one,' I said quietly.

He pulled out a very pretty, delicate teapot and poured the tea into two huge man-sized mugs. He reached over and opened a pack of biscuits, setting them next to the tea.

We sat and chatted so much that he didn't even notice I wasn't drinking it. It was great, just like the phone conversation we'd had, but in person.

He spoke about his hobbies and interests, as well as his strong passion for collecting horse brasses. He told me that he loved horseracing. He had a framed picture of a famous racehorse called Frankel on his desk. I learnt that he had grown up in admiration of his father, a farrier from Southampton. Working with horses all his life, his dad had his own successful business, which Sam had joined in with when he was younger. Sam liked London, but was originally from Southampton. He had been single for a short while. He had a younger brother and sister, both of whom still lived near home. He thoroughly enjoyed his job and had been in the army for seven years. And he definitely planned on doing his 22 years of service.

'I just love my job,' he said, with clear pride. I liked that. I told him that in all my years of recruitment, I had never met anyone who honestly loved their job and didn't moan about it. He didn't once talk about beer, birds or football. He loved animals, the countryside, fox hunting, and the brand Barbour. It was all so different. Yes, I hated fox hunting, but this didn't anger me. It was just good to have someone in front of me who had an interest. A phone suddenly went off and I prayed that it wasn't mine. It was. I hated my phone in that moment. It felt like the height of rudeness, having my phone ringing out, seeking attention on my oh-so-important date. I ignored it.

Sam interviewed me back, as we both pretended the phone hadn't rung. He asked me lots of questions about me and my life, and he seemed like he was interested. Maybe sometimes it was forced, maybe not. I enjoyed it anyway.

'Is that real?' he asked, pointing at my fake Mulberry, which I'd slung on the floor. This was so embarrassing. *I had to lie.* I couldn't tell a man who worked with leather that my bag was about as fake as the hair on my head. Suddenly, I started to feel very self-conscious about my wig. I went bright red. I felt inferior to this prince.

'Yes, it is real. What's that?' I asked, changing the subject, pointing at a chair. If I hadn't had foundation on, he might have noticed the burning sensation on my cheeks. He might have noticed my embarrassment.

When Saddler Sam spoke, he always looked very serious and in control, and knew exactly what he wanted to say. He had a dry sense of humour, which I liked. He made me feel more and more intrigued and interested in him, in his job. 'I'm good with my hands,' he said at one point, and it wasn't a sexual innuendo. 'Handmade, everything. Each stitch on a collar, bridal or saddle is handsewn and it takes hours. But it's the best quality man can make.' He had such a strong personality. His sense of style was old-fashioned and he had a traditional way of thinking. He talked about making tea, not buying it. His mind was programmed completely differently to mine, and he was utterly fascinating to me.

'And you live here?' I asked. I was thinking about the journey I'd had getting here. The different Tube stops, the walking distance between all of them. But actually, if this was going to work out, I was 100 per cent up for it.

'Yes, in the block. It's good because I don't have to travel to work.' Everything was so to the point with Sam, no messing around. I wanted to mirror his language, how he spoke, and the way he said things.

If everyone just spoke like Sam, I thought, *the world would be so much more efficient.*

'No excuses for being late for work then,' I said over-enthusiastically.

'No, never!' he stated, again, very seriously. 'Shall we go?' he said, walking out. I followed him enthusiastically, like a puppy.

We started to walk out of the barrack gates when we bumped into Pete, a friend Sam had spoken about over the phone. Pete was one of Sam's colleagues and close friends. Alongside him was a small horse. Actually, no, it was a huge Siberian husky dog. Dorothy started yapping at this dog, showing her teeth and snarling. Almost predictably, the situation worsened as the other dog began to mount Dorothy. Oh my god!

I didn't know what to do. I started to feel panic rise inside me. But I didn't need to do anything because Sam just pulled the two dogs apart with his bare hands. As the two dogs were separated, I wondered if bumping into Pete was planned. *Oh well, never mind, at least his friend got a look at me,* I thought. He seemed nice, and I was impressed that Sam didn't forget my name.

The snow had really started to fall at this point, and Hyde Park looked beautiful. We walked through the park and talked about him, me, work, home, friends, family, and life. We ended up right at the top of the park, and while in serious conversation, a strange-looking man ran out in front of us, a runner in the middle of December wearing Lycra shorts, a yellow see-through vest, and a sweatband. It wasn't so much what he was wearing that was odd, but the way that he was running. With his head up, bum out and chest puffed, he looked just like a chicken.

Time ran away with us and we ended up getting into a black cab and going to his local pub. Even the pub was tasteful, romantic, and perfect. 'Two Sailor Jerry's and Diet Coke,' he ordered for us at the bar. I sipped mine. There was no way I was going to drink the entire thing. It was way too strong. We talked and talked while Dorothy curled up by the fire in the pub. It got to 8.00pm and I was absolutely starving and needed to eat. 'Shall we get something to eat?' Sam suggested, as though he had read my mind.

I stuffed nachos, olives, pitta and hummus into my mouth as fast as I could get them in. As I ate, I was secretly daydreaming about Mum's takeaway that the girls had planned at ours that night.

'So, we're planning this big project at the moment. In pink leather, you'd love it,' Sam said.

'Tell me!'

'Okay. We want to make a saddle entirely out of pink leather. But it's doubtful that we're going to get the time. It'd be nice, though.'

Yep, I could definitely see it. Jordan would snap it up in a heartbeat for her range of bridal accessories.

And then he said it.

'Ideally, we'd make it for a Breast Cancer charity.'

An olive got stuck in my throat and I choked. I coughed and panicked and had to spit it out, as gracefully as possible, of course. I knew this date had been too good to be true.

My mouth opened and words came out. I hadn't planned for them. I would never have planned for them. Yet here they were.

'That's a really good idea. Just to let you know, I have recently recovered from ... well, what you were talking about,' I said, in a matter-of-fact tone. It had come out. Just like my diseased, tennis ball-sized lump. But there was no going back, so I just had to be a soldier and tell him about it. All of it. *The act has to go.*

An hour later, he had listened, nodded, sympathised without being patronising, and asked appropriate questions. He didn't ask about my breast, nipple, and lack of hair (that, I didn't mention). But it was out, in the open. This was my first date in seven months with a man who was half-decent, and I had told him. I didn't mention all the follow-up treatment I was still having or about to start – the Herceptin, radiotherapy. I didn't even want to think about a possible breast reconstruction. That could all wait for the future. But Sam seemed to take it all in. He didn't check to see if my hair was real or my body was still intact – neither of which were. His eyes didn't move to my chest, not even once.

We walked to the station, back past Burberry and Harrods with all the pretty lights. We stopped outside Harvey Nics. Dorothy, as always, was right in the middle of us, stopping any possible contact. The snow was now heavy, dripping down my face, and all I could see were tiny white dots in between my eyelashes. But I loved it. This felt like the epitome of romance.

He suddenly reached out for my hand, which felt amazing. Being touched for the first time without being prodded, injected, inserted, taken off, diagnosed, bandaged up, checked for bad news was wonderful. He just held my hand and he kissed my lips. I loved it. And then he gave me a gift – a handmade keyring, made out of leather and brass, with a heart in the middle. Each individual stitch was, to me, a sign of good things to come.

We said goodbye and I got on the Tube back to East London. I felt so happy, and for the first time in seven months, I felt at peace. I felt so alive and well. This man could *not* be let go.

CHAPTER 19

HAPPY

I was back at Walthamstow Tube station. And it was midnight. *My god, Mum's going to be worried*. I turned on my phone as Dorothy and I climbed the thousand stairs. The escalator was broken again. Five text messages came through. Okay, not so bad then.

Mum: *Having fun?*

Mum: *How's it going?*

Mum: *Let me know you're okay?*

Saddler Sam: *I'm so glad we met, and I would love to see you again.*

Mum: Annabel, *please let me know when you're coming home.*

Oh my god, Saddler Sam wants to see me again! I imagined the people on the advertising posters applauding me, flares and fireworks burning in the sky and ACDC's 'Back in Black' playing. I pictured all the passengers dancing with me, and a cabaret show starting.

Dorothy was pulling me through the station, most likely just praying for this night to end. It seemed this date night could not get any better for me. But oh yes, it could. Mum and the girls greeted me when I got home. They'd only had a *few* glasses of wine. Predictably, they interviewed me about my date. And they were loving all the juicy details: Harrods, the soldiers in the barracks, the leather.

'Was he wearing his uniform?' Glenda asked.

'No, of course he wasn't,' I said, as I started to eat up her biryani. This cold, leftover, half-eaten takeaway was the best thing in my life at that moment.

'Did you have a go on his horses?' Marie asked.

I laughed and said no. 'He's a gentleman and I really hope to see him again,' was all I said, and with that I took myself upstairs. Wig and lashes off, I fell asleep with a smile. ...

Three weeks went by, and I was now officially dating this lovely man. Over the course of this time, he went from Saddler Sam, to Sam, to Sammy. I liked it. It suited him. And my name became Annie. Goodbye miserable Annabel, hello happy and confident Annie. 'Annie Belasco.' My name, with his last name.

It had such a ring to it, I thought, as I walked past jewellers on my way to work, picking out potential engagement rings that Sammy could get me. I stopped myself before I got too far in to the fantasy. I didn't want to get this far and scare him off. I had to keep visualising the lobster in the cooking pot. And I had to keep reminding myself not to turn into that potential psychopath, which I knew could be around the corner at any minute.

But then again, it was like telling me not to buy eyelashes. I just couldn't stop thinking about it. I knew that I had to have a gold ring. It had to be gold. My grandpa gave my dear granny a gold wedding ring. And they were my true romantic idols. The perfect idea of love – Granny and Grandpa, hand-in-hand, always by each other's side. One without the other just never worked.

Sammy and I soon developed a routine. After work (every single evening), he would get the train to Finsbury Park and I would pick him up. He'd already met Mum and she had warmed to him straight away. Who wouldn't? I think Mum was really happy to meet Sam. She finally had someone else who could look after me just as well as she could. She thought he was polite and a gentleman, and she was right. He always turned up on time, he always looked smart, and he always had something for me. He fitted well into our family. It had been years since we'd had a man about the house. And just to have that extra person for security – who could run out to take the bins out, change a lightbulb, and all the things that we wanted to dump on someone else – god, that felt good.

He was loyal to his job, to his family, and to me. He never made me feel insecure about myself, not in the slightest. And I had never felt that before, not ever. Thoughts of you-know-what turned into thoughts of where we'd go for dinner. Where could we go on holiday? When would I get to meet his parents? Where, when, what, how?

We would spend evenings chatting in my room, talking about London, the traffic, our favourite TV programme *Gavin and Stacey,* our families, our friends, and our plans. We even started to use the terms "when we", "we could" and "that would be great for us".

Sam and Annie became "us". He asked me to be his girlfriend and I took myself off Plenty of Fish. My mission for finding love was complete. I had found it, and it was him. As time passed, I began to wonder about the hair and the breast conversation. It hadn't come up yet and as time went on, I began to wonder if he knew that I had no hair and I was wearing a wig. By this point, I had been to the hairdressers and swapped my old, reliable wig for a brand new one, one that was longer and darker. Sammy hadn't noticed and always just said I looked nice.

But surely he must have known?

*

While walking back from one of our favourite Italian restaurants in Knightsbridge one evening, Sam saw one of his friends walking by.

He was a big, meaty bloke, and they stopped to exchange greetings and news. After a few minutes of not being introduced, I was visibly pissed off. They had talked about work (so I had established he was a colleague), they had talked about leave and holidays, and about everything in between. But they had not talked about me.

'Why didn't you introduce me?' I said bluntly as we walked away.

'The world doesn't revolve around you,' Sam said.

I felt a flash of anger.

Oh shit. We were about to have our first row. I needed to win this.

'Yes, but after everything I've been through, you would think that you'd have the respect to introduce that person to your girlfriend.' I let go of his stupid arm.

'Really?' He wasn't looking at me.

'Yes! Really. I think that's so rude.'

'Well, you know what?' he shouted.

I couldn't breathe.

'Someone said to me today that they were surprised I was putting up with what you have,' he said. He spoke very quickly, almost like he'd wanted to say this for a long time. My soul died. My eyes fell to the floor, and my heart was swallowed up into the nearest drain.

The man I love thinks he's putting up with me. This was horrendous. I didn't have a reply to what he had said. I just walked away from him. Who was this man? No one could undermine what I was still going through. How could he possibly understand the year of chemotherapy, the year and a half of Herceptin, the pain of getting all the badness out of me?

My whirlwind romance was dead. I hated him. 'Dump him!' my head told me. 'Marry him!' my heart cried. I left Sammy in Oxford Street and made my way home. I felt so shocked by his outburst. He had never, ever made me feel insecure before. And there he'd done it, in one quick round of fire – BOOM. A gun had been fired in our relationship, and everything was ruined. Walking up the staircase to Walthamstow Tube, I prayed that my phone would go off with an apologetic text message from Sammy. *I'm sorry, I didn't mean it. Come back!!!* But nothing came through.

I was angry, mainly because of all the hard work that had gone into removing this negativity from my head. And now I felt like I was nothing more than a hindrance to this guy's life. And he was too embarrassed to tell anyone that his girlfriend had been going through a life-threatening illness.

No texts came through. I just quietly went to bed, to sleep it all off.

I woke up and it was Sunday morning. There was a text waiting on my phone, like a stocking on Christmas morning.

Sammy: *Please meet me at the station. I want to work things out.*

Thank god, I thought, looking at Dorothy, who was perched on the end of my bed, staring back at me.

I agreed to meet him at the station. Although I felt a lot better after our little tiff, I was still pissed off, so I needed to show it. I didn't wear any make-up. I wore just a tracksuit, brought my fake Mulberry, and took Dorothy with me. And I turned up late to meet him (I didn't do performing arts at college for nothing). But the sadness I felt was completely real.

Sammy stood there looking as fearless as a daisy. He apologised sincerely and handed me a beautiful postcard of a white horse and two people, a couple, riding into a meadow. He said it was us escaping hell together. This meant more to me than a real Mulberry. This felt like love, real love, and we made up quickly. We spent the rest of the day arm in arm, hugging and kissing, chatting as normal until a conversation turned to my next Herceptin appointment on the following Friday afternoon.

Why don't I come with you? Sammy asked me through text.

This felt like it was a bit too soon.

My Herceptin appointments were for me. They felt like my time, my space, my therapy. I knew what to expect and who would be there. It was my comfort blanket in a rough time. If ever I started to panic about anything to do with my health, I just looked at my calendar with the massive pink ring, circled around every third Friday of the month, and I would feel better.

I would walk in, straight from work, park myself down, and talk to my friends that I had made there. Herceptin was a shorter treatment than chemotherapy, but administered the same way, through the port in my chest.

Those Friday afternoons, I would assign myself to working "from home". I would bring my office into the chemotherapy ward. I'd place my laptop on the water tray in front of me, notebook and pen beside it, and I'd prop my back on a pillow. On one occasion, I even managed a 45-minute conference call without being interrupted. I would also use the desk in front of me (sorry, the food tray) as a dressing table.

I would lay out all my make-up and my wig. I'd get my bathroom mirror out and do my face. I would brush my wig and make myself beautiful, ready for my next date in the evening with Sammy. The nurses would laugh and other patients would join in, asking about my huge and ever-growing collection of make-up. I'd always offer to do theirs too, if they wanted and felt well enough.

But it wasn't all happy and fun. It was sometimes completely miserable and dark.

On one of my sessions, I met a woman who had to have chemotherapy while being pregnant. She was such a brave woman. She later gave birth to a beautiful baby girl and named her Iris. Only I knew this, and I didn't share it with any family or friends, because it wasn't their business.

Really amazing things would happen like this all of the time, but I would always keep them to myself. It would prove to me how strong the human body is. This woman was pregnant and being filled with poison to destroy her immune system, and yet her little innocent foetus stayed comfortable in her womb, not having a single clue what her mother was going through. And they both survived, happy and healthy. The word resilience doesn't even begin to sum it up.

So this was my space, my time, and my treatment. I didn't know if I wanted Sammy there. What if the reality of all this shit that had happened, and was kind of still happening, scared him off?

I didn't text back that morning or that afternoon, and I ignored his call in the evening. I just didn't know if I wanted to drag him through the mud and expose him to this world. Maybe I shouldn't have deleted my Plenty of Fish profile so quickly. Maybe I shouldn't have told him straight away about everything. I just couldn't help but think about what might happen if he came with me. What if someone recognised me and asked about my wig, my breast, my three eggs preserved for the future?

'What if you give him a chance and let him make his own mind up?' Mum had said that evening, as I ignored yet another call. I couldn't let this poor man suffer because of my paranoia of rejection. We had got this far at the right speed, and the only one creating an issue was me.

My next Herceptin appointment arrived and we'd done a deal. We were doing our big reveals. Sammy was coming to Herceptin treatment and I was meeting his parents afterwards. After that, there'd be nothing that we couldn't weather.

*

'Confirm your name and date of birth. Where does the needle go?' 'Annabel Walsh, 20/12/83, my chest. *And this is my new boyfriend,'* I said, beaming ear to ear. I'm not sure if the nurses heard this bit. They didn't react, but I suppose they were quite busy with their jobs.

I had warned Sammy that I had a port in my chest and that my medication was administered through it. The Sammy I know goes through periods of looking serious, being very dry-witted, and sometimes just saying nothing. As he stood by my side, he said nothing. *Good, I thought, this was normal.* He looked serious as he stood there, holding my hand, and everyone was looking at us. I loved it.

I lay back on the hospital bed as the nurse inserted the needle into my port in my chest. I was completely numb in the area but the needle piercing the skin always made a huge CRACK. My legs always went up, an involuntary reaction to the insertion.

And then, SAMMY FELL DOWN.

He was on the floor! My soldier was trained for war, and had fainted at the sight of a needle. As quick as anything, the angels urgently gathered around this chaotic scene and tried to wake Sammy up.

'SIR, SIR, SIR, SIR?' An alarm cord was pulled and a doctor rushed in.

He'd seen the needle and just gone out cold. Everyone was staring and pointing and watching the drama – they loved it.

CHAPTER 20

Meeting the Fockers

'God that was awful and embarrassing. I'm so sorry!' I had heard this a thousand times since Sammy had fallen, and it was getting on my nerves. I switched off, listening to his Lily Allen CD, and thinking about how on earth I was going to make a good impression on his parents. The satnav claimed there was two hours to go before we got there, which was good. It gave me loads of time to prep myself. This was a massive deal. Some texts came through. Karen: Good luck just be yourself.

Mum: *Have fun and don't worry.*

Ciera: *Make sure you tell them that I've been on holiday in the New Forest.* – God, it had to be about her again, didn't it!

Theresa: *Enjoy meeting the fockers. Lol.* – LOL? Has she lost her mind? It was probably the new influence of her new boyfriend kicking in.

'PULL FORWARD, YOU PRICK!' Sammy screamed at another driver.

He suffered a little from a thing called road rage. I joked that I was going to get him a Pass Plus driving course for Christmas, extra driving lessons to boost his confidence. I always had to remind myself that he wasn't used to London. He was from the New Forest, where the local traffic was the cows and the sheep. Mine was the number 56 bus and a 10-ton lorry on a backstreet. That's got to make a difference!

I removed all the irritating text messages as I sat there. *Delete, delete, delete.*

'What are you doing?!' Sammy asked, grabbing my phone off me while negotiating the M3 corridor during rush hour, dangerously swerving a McDonald's lorry.

McDonald's, how I miss you.

Since I had met Sammy, I'd really had to tone down my cravings for carbs, for calories, for indulging. All I could think about was food, all of the time. If you-know-what wasn't hard enough to deal with, the after-effects that the steroids and sickness left me with were an utter nightmare. I was fat and I couldn't lose it, no matter how much I tried. My body was just used to eating five times the amount it needed.

I was thinking about food when I needed to be focusing on the potential mother-in-law. What was her name again?

'It's Anne! How can you forget that? It's literally your name!'

Hmmm, yes, it is. And if we get married, we're going to have the same bloody names!

Don't say that, don't say that, don't say that, I told myself over and over again. I changed the subject.

'And what does your dad do again?' I quickly checked over my revision.

'He's a farrier. He puts shoes on horses, like a blacksmith,' Sammy replied, slightly abruptly. He'd reminded me about it about four times. God, I hated meeting the parents. I dreaded a silent – or worse, clingy – mother-in-law or a dominant – or worse, perverted – father-in-law.

'Or they could be really lovely and welcome you,' Mum had said, forever the optimist.

They need to like me. Please let this happen, I prayed. What if Sammy was a proper spoilt mummy's boy and his mum hated me? What if his dad asked me questions about being a blacksmith, or was it a farrier? What was the difference? What if they knew I was wearing a wig? Imagine if his sister had an amazing cleavage and I couldn't stop staring at it, wishing it was mine. Then they'd think I was a lesbian and I only wanted Sammy for his leather. I suddenly became terrified of the entire thing. I wanted to turn back around and go home.

I started to lose phone reception because we were down a long, winding road. It was getting darker, just like something out of a fairy tale. Except maybe there wasn't a happy ending at the end of this one.

'We're here!' Sam announced.

I didn't speak. I just gathered my things and got out of Sammy's immaculate car. Where the hell were we? Their house was huge. It had gates, it was hidden away, and it had more land than the local park in Walthamstow. My god.

Sammy walked past the front entrance, round to an unlocked back door.

'Can you imagine doing that in East London?' I later said to Gudrun. At one point, we'd had four locks to get through just to our shared entrance hall at university, and here they were, with this huge place, with a back door that was unlocked!

Sammy walked right into a big, bright, hot country kitchen, with pans bubbling. There were at least 50 different kitchen utensils hanging down from the cupboard doors. He pulled up a chair and sat down. I just stood there, not knowing what to do, but then his mum bounced over to me with a huge smile and a hug, giving me the warmest welcome I could have hoped for. Then Sammy's dad shuffled in. He was an older, Father Christmas-looking man. But his features were the spitting image of Sammy.

'Hello, I'm Stephen,' he said, kissing me on the cheek. And then there was Clare, Sammy's sister.

'Hiiiii,' she said pleasantly, but I had a feeling she had already met a few girlfriends of Sammy's. I wanted her to like me. I had to get to know her, so I could ask her about Sammy's exes. If anyone would spill the beans, it would be her.

And then walked in a bouncy, wide-eyed rabbit-like man, the very friendly and approachable brother Peter.

'Hi Annie, I'm Peter,' he said, shaking my hand. He had good eye contact. He was very sharp, just like his brother and his dad.

God, it's so hard not to assess them like candidates!

A Diet Coke was put straight into my hand. It saved an awkward conversation where I'd have to announce, 'No actually, I'm the only person in England, the UK or the world that does NOT LIKE TEA OR COFFEE!' They'd made it easier for me from the start.

I noticed that they had one of those old-fashioned tea pots bubbling over on the cooker, the ones you see in those adorable Janet and Allan Ahlberg books about babies and their parents. It was so tasteful. I really wanted to look around the rest of their house. I wondered how many bedrooms they had, what the décor was like. Where was the toilet? That was always the best way of getting a nosy around someone's house, I'd found. However, with this one, it could be harder than just a simple exploration. The bigger the house, the nearer the toilet could be, potentially. I imagined a house this size would have at least two, if not more.

I was starving and it was dinnertime (at last!). We all sat down to one course, but size-wise, it was really a five-course meal all served up in one big go. They served chicken, potatoes, vegetables, pasta salad, cheese, bread, and not to mention cakes. My god, the cakes were good. They were all homemade by Anne, who had just whipped them up after work.

I couldn't think of anything worse than getting home and cooking. How on earth did she just whip up five different desserts? But I didn't care about the logistics. I just shoved more chocolate biscuit cake in my mouth and shut up. This was going to be a decent weekend.

The Belascos were the polar opposite version of my family. They were very informal, whereas my family could be more conservative, more formal. It was a nice balance to have. Mum's Sunday lunches were polite, guests would ring the doorbell and take their shoes off at the front door, everyone took their turn, eat, talk, and to help out. Meal times in the Belasco household were a mixture of fun and chaos; everyone spoke over one another, and even had a punch-up about the washing-up. The kitchen was the heart of the house, like in children's books, and there was always something to talk about.

The conversation flowed around the table. Clare wanted a new car, Peter wanted a new girlfriend, Stephen couldn't find his spanner and was blaming Anne, who was looking at me with raised eyebrows, as if to say *this is my lot.*

'ANNE, QUICK, WE'VE GOT ONE,' Stephen suddenly shouted out at Anne. Anne dropped her fork and ran into the front room, only to return to the kitchen with a rifle. A RIFLE. She loaded it up and BANG.

'Damn, didn't get it,' she said as she slowly sat back down. She had tried to shoot a squirrel. Everyone continued the conversation, as though this incredible and shocking incident hadn't just happened. *Mum's got a John Lewis loyalty card and Anne's got a rifle!*

The conversation quickly turned to me. They asked me where I was from and what I did. I talked about East London and Walthamstow. 'You know that band, E17, from the 90s?' They nodded. But the conversation about me ended right there. I wished Sammy had told them about my situation. But how the hell would either of us even begin to approach it? I felt like the entire weekend was separate to my life. But that was good, because I was about to start an intensive six-week, five-days-a-week radiotherapy course.

CHAPTER 21

RADIOTHERAPY

Two months after my chemotherapy had finished, I was about to start radiotherapy, every day, five days a week, for six weeks. Each time I'd receive just three tiny minutes of radiotherapy. 'It's a walk in the park,' Dr P had said, describing my next ordeal.

It might have been, but I was finding that my mood was getting worse. One minute it was high, and the next it would be low. A story, comment, or even word would push my good mood to the edge of a cliff. But then a single compliment, a positive story or seeing a happy face could make me feel great again. It was weird. The ups and down didn't feel like me. The only thing I was certain about was that I couldn't trust my mood, whatever happened.

But I needed to focus on radiotherapy. It was at the same hospital, so it'd be the same journey. There'd be the same patients, but different angels. I had to do something to change the daily journey, so I took the bus. I was too tired to drive my new car without the risk of having a minor scrape or potentially writing it (or me) off. On the bus I could text, email, and use the internet all the way there and back without interruption. At least that was something. It all felt like such an effort for such a small amount of time. It was literally two to three minutes per session. But the psychological baggage being dumped onto my unsorted pile of anxiety and worry made it a much bigger deal.

'It will all be worth it in the end, gorgeous,' Sammy had said to me. *An all too familiar saying,* I kept thinking. So many people kept saying the same thing to me. *It bloody better be worth it.* I could get through my treatment and yet this disease could still come back and kill me. Then it wouldn't be worth it, would it?

As my mood began to sink, I thought about Sammy's words over and over again on the bus to Bart's. I popped another co-codamol to get rid of the pain in my arm and to drown out the voice of doom my head.

The routine at my radiotherapy sessions would be to arrive, always at 8.40am, and check in. I'd drop my bags off and get changed. And then I'd wait, talk to other patients about whatever, and then go and lie on a bed while they zapped me. They targeted my neck, chest, and right-hand side of my body intensively, every single day for a few minutes at a time. And then I would go home. And then back to work. It was beyond exhausting. Day in, day out – *zap, zap*, laptop on, work. Over and over again.

I didn't even know what the radiotherapy was doing. I hadn't asked because I couldn't handle the answer. Neither could anyone else. At least, not when I was around. I had finished chemotherapy, I was alive and well, and had an amazing boyfriend. I just couldn't let my mental health issues creep up and scare him off, scare my family off, scare my friends off.

In between radiotherapy and work, there were talks of the dreaded 'R' word. It was 2010, and there was a recession.

Rumours flew around corridors at work, and group emails flew back and forth. Colleagues started dropping like flies all around us. 'It was always expected in a recession.'

'Who do you think will be next?'

I didn't care. It didn't faze me. I felt like shouting, 'Make me redundant!' I'd beaten you-know-what; I could handle anything. But that definitely wasn't true. I couldn't handle my tiredness and worrying any more. Luckily, this was my last week of radiotherapy. As the days and weeks had gone on, the mental torture of sitting in that room had become very intense. Despite not wanting to, there were always conversations that I overheard. I didn't want to hear their stories or tell mine. I already knew that everyone around me was deteriorating, losing their motivation or, even worse still, not even turning up for their appointments. And I didn't convince myself otherwise; I knew that they were dead, killed by this horrible disease that had already taken so much from their lives.

I always wished that certain people would turn up. I wished the doors would open and they would walk in, just a little late ...

'BERNICE!' My mind recognised the name and my mouth came out with the right words. It felt like Christmas, my birthday, and Valentine's Day all rolled into one. It was like every celebration I could think of. I was just so happy to see her.

She tottered in (just like her daughter had the last time I had seen her) and sat down right next to me.

Bernice always spoke in a whisper. She was from Glasgow and I absolutely loved her accent. It was comforting; it reminded me of Mum's sisters-in-laws, who were all from Ayrshire in Scotland. It sounded kind to me, comforting.

She talked and talked, and I listened. I was praying I wouldn't get called for my appointment as I just wanted to be with her. She was grieving for the loss of her daughter and had also discovered that she herself had not just one form of the disease, but two. It was comforting, for me at least, to see and talk to her. She was proof that the absolute worst thing in any person's life can happen, but life just goes on. Bernice was called in at the same time as me. She said goodbye and then she had to go. I wished her well and she said the same to me. That was all that needed saying. I felt a kind of sombre happiness as she left me.

As the theatre stage was set for my dose of radiotherapy, the light went off and the radiowaves kicked in. They hit my neck, my chest, and my shoulders. I lay there, just thinking, obsessing, and stressing out. My eyes glittering with tears, the words just came out – the ones that I didn't want to say. I asked the nurse, 'Will it come back?'

Instead of answering the question, she suggested that I speak to a consultant. I hated being ignored and dismissed. The nurse had qualifications in medicine, my bundle of notes, and, above all, access to the answers, but she couldn't say a thing.

My mind filled with terror. The paranoia that kicked in was unbearable. *Why didn't she answer me? Did she know something I didn't? Why had I not asked before? I've just gotten over it and met the love of my life, and now it's going to come back and kill me!* 'I CAN'T HANDLE THIS. I CAN'T HANDLE SITTING IN THIS ROOM, FEELING LIKE I'M WAITING TO DIE. I DON'T EVEN UNDERSTAND THE TREATMENT I'M HAVING. I NEED YOU TO TELL ME IF I'M GOING TO BE OKAY!'

Wailing and crying, I was taken to a consultant a few minutes later. I hadn't met him before.

It's so strange – here I was, in front of a complete stranger, talking about life and death, and it was all so perfectly normal to me. The consultant was a kind-faced, softly spoken man. He reminded me of my grandpa. He also reminded me of Sammy. I warmed to him straight away.

He spoke quietly and slowly so I could hear his words through my sea of tears. 'In my opinion, because of what you had, I don't think it's likely to come back,' he said very calmly.

"Not likely" was a term I was always going to have to live with. No one was ever going to say "never". No one was ever going to give me permission to live my life without the fear of this evil motherfucker coming back. But I just had to record in my mind his positive words. I trusted him, and I trusted what he had said. I felt calmer. Everything seemed less red and anger-inducing.

Later, I sat on the bus on the way back home and I was exhausted and tired. I had dozed off a couple of times on the bus on my journey home. My journey would often involve boarding the bus and staring into space, thinking about nothing. I'd then start blinking a lot. Gradually, I'd allow my eyelids to stay closed over my bloodshot eyeballs for longer and longer, until I entered full-on sleep mode. 'Make sure you put your phone away, out of sight. You don't want to get mugged,' Sammy had warned me when I spoke about my sudden falling asleep syndrome on the bus.

I'd sniggered disapprovingly at such a ridiculous statement. It didn't occur to me that anyone would have so little a heart to mug someone who had just finished off chemotherapy and now had to go through radiotherapy. I didn't even think about the fact that people wouldn't know this. I was self-centred and self-obsessed. The way I saw it, the world owed me a favour and I was claiming it back.

CHAPTER 22

THROWING A SICKIE

Sammy had always talked about his regimental army summer ball, an extremely exciting event that happened once a year. The soldiers work hard, contribute all year round to the bill, and then have one hell of a party.

And he had asked me to go with him.

'I'M HIS DATE!' I squealed at Mum, Marie, and Glenda one Friday night. Friday night was hair-wash night for my wig. I had nailed the upkeep and maintenance of my appearance by this point. Standing in the kitchen in the middle of their get-together, I was confidently and aggressively washing my wig in the sink. This was a huge deal and I'd made sure that everyone knew about it. However, I wasn't going to let my excitement and desperation to be a part of a power-couple ruin things. I had to do my research and get it right. Army balls were a political deal from the outset. First and most importantly, there was a dress code. An unofficial dress code, but everyone still knew about it.

'So what about the dress code?' I asked Sammy as casually as I could. 'What sort of thing do the women usually wear?'

'Cocktail dresses,' Sammy answered.

I paused.

I'm from London. I've never worn a cocktail dress, and a cocktail for me is a fishbowl in Benidorm filled with alcohol and fruit juice. 'Okay ... what length?'

'Below the knee.' He shrugged.

'Okay, and ...?' I pushed for more. This was my first ball as an army wife. Well, girlfriend. And I didn't want to fuck it up for him or me.

'Oh, I don't know. Anything below the knee or over the shoulders. And something that doesn't look too slutty.'

Okay, I've got it. Crisis averted.

'You'll look beautiful whatever you wear,' Sammy said kindly. Nice thought, but untrue. I couldn't show my chest or my legs, nor could I have an up-do hairstyle. Not to mention that there couldn't be even a peek of shoulder. Sexiness was out the door. I might as well have just worn a bag over myself.

The search for the dress started, and it was not an easy task. Being a Londoner meant that I wasn't used to cocktail dresses and dress codes. Living in London was always about just finding a dress that I liked, that fitted, and that I felt sexy and comfortable in. Many shops and an internet trawl later, I found a range of beautiful dresses. Some had just one shoulder or were strapless. One was even a halter neck. But they showed legs or breasts, and I needed one that would cover both. Just like a nun. Everything within my price range and age group was completely inappropriate. Reluctantly, I upped the budget and depressingly lowered my style standards. I eventually found a dress. It was perfect. It didn't draw attention to my legs or my chest, and it was baggy around the belly. I named it my "mastectomy dress".

It was black, below the knee, and over the shoulders. It was also a size 18 (the tag could be removed before anyone else saw) and it was still a bit tight. But I didn't look like I only had one breast. With a bit of extra make-up, I could look alright. Sammy's outfit was fine; he could just wear his suit. He stood next to me and we looked in the mirror. He looked so incredibly handsome and just perfect. I imagined the lights going down, the trumpeters playing their fanfare, and a master of ceremonies announcing our arrival.

'Ladies and gentleman, please will you stand for Beauty and THE BEAST!'

The night before the ball, I pulled my size-18 dress on over my body. God, it looked like a big black sack. As I stared back at my reflection, I became quite upset with the image in front of me. I wasn't classy or glamorous or any of the things I had always aspired to be. I sat on the floor with the black material all around me. I hated that this illness had taken my physical health, mental health and stability, and now it had taken my looks and my style. I barely felt like a woman any more. I looked unrecognisable. I was pale, fat, and completely covered in black. I looked like I was going to a funeral. I looked like a black cloud that would piss on everyone's day. I wasn't Annabel any more. I was supposed to be 26, yet I didn't look a day under 50.

But I had to do this for Sammy. I might have looked like shit, but I could play the game and make him proud. Forcing a smile onto my face, I redid the smudged eyeliner I had messed up thanks to my crying. I really didn't want him to think I was still suffering, a year on from my ordeal.

*

It was the morning of the ball and we woke up in Sammy's room, overlooking Hyde Park. The view was beautiful, and everything just felt so peaceful and serene. Sammy was pouring out his morning tea and sensed my unhappiness. I was excited for the ball, but I just still felt so unconfident.

He pulled out an envelope and gave it to me. 'It's a Harrods MAC make-up voucher, and I've paid for you to get your make-up done for the ball.' If I wasn't already deeply in love with this angel, there was no doubt about it now. I needed to marry him. 'So hurry up, don't put any make-up on, and go to your appointment,' he said, ushering me out of the door, not realising I had slept in my make-up every single night since we'd been together.

It was such a lovely appointment. I explained to the people there that I wanted to look exactly like Jordan but a little subtler, and that I needed my eyebrows sorting. Actually, I just needed them to actually exist. The girl did a brilliant job; she gave me dark eyes, brows, light cheeks, and great lips. I felt like me again. I felt ready.

Several hours later, I pulled on my black sack once more and we made our way down to the mess, the place where the soldiers had their drinks. It was absolutely breathtaking. There were round, beautifully decorated tables, with candles and lights. There was a band set up for later. The men were in red and black suits and the women were in black and red dresses, and they all looked so glamorous. I could hardly believe I was there.

We sat down to our meal and I spied the buffet. It was not a buffet I was used to, with tuna sandwiches and rolls. It had six types of meat, fish, salads, prawns, mussels, soup, and a whole table dedicated to cheese. And don't even get me started on the bar. Soldiers downed bottles of port, while their wives and girlfriends were drinking rosé and whisky.

Chatting to the army wives and girlfriends was a joy; all they spoke about was engagements, marriage, and the politics of army housing. I couldn't wait to be part of this world, to have conversations about my house and my marriage and my husband and my life. The band started, the raffle commenced, and Sammy ended up winning £500. We danced, we talked, and we laughed. I felt so alive and happy enjoying myself in this new world with this wonderful caring man, that I forgot about everything else. I was drunk on love.

*

Oh Christ alive, Mary, and Joseph. I opened my eyes slowly. This wasn't surgery. This wasn't chemotherapy. This was the hangover from hell.

I called in sick. 'So, I won't be in on Monday!' I explained proudly to my boss in a cheery tone.

Sammy thought this was an absolute disgrace. The ball had been on a Saturday and I was signing myself off for maybe an entire week.

'Because you mixed your drinks?' Sammy asked.

'Yes, I did, and it felt fucking fabulous! I've got a hangover and I deserve a sickie!'

I looked at the mess on the floor, including my bra on one side of the room and breast prosthetic on the other. I drew in a deep breath and asked, 'So when did you first know that I didn't have an even chest? That I was missing a breast?'

'Straight away. As soon as you told me, I presumed you'd had a mastectomy. It wasn't on my list of top five worries,' he said, with a shrug.

God. He had accepted me for who I was completely, and how bloody brilliant was it that he knew all along? *Maybe I could start inching the wig off?*

*

Recently, Sammy had suggested that maybe we should venture out of London to do something slightly different. *YOU'RE GETTING ENGAGED!* a friend had texted me when I told her about it.

I'm really not, I had replied, thinking *please, please let me get engaged.*

Sammy had said that he would drive us to Windsor in Berkshire. I had been once, as a child, to see the castle. But it was a distant memory, and I wondered if it was going to be replaced with pure happiness or bitter disappointment.

We travelled to Windsor and had a good time on the way there. I really couldn't walk very far though, because I was so tired. Co-codamol, my dear friend, helped me with that. I was taking them regularly, just like mints.

Sammy and I reverted to our favourite pastime – eating. We sat in Bella Italia with the backdrop of the castle behind us. Everything was perfect again. In the months we had been dating, I had given him my all and he had given it back to me. But I needed to tell him my big secret. Not the one about my breast. He didn't care about the chicken fillet shoved in my bra, and occasionally he would make jokes about it. I liked that. But the hair? That was different. If I was going to marry this man *(please god, let it be true)* then my hair was quickly becoming something I couldn't hide from him.

After the chemotherapy ended, my hair had started to grow back. I'd been thrilled. I just needed it to grow a few inches longer to get away with a pixie haircut. It would be a dramatic change for Sammy, to see me going from having long, brown, shiny locks to Sinead O'Connor-esque hair. So he needed to know in advance, to be prepared.

'I need to tell you something,' I said, without looking directly at Sammy. 'I'm wearing a wig.'

I looked down at my burger and chips and shoved some into my mouth so that I couldn't say any more.

'Yeah, I know,' Sammy replied very seriously. And nothing more was said on the subject.

I can't explain the shock that hit me. He had known for weeks and months that I was wearing a wig and he hadn't said a single thing about it. If I'd had any doubt before about him, it was all gone in that moment. He'd never had an issue with the wig or the breast. He liked me for me, not what I had been.

But my dreamy smile and "marry me" face soon disappeared as things rapidly went downhill. Sammy had brought me to Windsor for another reason, other than just to have a nice day out. He also had something major to tell me. He had been posted back to Windsor Barracks with immediate effect.

'It's a fucking disaster. What am I going to do?' I asked anyone and everyone who would listen to me go on about it.

'Well, he is a soldier ... didn't you always know it was a possibility?' came the reaction from most people.

I didn't want to hear it. I couldn't lose this man. He had saved me from myself. My life, my soul mate (or whatever it was that people in love always said) – that was what he was to me. I just couldn't lose him. But he would move back to Windsor and I would be in London, too fat and knackered to see him. It was too far away for us to continue the way that we had before.

'It's an hour and a half up the road! He's not going abroad!' Mum tried to reason with me.

I didn't care. It was still a distance.

The distance had to go.

CHAPTER 23

Girls Just Want to Have Fun

Sammy was not keen on the idea of me moving to Windsor at all. We hadn't been going out too long and he said he didn't want to rush things, to take things too fast.

And also, I didn't want us to move in together and then for it all to go horribly wrong, just as Sam was about to start his new job.

'If things went wrong with us now, it would really cause a massive problem for me at work, and I just can't let that happen,' he'd said.

I was beyond fuming. So he had been promoted, so what? Why was he being so selfish? *He should leave the army. He should put me first, leave and get a job in London as a saddler, so I could attend all my appointments and still see Mum and Dorothy.* It felt so simple to me. That night, we had a huge row with a lot of swearing, a lot of upset, and a lot of distress. 'YOU are selfish!' he shouted at me.

'No, YOU ARE!' I screamed back at him.

We had a strong, passionate relationship, but we both also had a lot of fire in our bellies. We were angry and full of temper. He would say no to me a lot of the time and that was one of the reasons why I liked him. And I would do the same to him, keep him in check, and that was why he liked me.

Sitting on the bus back and forth from work, I would think over and over about my dilemma. I wanted to marry this man, and I couldn't have him moving back to Windsor without me. I had to run away with him. That was the only solution I could think of. As we drove past Tottenham one day, there was a lot of noise. There were women in funny coloured wigs standing outside Boots. They had banners and cupcakes, and were shaking huge buckets of money. 'RACE FOR LIFE. Race, run or walk, five or ten kilometres to raise money for cancer!'

I thought about how resistant I'd been towards charities and campaigns, especially when I felt there was a "forced fun" element in whatever they did. I definitely still didn't approve of marzipan nipples. But I was becoming more educated around charities and what they did. Through talking to patients having similar treatment to me, I realised that not a single one of them had anything negative to say about charities.

Over time, I realised that my resistance was just me being overly defensive. I began to see all the good they did – the funding, the counselling to patients and families, the help. I even wondered if I could be a good example of a survivor. *I should raise money,* I started to think. I needed to give something back to the people who had helped me, through all their fundraising and research. Here I was, alive and well, and I absolutely had something to prove to the world.

That's it, I decided, *I'm going to run.* Sammy reluctantly agreed to train me. Though the dream seemed so much fun, the reality was that I had not walked faster than a quick punt to the toilet for months. Actual running was something I could barely remember doing.

I had told my dad about my intention to run the Race for Life, and he was very supportive of the whole thing. He bought me a treadmill, which was delivered to Mum's house and put to use in my sister's old bedroom. I had promised Mum that by the time Polly's new baby was born, it would definitely be gone. What I didn't tell her was that I hoped Sammy and I would be moving to Windsor one day, and that the thing would be coming with me.

Every evening, after a 12-hour day, Sammy would drive from Knightsbridge the whole way around South London to East London ... during rush hour. We would then battle with my attempts on the treadmill, argue about how I was standing on it, how far I could do, if I would be fit enough. Being on a treadmill was one thing. But running outside was another thing. And with a wig on top of that!

'Ditch the wig!' Sammy urged. But no, my vanity meant too much to me. I tied my wig hair back, and it felt like a weird bale of hay on my back. But it was at least better than having nothing there.

I felt so motivated to do it. But the training became a constant stress for me and Sammy, and neither of us were getting anything out of it.

After another evening of sweat, and tears, I checked my Race for Life sponsorship profile that I had written up the week before. 'I am running for me, and for all those people with cancer just like me.' It was short, and it wasn't a sob story. I couldn't bear sob stories. I didn't like the "single mother, council house, terrible childhood" reasons for why someone should win, like the stories that contestants on *X-Factor* came up with. I wanted to make a point, but I also wanted to earn some money and give something back to these incredible charities, which were part of the reason that there were advances in the field and the success rates were increasing.

I wondered what my target would be. 'Put £600 and be happy with £300,' Sammy advised. I did think that was a bit ambitious. After a year of basically ignoring all charities, turning the TV off when the ads came on, boycotting Boots and Topshop, and refusing to darken the doors of any shop that had a pink ribbon outside, I strongly doubted people would buy in to this. The night before my Race for Life, I checked my sponsorship profile, slightly worried (okay, maybe very worried) that I hadn't raised a single thing. I'd been putting off checking the total amount.

As the page loaded, my heart raced. And then ... I had raised nearly £2000! I was extremely shocked, but so touched by it. People were so kind with their donations, but more so with their comments. They used words like "inspirational", "survivor", "positive person". I would never have used those words personally, but seeing them on the page like that, written by other people ... I just knew they were right. I was a survivor.

*

May 2010 came around faster than I thought. The race would take place in Regents Park, London. Sammy woke up in a terribly frantic mood, worried about all kinds of things. He, Mum, and all my friends met in East London and we got the Tube to Hyde Park. The atmosphere outside the Tube station was incredible. My parents and all of my friends had turned up to watch me do this. The sea of pink T-shirts was overwhelming. The weather was warm, and everyone was just happy and supportive of one another. I approached the starting line, my number banner on the back.

There was a space for a loved one's name. Mine said: "*I'm running the Race for Life for: ME*".

'Girls Just Wanna Have Fun' started playing over the park. My nerves kicked in, and it felt like someone was twisting a spoon inside my stomach. I felt so hot. Sammy had joined me at the starting line. I pulled my wig off.

'It's coming off. I can't do 5k with that bloody heap of hay on my head!' I said. Everyone cheered as they saw me take it off and hand it to him. I felt very emotional as Mum looked at me, standing there without my wig in broad daylight. We both tried not to cry, but I did. Five kilometres. Christ. This was going to kill me.

'I can't do this,' I said to Sammy, looking around at all the pro-runners, the sports gear, and the Nike Air Max trainers. I was nothing like them.

'Get to the bloody front!' he ordered, smacking me on the bum for motivation. As the atmosphere built up, he set my iPod to 'Keep on Running' by Spencer Davis.

A horn sounded. We were off.

It didn't take long for the pain to creep up on me, but I kept going. I made it to one kilometre. I was soaking up the atmosphere. Two kilometres. Women were running past me, patting me on the back and showering me with compliments. They'd seen my hair, or the lack of it, and they'd seen my name badge on the back. They were congratulating me for it all. Four kilometres. I could see the finish line. Sammy was shouting. 'Come onnnn!'

I felt like Kelly Holmes in the Olympics. My family and friends were all shouting, waving, and screaming with joy. And to my amazement, I broke into a small sprint just a couple of steps over the finish line.

I did it. I've raised over £2000 and I've finished it. I did it!

'This is one of the best days of my life,' Mum said, hugging me. I knew how much this meant to her. This was one you-know-what appointment that I didn't want to protect her from. I wanted her to be in the middle of it, soaking up the magic of it all.

My sister couldn't be there because she'd had her baby the day before. Her name was Lily. She was beautiful, with dark hair and eyes. She was a very bonny baby, and I just knew that she'd quickly become her sister Poppy's best friend. We sat down to a celebration meal with both our families and friends. The chatter was all about the race.

We all felt euphoric. It was a release for everyone. All the fear and upset and anger had been washed away by this Race for Life victory. I had done it. My sister had given birth too, because life really does go on, no matter what happens. The chemotherapy had taken the badness out of me, and only the good was going to remain.

Now all I needed to do was to convince Sammy to move in with me.

CHAPTER 24

Home Sweet Home

'It would just make so much sense petrol-wise. Most weekends, the trains are cancelled, especially if the Queen is at home. And think of Dorothy. She wouldn't know if she was coming or going,' I said to Sammy one evening.

My rationale for why we should live together was becoming more and more frantic. Sammy raised an eyebrow, unsure why Dorothy had been brought into this. 'Plus, my radiotherapy's over, and it would be a fresh start for us, away from all the treatment!' Actually, this one was true. After 21 months of treatment, we really did need a bit of a change now. I wanted to be away from London, to meet new friends, to start again. This definitely made sense. Plus, I had been living with Mum for nearly two years. I needed my independence back, and so did she. ...

It was Spring, 2011. And I had finally convinced Sammy for us to move in together after what seemed like an eternity.

'It'll only work if you listen to me. I will sort out somewhere for us to live,' he said. Fine by me. I couldn't give a damn if we lived in a cow shed, as long as we lived together.

'It is *basically* a cow shed,' Danny had said to Sammy one evening. Their names were a little bit similar, which got rather confusing when talking about them both in one conversation. It was rather irritating to the receiver. *Sammy, Danny, Danny, Sammy.* Danny lived in a small cow shed in a small village in Acorn town. It was about five miles from the town centre in Windsor. It was close enough, but it still felt very far away. And it was right out in the woods.

The Cow Shed, as I started to call it, was actually a small conversion which sat on the land belonging to Gertie and John. Danny was in a pub one night and had got chatting to the couple. Four real ales and a packet of peanuts later, a verbal contract was made and keys were handed over to us straight away. This seemed to be how things worked outside of London, apparently. There were no guarantors, no references, just a verbal agreement over a few drinks one evening. It was a simple life. And this was definitely a simple property.

Danny had suggested to Sammy that we take up this new place "as a favour to Gertie and John", who really could have done with some tenants. We went to visit the house and talked all the way there, playing house. We talked about decoration styles and discussed nights in and out, and what living in the countryside would be like. We drove down a country lane that went on for miles. How on earth would we call a cab, get a takeaway? They'd never find us. God, my map reading skills needed to improve. Thank Christ I drove a car. We finally pulled up after a lot of complaints from Sammy.

'These mud tracks better not fuck up my suspension,' he said grumpily.

We pulled up to locked security gates. There was a sudden loud noise in the air. Perhaps it was barking. No, howling. We spotted a bunch of beautiful, red, white, and brown dogs. Birds – huge ones as big as the dogs – flitted around and a larger than life woman ran up to us, carrying a pig in her arms.

It was like something straight out of a fairy tale. 'Don't mind the pig.

And I'm not talking about John!' the woman said with a chuckle, referring to her husband. Gertie and John were both completely lovely. They had lived in Acorn town all their lives and had slowly built their own empire. They quickly lead us into their huge, *Downtown Abbey*-style kitchen. Gertie and John talked about their house, their kids, the animals, Windsor, London, New York, Paris, Milan, and Barbados. They talked about their housekeeper and swimming pool. It might sound like they were bragging, but they were just eager to talk and were quite humble about it all. They had earned this life and they were totally living it. They didn't ask much of us. But that was fine, I was used to that.

We nodded a lot, coming out with 'Yes', 'Oh! Righhhht!', and 'Oh, of course!' every so often. We heard endless stories of how they'd made their fortune. We were eventually taken around to our love nest, the Cow Shed. We couldn't all walk in at once because there was a small corridor that led immediately into the living room. So one by one, we trotted in.

We piled into the tiny living room. It was completely empty. Gertie and John said something about having "table and chairs thrown into the deal". The tour took us all of three and a half minutes. The kitchen was functional, but unclean. It had all the appliances a kitchen needed, but they were definitely not from this century. The bathroom was fine and the bedroom – well, it would work. 'And that,' Gertie said, pointing outside, 'is your view.'

We turned to look. I saw a lake, with birds sitting and nesting. There were chickens pecking around the lake and a small boat tied up by the side. Big, huge, beautiful willow trees towered over the water. And there were huge manicured gardens and fields lining the lake. It was absolutely stunning. This felt like the place for relaxation, for peace, for romance, and for recovery. This was my place for love and remission.

'This place is small. It's dingy, and it's dirty!' Sammy said to me, while we were having a private whispering moment.

'No, it's cosy. It's private and it's a nest!' I hissed back, as quietly as I could. I was completely sold.

I could just see myself running around in an apron, feeding chickens, and baking some sort of proper meal for Sammy after a long day's work. 'How much?' Sammy asked boldly, demanding a figure from Gertie, who clearly controlled the purse strings. They agreed on the rent and the move-in date. My favourite part was when we discussed who would feed the chickens and when.

Our dream was getting nearer and nearer.

*

'I think these might be yours?' Sammy's dad Stephen said to me, giving me direct eye contact.

The worst had happened. Sammy's dad had a pair of my knickers in his hand. He had been helping us move into our cottage, which we were no longer calling the Cow Shed, not now that we'd moved into it. Somehow, the knickers had fallen into the back of his van. 'ANNIE, GET A MOVE ON!' Sammy shouted. God, I was useless at this moving malarkey.

Mum was overly emotional, and so was I, but we were both glad we were doing it. I was moving forward with my life, even if I had forced my boyfriend to live with me. We spent weeks playing house and setting up our home. Sammy'd brought his pride and joy, his horse brasses. He'd also brought the picture of the racehorse Frankel, all his little things from his previous life. I'd brought a load of diamante mirrors and fluffy lamps. It was a very equal mixture of mine and Sammy's personalities.

'It's like a Norfolk pub crossed with an Essex mansion,' Sammy had once said on the phone to someone. I had laughed; this was definitely the best way to describe the inside of our cottage.

I was getting right into this country life stuff. But there were some things that needed to be done first. I had to plan my week entirely.

Every meal had to be planned to a T. With a full-time job and the closest Tesco six miles away, you just didn't have time to forget the fucking tuna off the list. So meals were always planned. I would get up super early to leave for work.

I had recently been promoted to manager within the recruitment agency and I was thriving. I was enjoying it. I no longer woke up first thing in the morning and dreaded the day ahead. I got up at 5.00am and let the chickens out, took the mince out of the freezer, got into my BMW 1 series, and did 60mph on country lanes. I would come home at night, kicking off the heels that I could now bear to wear again, and cook my man a meal. Then I'd wash up and we would watch TV together. This was the life, as far as I was concerned. I was happy, in control, and I had my independence back.

I love my morning updates, Mum had text me.

We always kept in contact, texting one another all the time. We'd done it ever since I was at university. I would write everything down and just send it to her. I always found writing so much more efficient than a phone call and besides, we couldn't really speak as the reception was terrible where I lived. But that was fine. We would still see each other at least once a week, as we were only up the road. I didn't want to be on my phone chatting anyway.

I emailed Karen: *It's so nice not having any reception here. You feel liberated without your phone.*

Sounds like a bloody nightmare! Karen replied, clearly shocked.

My friends took turns to come and visit me. And like most tourists, they saw it more of a novelty than something permanent: Annie in a country cottage in the arse end of nowhere, reading the *Berkshire Lady* in her spare time. But I felt safe. No one knew me and I felt like I was starting my life all over again.

My annual check-ups had also been moved to the local breast unit in central Windsor. And they were a very different experience to those in London. They were infinitely slower, and had more of a front-room atmosphere than a proper frosty waiting room. I had registered with a new doctor, Dr Dickinson, who I fell slightly in love with because of her sheer sense of humour and bed manners.

As I sat with Dr Dickinson at one of my appointments, I remembered my breast nurse, Helen, telling me that you-know-what would change me, change the way that I lived my life. And now I knew she was right. I was happier now, more positive, and I felt a sense of gratitude for my life that hadn't been there before. I no longer felt the need to go out and get drunk all the time. I realised that I didn't need a man to define me, didn't need to sleep with someone to feel self-worth. I had a partner who saw me as his equal, who was my good friend. All I needed now was to turn that partner into a full-blown husband.

I had always known which engagement ring I wanted, even from a young age. What can I say? I was a young girl with dreams. It was an in-your-face princess cut, gold, square diamond. And an image of it was saved in maximum resolution on Sammy's computer. The summer months of 2011 came, and I started to blossom. I had joined the local slimming club in an attempt to pull myself out of the hold of all those steroids. My hair was growing back and looked great topped with real hair extensions. I felt attractive and confident again – like during the Benidorm days – but with actual class and sophistication. I'd got my life back.

CHAPTER 25

PUT A RING ON IT

Sammy and I booked a holiday to Gran Canaria. We didn't have much money but wanted somewhere cheap, lively, and fun, though I knew I'd most certainly not be sunbathing ever again. The thought of it made me feel sick. But that wasn't the point. It was about us going on holiday and enjoying our freedom together. We arrived at Gran Canaria at 2.00am. The flight was cheap because of the time we landed, just as it started to get busy in the town centre. It was really exciting. It was like a cheaper, tackier Piccadilly Circus. This was right up my street. We dumped our bags and went out onto the balcony to decide where we were going to go out. This holiday was seven nights long and we couldn't waste any of them by staying in.

'Annie?'

I turned around and saw Sammy on his knees. Because of his height, it still looked like he was standing!

My heart stopped – and then started beating at a mile a minute. A thousand thoughts came to me all at once. He quickly produced a box. I felt sick, but happy. I was excited and tearful, shocked and ecstatic.

The man of my dreams was on his knees, on the first night of our holiday, asking me to marry him. Here was my prince on a balcony, with a ring in his hands! He opened the box slowly ...

'Annabel Walsh, will you ...'

I looked down. The ring was silver. Oh my god, the ring was silver. He'd got it wrong.

Okay, no, it's fine. Forget it, and smile. '... marry me?'

Pause, I remembered. My granny always said that I had to pause.

'YES, PLEASE!' I shouted, crying and hugging him. He beamed. I loved it when Sammy smiled. His blue eyes got wider and his cheeks got rosier. But he didn't do it very often. I knew he was bursting with happiness at this moment. 'I'M ENGAGGGGGEDDDDD!!!' I screamed down the phone at Mum some moments later.

'Oh, Annie, that is truly wonderful. I couldn't be happier!' Mum said. Afterwards Sammy and I stood out on the balcony, looking at all the pretty lights in the town centre. I wished there had been someone there filming the moment so we could watch it back forever.

I'd endured hell for the past year, but now my life had turned into the dream I'd always hoped for. We were far too excited to go to sleep, so we hit the town at 3.00am. We walked through the streets of Gran Canaria in our own buzz. I was 27 and engaged. I was proud to be engaged to my soldier.

And it turned out that he'd actually got the ring right! It actually did have a gold band like my granny's. Now that I could see it properly, in better lighting, I'd say that it was gold with a princess square cut diamond. Traditional, just like Sammy. We got drunk and stupidly tried to ring all the important people in our lives to share our happy news. We called Sammy's mum, my sister, my granny and grandpa ... the list just went on and on. 'Right, stop now. It's bloody 5.00am,' Sammy said, when I tried to go downstairs and tell the hotel manager.

We woke up the next day feeling like everything had been a dream.

We had drunk for hours but we weren't hungover. We had too many happy hormones swimming around for a headache to ruin it. We walked down to the beach. I hadn't swum in the sea for years, so I stayed back and watched as Sammy went diving in. All I could see were bodies in the sea – young, old, fat, and thin. Some were in bikinis and swimming shorts, and some were in T-shirts. They all looked so happy and free. Sammy shouted over for me to come in. *Could I?*

Bra on or bra off?

No, I couldn't. Not in the sea, where everyone would see that I was a freak. No, I was not doing it.

'YES, YOU ARE!' Sammy pulled me in and held me tight against him. It was such a nice feeling, with the freezing water against my body and the burning sun on my face.

'You really are the perfect man,' I said, kissing him, the sun in our eyes. Following this, we spent most days in the sea or the pool, and most nights in the nearest Irish bar, where I'd spend time talking about the wedding.

We wanted – or I wanted – to do so much that we actually found it easier to eliminate what we didn't want to happen. We compiled a very fun list: The Not Happening List.

1. Not marrying abroad
2. Not marrying in a religious setting
3. Not scrimping on booze for the guests

We agreed on everything (Sammy had no choice but to listen to me).

The holiday was done, the ring was on my finger, the diet was ruined, and I was the proudest woman in the world.

As we got back to Gatwick, Sammy disappeared into WHSmith and returned with a stack of bridal magazines. I could now officially be one of those women that I saw every morning on the Tube, suited up on the way to her perfect job, living her perfect life with the perfect ring on her finger. I'd be the envy of the whole carriage!

We started the wedding preparations. Who would we invite? Everyone, I decided. When was the wedding going to be? Not in the school holidays; that was too expensive. Not at Christmas, too many distractions. May? No, definitely not then. There were seven family members' birthdays in May, so it was an expensive month anyway.

October, then? Yes. The date was set for October 2012, the following year. Eleven months and counting. And we knew before we touched down in Gatwick Airport who was invited and who was most definitely not. We didn't want to invite children, but what about our nieces? They had to come.

Sammy started telling anyone who would listen about the effort he'd put into the proposal. 'Went to every jewellery shop ... met an actual designer ... chose the diamond ... had to walk through Windsor high street with the deposit. In cash. In my pocket ...'

The ring was perfect. *He* was perfect. True to his word, he had stuck to every detail I wanted in the ring. I'd plastered it all over the screen he owned in the house.

Soon it became too much, though. Every time he told that story, I wanted him to stop. I started to feel very guilty about my persistence on getting the ring right.

Everyone was very excited for us, though, and I loved all the attention that I was getting. I thrived on it. That evening, after yet another engagement celebration, I started to think about what married life would be like. Especially to a solider. And although we were set on marriage now, we'd never had the conversation about babies. We were both becoming increasingly broody. We'd find ourselves cooing at birds' nests and sympathising with parents struggling with babies on the plane. I needed to talk to him about starting a family.

One night, as we were lying side-by-side on our bed, we were both silent, just thinking about how far we had come and how happy we were.

I started talking about fertility. Sammy was pretty oblivious to the fact that we had a potential relationship-altering conversation coming up. I adopted his confidence and dived straight in, like he had in the sea on our holiday.

'You need to realise that, actually, it might be very difficult for us to have children,' I said to him, nervously. He paused and looked at me. 'I don't see why it would be, Annie. Your system still works,' he said, referring to my periods.

'Yes, it does, but I just want to know that you'll still be there if I, well … *we,* can't have children,' I said to him, feeling slightly sick. Suddenly that decision to freeze my eggs three years ago was so important.

I realised that pussy-footing around wasn't going to be good enough on this topic. I poured my heart out. I told him about being pressured into making a decision very quickly, the process, the operation to remove my eggs. I told him about my constant swaying between not wanting to have children and picturing them as a possibility in the future. There I was, with the man I loved, thinking about my life and my future. Would Sammy still be into me if I couldn't give him a baby?

'Of course I will!' Sammy said to me, after I'd explained everything.

It was then that I realised how scared and cautious I had been about approaching the subject with him. In my head, Sammy was a young man, wanting to start a life with his new wife and create a family. The idea that potentially I might not fit that bill for him terrified me.

Sammy could see past all the negativity, my lack of hair, and my low self-worth regrading my femininity. I really appreciated that. I had opened up to him and he had accepted it. We didn't take the chat any further.

But there was always the next mission to think about. This time it was the wedding dress. I wanted something amazing, something that would catch everyone's eye, something that would make me feel like the queen I always knew I was.

'I can't wear that, I can't wear that, and I definitely can't wear that!' I exclaimed, as Karen started the search. I ripped out pages of white dresses from the many, many wedding magazines we had all over the floor. I'd hired a wedding organiser. My oversized, unfilled diary was now bursting with cut-outs and pictures. There were no Disney-like dresses. They were all very Jordan-marrying-Prince-William.

'Look at how awful Jordan looks,' Polly had said, pointing at a picture of her latest wedding.

How dare she! I strongly disagreed. I looked at the picture. There she was, with mahogany skin and long, curly back hair, wearing a gigantic diamond white-meringue dress, covered in diamantes, pearls, and other gorgeous embellishments. I saw another shot of her entering the church smiling, breasts first, as always. She looked amazing. I needed to be like her on my wedding day. I needed to be the epitome of perfection.

I needed breasts. Two years after my you-know-what, my delayed reconstruction was finally on my doorstep. It was ringing the bell frantically.

We had to return to London, to the hospital in East London where I was originally diagnosed. But this was an exciting feeling. I was about to get cosmetic surgery. I had a new purpose.

Finally.

CHAPTER 26

THE BOOB JOB

It felt strange being back in my old haunt in East London. We went to the same hospital where I had been diagnosed and had later had my mastectomy. I felt scared. I had no idea what to expect, and I hadn't enjoyed my experience with hospitals before. But I also felt excited, thinking about what might come from this.

Mum and I attended my breast reconstruction consultation, just like old times. Waiting in the room, I had a nervous energy. I couldn't stop tapping my legs or clasping my hands together. I just wanted it to be done.

I pictured the doctors and nurses all staring at the bling on my finger. I fantasised about the nurse calling out my new married name: 'Annie Belasco!' I let myself pretend that that was what they said when they called out my real name.

'So, there are two options,' the consultant said, putting a diagram of a one-breasted mannequin on the white wall behind us. 'The first is autogenous reconstruction. Here we use tissue from your bottom, stomach or back, depending on the greater mass. If we use tissue from your stomach, we call this a "DIEP flap". The second is prosthetic reconstruction. Here we insert an expandable implant in the breast area. Over a period of three to six months, we then use a pump to inflate the breast. This will need replacing after 10 years.'

The "we" he was talking about was the team at the reconstruction unit. "He" was Dr Chinwabee, a very tall African with a heavy accent, who made no eye contact. His manner mimicked The Judge's, but with less menace. I wouldn't have much time to get to know him, but from judging from his CV (basically his long introduction to us), it was clear that he knew how to create a great pair of boobs. He was the man. He was my new hero. I wondered if he knew Jordan ...

'So, it's a fairly big decision to make. Come back and see us in two months and we can go through it all again.' Two months? My mouth dropped open. There were only 11 months to go until my wedding. In two months it would be nine. I had three months to order and have a dress made. This was worrying. I didn't even want to think what this would do to my wedding schedule. This time frame was not going to work. It didn't suit me, but I didn't want to speak up, to piss him off, to have him write the whole thing off. How was I going to handle this?

I started scrabbling around in my handbag, looking for my co-codamol. I changed my mind and decided to say something. Taking my hand out of my handbag, I looked up and spoke. 'Okay, I think I've made my mind up already!' I said enthusiastically, nodding.

'You say you "think". You must be clear, you must be sure,' Mr Chinwabee said very seriously.

'I am sure. And I can't wait two months,' I said, with urgency.

'Hmm.' Mr Chinwabee was clearly not impressed with my quick decision.

I had to get this situation sorted, quickly. I couldn't state the obvious, that I felt that time was running out for me, that I had things to do. So I thought back to my recruitment training. I thought about selling a new role and a better work / life balance to the candidate.

I thought about my tactics when getting them a pay-rise and fewer hours. I thought about how I'd convinced poor blokes all over London to go on a date with me, on the exact weekend I wanted. I was the barrister, and Mr Chinwabee was a jury member who I had to convince.

I wanted breasts. I wanted to feel feminine again and look nice for once. I didn't want to have to carry around the chicken fillet and hide my huge scar. I wanted a big breast to match my other one. I wanted the DIEP flap option, which would take fat tissue from my stomach, resulting in a free tummy tuck as well. And then he'd transport all that fat to the breast area, to form the ideal breast. I wouldn't have a nipple, but right now that could wait. That was fine. I could deal with that. I just needed the shape, and I needed it to be convincing.

I talked and talked and talked. I don't know where it all came from, but I was able to confidently talk about my concrete, "100 per cent book-me-in-now" decision, one that had actually taken me months to come to. And yes, I was most certainly fully aware of the ins and outs of the operation, the process, and the recovery period. Somehow, it worked. Signing the declaration form, I felt like a winner. And I knew that in the months to come, I was going to feel like a woman again.

CHAPTER 27

BRIDEZILLA

'We are not getting married in Windsor Castle. Have you lost your mind?' Sammy screamed at me.

Of course I have! I thought. *But doesn't every woman?* 'BUT YOU'RE A SOLDIER! TO THE QUEEN! MAKE IT HAPPEN!' I wailed down the phone. The phone went dead. The doorbell went off, and Pizza Hut and I had yet another date.

This episode of my life had turned into another mission and I was obsessed. I wasn't thinking about work, home or my upcoming operation. I didn't have anyone with me. Not Sammy, not Mum, not Karen. I vaguely listened to occasional ideas they sent my way. Maybe I should invite so-and-so to the wedding? Maybe we could include this song on the DJ's playlist?

I didn't want to lose sight of my mission. I didn't want to get ill like I had before either. The whole day had to be pure and perfect.

I hadn't seen Karen in around eight weeks by this point, and was starting to feel slightly guilty. Maybe she wanted to come wedding dress shopping with me? Maybe she wanted to help me choose the food or the venue, or think of a reading that she could do?

'Maybe you could come to Brighton?' she asked. That was definitely not an option. I had a boob job in two weeks, a moody fiancé, and a wedding to plan.

So far I had chosen my dress designer, but not the dress. I'd chosen the theme. During rare calm moments over the last couple of years, I had always imagined listening to Enya, with white flowers all around me. It had to be white, pure, virginal – yeah, yeah – and glamourous. Jordan had had a white wedding theme, and so had Kate Middleton and Prince William, so it would probably go down well.

And yes, I would walk down the aisle to 'Anywhere Is'. My eyes welled up with tears as I thought about it, as I made notes furiously and updated my Excel spreadsheet with timings.

I had to work really hard to not think about my operation. I distracted myself with the wedding planning. I would spend my days at work, researching, Googling, getting links for flowers, photographers, venues, food, speeches for the best man. And I would spend every evening calling people. I'd leave messages. I called two, three, four make-up artists living in Devon. 'Of course a £500 petrol fee is fine with us!' I said to one.

We also had a budget sheet and an actual bank account for the wedding. We booked a venue and paid the deposit. A menu was drawn up, the guest list was finalised, excuses for not inviting certain people were rehearsed and families were told about all the details.

I invited a lot of different people from different episodes of my life. There were three categories of people on my own guest list: before my you-know-what, during my you-know-what, and after.

Every single person attending our wedding would know what a big deal this was for us. After all I'd been through with my illness, it would be such a great celebration. My maiden name would be dead and buried and my new name would represent the cured, healthy, new me. I didn't want the bastard disease brought up once on my wedding day. It had to be over. I had to draw a line under it.

But there was a problem. Every day I was getting more and more stressed out and worried. And I knew exactly what shade of white the ribbons on my invitations were, but I didn't have a clue what the date was or how much medication I had taken on that day. And to make things worse, I was dreading my surgery.

But I didn't tell anyone. I had rushed through my appointment because I didn't want to hear any negativity. I didn't want to hear the risks and complications that were involved. But I was terrified. I'd made such a quick decision and put my wedding before my health.

And yet I kept my feelings to myself. People didn't need to know. I got through it with a combination of medication and keeping lots of company, and avoided the subject entirely.

My medication was Sertraline, full dose, 200mg a day. This treated my anxiety, but it didn't do anything to help the increasing number of panic attacks I was having. So I had to add to my medication shopping list. I went back to my doctor and explained that I "needed something stronger". Diazepam became my new friend, accompanying me in times of need, calming me down.

I went on the odd night out with Theresa, my dear friend who had bravely shaved my head for me with nothing more than a razor and some whisky. But we always ended up talking about my wedding and nothing else. I spent every weekend at wedding fairs. Sammy would come if there was free cake, but otherwise he wasn't very interested. I had even started referring to myself in the third person as "the bride".

'Why are we even here? You've booked half of Berkshire and this is in Essex!' Sam shouted at me at one wedding fair.

'You never know! I need options!' I was furious. Why was he being so negative about my special day? I picked up dozens of flyers as we left.

My blood was now free of illness and now it felt like it was filled with confetti and cake.

We were getting married in Berkshire. Sammy had told me that traditionally people got married in the bride's hometown. However, I had worked out that if we did that, there wasn't a single route we could take to the venue / church without travelling along a street filled with bad memories. I did have some nice memories of London, especially East London, which was the place of so many of my new beginnings. But I couldn't face any kind of reminder of what I had been through. I couldn't face the memories of travelling on the underground to and from hospitals. Or – god forbid – the memories of that tanning shop I used so often.

So we weren't going to have it in London, or in Southampton where Sammy grew up. We decided to keep it fair and simple and marry halfway between both of them – in Berkshire, our new home which we loved. Two weeks later, a relieved and enthusiastic Sammy went off halfway across the world for two weeks with work.

'BYE!' he shouted as he tooted his horn and sped off to Heathrow. I had an empty cottage and a head full of co-codamol.

Sitting in our little nest, I could see blue tits hoping about in front of the lake. There were lots of little creatures bouncing around from place to place. They looked so happy and so free.

I put the TV on, watching a tennis match to distract myself. Back and forth the ball bounced. I tried to work out the circumference of the tennis ball, to try to see if the lump in my breast had been the same size.

It didn't work. I clicked over to *Big Brother*. 'Get ya tits out for the lads!' I heard a loud voice bellowing from the TV. I grabbed the remote control and quickly changed channels. *Country File* came on. A young farmer showed some school children how to bottle-feed lambs. 'The mother is refusing to let them latch onto her teats,' the farmer explained.

I switched off the TV. I was getting more and more anxious and angry for no reason. Trying to distract myself, I checked my voicemails to see if DJ Dave had come back to me.

Watching the blue tits continue to hop about, I listened to a voicemail. 'Hi, Annabel, just wondering if everything was okay, as we were expecting you in Birmingham today.' My boss Carl had left a quiet message on my mobile. Oops. Work was literally the last thing on my mind and we'd had a very important, "no excuses" meeting to attend that day regarding redundancies.

Immediately, I felt guilty, but then soon after I felt annoyed. Why was he ringing me all of the time? I hated my work mobile. There it sat, on charge in the corner of the room, just waiting to ring. There was always someone wanting to get hold of me. It wasn't a phone; it was a hostage device, a tracking tool. My brain just didn't have space for anything other than painkillers and my wedding. And all these people getting in the way were a constant distraction that I didn't need. There were constant reminders of breasts everywhere, from blue tits on the lake to tits on the TV. I didn't want to think about my own.

My phone beeped again and a text message from Sammy came through. *Have you ever eaten a Fray Bentos pie?*

I deleted it straight away. I wasn't in the mood.

We had a chat later that night. Sammy suggested that I turn my attention to my major operation the following week.

He was right. All my attentions had been focused on the "wedding of the year", as my dad put it. Actually, that just pissed me off. *No one gets married any more,* I thought. *I'm the first in our age bracket in this family to get married, and people should be happy, not taking the piss.*

The truth was, the reason I didn't want to think about breasts and chests was because I couldn't imagine myself with a fully formed chest. It had been four years and the last time I'd had a proper chest, it had been diseased and could have killed me. I pictured it like Mum's old vine growing up the back of her house – diseased and dying.

I was just really scared and didn't know what to expect.

CHAPTER 28

AND IT GOES ON

'We are not going to give you the chop!' Carl announced, with a forced happy voice, his huge white veneers shining at me. *Maybe I should get my teeth whitened for the wedding?* I thought. I wasn't being made redundant.

'SO? Are you pleased?' he asked, clearly frustrated by my non-reaction to his great news. I was just sitting there, thinking about the fact that his big, boob-like stress balls had disappeared from his desk. 'We're restructuring the team,' Carl continued.

I winced. His mobile was ringing *really* loudly, yet he just ignored it, letting it ring. It felt like a jackhammer to my brain. Why did people always do that? Why did people attend meetings with their phones on loud? People always had calls coming in with some stupid ringtone. It was so frustrating. And then they never turned them off either; they just let them ring.

'70 per cent of the team are gone, and you are one of those who were chosen to stay,' he said, like he was Simon Cowell selecting me for boot camp on X-Factor.

The phone started again. It was making me anxious. I kept looking at it, and then at Carl, and then at the phone, and then at him. *ANSWER IT, YOU BASTARD!* I pleaded at him with my eyes.

'So? Are you pleased, Annabel?'

'Yes, I'm delighted, thank you!' I managed. 'Now, I need to talk to you about my wedding and my annual leave entitlement.'

I didn't give a shit about work, redundancy, or whatever the hell was, or was not, going on. I had totally missed this whole recession thing. What I really wanted to do was to ask Carl about the kind of breasts he liked and if he thought I could do with a pair of them. I doubt I would have got an answer that mattered, because Carl was definitely not on the heterosexual train. He had a young Italian boyfriend and was only interested in meatballs.

Sammy was now back from the US. We'd been to visit our wedding venue and he loved it. It was a hotel in Berkshire, a Victorian building with modern interior and big, grand staircases lined with portraits of previous kings and queens. There were chandeliers dripping in crystal, and diamante handles in the toilets. That was us. A Norfolk pub crossed with an Essex mansion.

We didn't want to marry in a church. We definitely weren't religious, although I had chosen the "spiritual" option in one of the drop-down options on my dating profile. And yes, I was. I loved clairvoyance, crystals, and, of course, angels. Yes, I definitely believed in angels. When you're faced with life and death and aren't religious, you have to turn to something. So mine was finding and believing in special people: the nurses, Mum, Karen, Dorothy the dog, and, of course, now Sammy. He made me believe in angels, without even knowing it.

March 2012 came around, and I was back in East London. It was the night before my reconstruction. Sammy and I stayed at Mum's house. It felt strange but comforting being back at my family home, especially with Sammy along.

Predictably, Mum made a fabulous pre-op dinner. It was gratefully received. The chat was all positive – no negativity allowed. We just sat talking about the good things. The conversation was mainly about the wedding again. I did most of the talking, bringing up the same subjects over and over again, and I never got tired of them. Like the flowers. There could be no green there, no pink or red, no yellow. They had to be white, pure white, virginal white, like Jordan and Kate Middleton. Any colour added into my wedding theme was considered to be a disease, just like the lump in my breast.

'No colour, just white!' I had barked down the phone at my wedding planner.

'Annabel, just leave it. The wedding is months away and your operation is tomorrow,' Mum said.

She was right, but I'd better not see any colour at that wedding.

CHAPTER 29

RECONSTRUCTION

Sammy, Mum, and I drove up to the hospital in Essex, to the plastic surgery unit.

> Jenny Murry,
> Dad

We were greeted by a group of angels the next morning. Sammy had told them that he and Mum were joining me.

One young nurse called Rebecca showed us around the department, the ward, the toilets, the showers, the beds, the corridor, and the High Dependency Unit (or HDC, as it was known to everyone else). I was a little bit confused about why there was a massive, aquarium-sized fish tank in the middle of the ward, and only three beds around it. 'Where you will be while you are recovering initially,' one of the nurses said.

Wait, I'm going to have to stay in hospital for a while?

My heart dropped, my head started spinning, and I started to panic. I had thought this would be like the mastectomy, where I would have the operation and two days later, I'd be on my way. I should have listened to Mr Chinwabee when he was talking to me. I should have done my research and given myself the two months' reflection period as he had advised. I should have actually thought about what was going on. I could feel a tantrum coming on, a panic attack. My chest filled with terror. I had to control this.

These emotions have to go. I slowly got dressed into the brown gown while one of the kind nurses spoke to Mum and Sammy for ages. What on earth were they talking about? I spied my hospital notes – my old, reliable, favourite read: *Dah dah ... right breast ... dah dah ... young woman, 27 ... dah dah.*

It did not say you-know-what anywhere. Absolutely nowhere. It had been scrubbed from my life. I rustled around in my bag, quickly looking for my co-codamol as the nurse and consultant walked out of the room. Three boxes fell out just as Sammy and Mum came back into the room. I was so embarrassed. Mum stacked them all up into a big tower while telling me they wouldn't be needed as the nurses were more than capable of prescribing medication "that you actually need".

I felt like a little girl being told off. They then sat beside me as they explained to me what the nurse had told them, something about how my operation was going to be very intense and long, and that they would be called as soon as it had been completed.

I heard a familiar voice. Dr Chinwabee, the daddy of breasts, was here. And he was coming to see me. I sat up, pushing out what was left of my chest. He also had Gurpreet with him, the nurse who had been with me throughout my entire journey. I smiled and said a rather too fake 'Hello!'

He muttered something about my gown and rustled around for a pen. I laughed to myself, remembering Dr P and his pen. *Please don't drop it, please don't drop it.* But he didn't, thankfully.

Nurses gathered around Dr Chinwabee. One of them started drawing lines on me.

My god, this was taking a long time. I couldn't feel the pen on my body. I could just see eight pairs of eyes staring at different parts of my completely naked body. It was like a big, medical Medusa was just staring down at me.

'Look at me!' I said to Sammy and Mum, full-frontal naked in the middle of the ward with a thousand lines and dots all over me. I thought it was quite funny; they definitely did not. So I put my brown gown back on and said goodbye.

I didn't like this bit. I watched the angels go back and forth, saying nothing to me. Occasionally I would hear a blood pressure machine being turned on and then off again, but other than that, there was nothing.

I could hear someone crying. Was it Mum? A nurse? Or another patient? I had no idea.

The angels appeared and asked me to remove my engagement ring. I didn't like this at all either. I hadn't realised how much of a security blanket it had become for me. It was my cure for you-know-what, my statement that I had found love. But it had to come off. For now. I didn't get the opportunity to walk into the theatre this time. I lay on a trolley bed for what seemed like hours, waiting to be put under by the anaesthetist. Finally, it was my turn. I counted down.

5 … 4 … I looked down at my chest.

3 … There was no Enya singing in my head. Why?

2 … 1 …

*

My head was awake, but my body was not. I couldn't open my eyes. I could just hear words floating around me. It was like a bad dream. I drifted in and out of consciousness. I could hear the beep of the blood pressure machine.

Beep.

I could hear Sammy talking.

Beep.

I could hear Mum talking.

Beep.

Sammy was talking again.

I opened my eyes. Lots and lots of people were in the room but I couldn't see Sammy or Mum. I didn't recognise anyone. I felt completely alone, like a foetus without the womb to protect it from the rest of the world.

'Annie?' a quiet voice said. I didn't know what was happening or where I was. The sensitivity, headache, confusion, and pain were so incredibly intense. I didn't think I could be in so much pain without dying. That's it. Maybe I was dead. Could that final operation have been the final blow to my poor, young body? Perhaps I had died and gone to heaven and the nurses were actually angels this time around.

'Annie, it's me.' A recognisable voice. I knew who this was. It was my Sammy. I couldn't smile, but I really wanted to. I really wanted him to know that I recognised him and felt comfort from his voice.

I fell asleep again, waking up with Dr Chinwabee and his angels gathered around me. I was more conscious this time around. I felt unsure if the morphine was masking the truth, but he actually appeared to be smiling. 'The operation was a success, although it took us a lot longer than we anticipated. But the breast will take good shape accordingly.'

Dr Chinwabee was probably talking to Mum or Sammy. I wanted to listen, to understand and follow what he was saying, but I had completely lost all sense of time. I was sure by now that two days had passed, but maybe it had been longer than that. I had no way of knowing.

The operation was supposed to take four hours and it had taken 11. I had no idea that a general anaesthetic even worked for that long. My body had been completely unconscious for 11 hours. No wonder I'd felt like absolute shit when I'd tried to wake up. I was so confused. It felt like I couldn't differentiate between my body and head. I knew who Sammy and my family were, and I knew they were there for me, but I couldn't get comfort from anyone or anything. There was constant aching pain in my stomach where the fat had been removed. Consistent and constant top-ups of medication, morphine, antibiotics, co-codamol all kept my pain under control, but it was always there, lurking in the background, waiting to pounce.

I couldn't eat, drink or sleep comfortably. I slept a lot, through the pain. I sipped water through a straw like a toddler, doing it all lying down. Sammy kept travelling back and forth from Windsor to check on me every single day.

He would get up at 5.00am, let the chickens out, and go to work. He'd work until 1.00pm, then drive all the way to East London. He'd pick Mum up then drive straight to the hospital. He would then see his sore, weeping fiancée, who sometimes wouldn't even speak to him because of the pain. And then he would repeat the journey back and work into the night, to make up for lost time. The exhaustion must have been appalling. I could barely imagine it.

'I feel so awful. When will it stop?' I cried to Mum as Sammy took one hand and she took the other.

'You are gorgeous, and we both love you,' he said.

I now realised why I was in the High Dependency Unit. The physical pain was worse than the diagnosis, the treatment more brutal than chemotherapy. And my state of mind had suffered the most, like a cabbage slowly deteriorating, as the drugs worked their magic. Sometimes I didn't even speak because I didn't have the energy. 'It's so bad,' I said to my dad, when he visited me one morning. It had taken him a whopping four hours to get to me from Watford via trains, but it was a welcome effort.

'Once you make the transition from the High Dependency Unit to the ward, you'll start to feel better,' he said, eating the grapes and

Ferrero Rocher he had bought me. He hadn't needed to get me anything. Him being there, making the effort to come and see me, was comfort enough.

'Why don't you turn your phone on?' he suggested. 'Your friends will have been trying to contact you.' Turn my phone on? Invasion? Contact? Tracking? Harassment? No. I couldn't. I needed the peace and quiet.

The tea lady cottoned on that it was now day four and I hadn't eaten anything. The more medication I took, the more I was being sick. I couldn't hold anything down, and I couldn't open my jaw wide enough to eat. Four days on and a square, squashed, grey-and-white sandwich was parked on a tray under my nose. The smell was unbearable and I either hid the food or openly left it alone, showing them that I couldn't eat it. I joked to Sammy, suggesting that he eat it for me. Sure as anything, he did, but even he was repulsed. That cheered me up a little, but soon I was feeling low again. I still hadn't seen my chest. I wondered when the big reveal would be, and I wondered if it was worth all of this.

'You have to bear in mind what they said in your consultation, Annabel. It's going to take weeks, maybe even months to heal and form properly. You need to be patient.' Mum knew "patience" wasn't part of my vocabulary.

When Dr Chinwabee finally did his rounds that day, Mum and Sammy had already left. I was on edge waiting for him. I felt so impatient, I could scream. But I couldn't scream. I couldn't shout. I could barely speak louder than a whisper.

Finally, he and his angels appeared. The curtain whizzed around me. They all filed in, like a football team having their brief before a match. Filled with knowledge, they talked about me like I wasn't there. And then they interviewed me, asking me what I was going through.

'So, the way I would describe it ...' I started to say, very slowly and very quietly. The angels huddled closer, almost merging into one creature, trying to understand what I was going on about.

'Yessssssssssssssssssssssssssss?' they said together.

'There's a dark cloud that comes when I open my eyes, and when I close them. I have pain from my fingertips to my toes. I'm depressed. I'm ill. I feel like I want to die.'

Dr Chinwabee laughed.

He *laughed*.

I wanted to shoot him. I wanted to get Sammy to hire me a gun so I could *shoot* him! There I was, lying there with a fucking catheter in my arse and a drip in my wrist. And now I was suffering from genuine suicidal thoughts AND HE WAS LAUGHING AT WHAT I WAS SAYING. I wish I could have screamed something at him, thrown something at him.

Instead, I painted on a smile.

'It's fine, many people feel the same. And you will feel better tomorrow,' he said to me. The nurses huddled back out, whizzing the curtain back around the rail, and I was left alone.

CHAPTER 30

NOT OUT OF THE WOODS YET

I didn't feel better tomorrow. Tomorrow came and I still felt like death. Sammy and Mum continued to make the journey to see me. Sammy was becoming physically exhausted with the six-hour round trip every day. Mum was emotionally exhausted. I learnt that Mum had started sobbing in the corridor one day. Sammy had put an arm around her, telling her it would all be okay. I felt guilty putting her through this all over again. But I also felt glad that she had someone to lean on. I was glad that Sammy was there for her, that he could reassure her during the times I couldn't.

I liked Mum and Sammy's relationship. They supported one other. She understood him and admired his strengths. He valued her opinion and appreciated her kindness. They were a solid team, always backing me up whenever I needed it.

The corridor doors opened and a voice that I thought belonged to Sammy travelled down to me. I drifted off into a daze and started to fixate on the curtain, waiting for it to be whisked open and reveal my beautiful husband-to-be's face. I imagined that the interlocking shapes on the curtain were the shape of me and Sammy kissing. We had kissed on our first date. That kiss had relieved my pain. I wished I could kiss him again.

'Hiii!'

The curtain opened. It was not Sammy. It was a bouncing, puppy-like man called Martin. I knew this because he had a name badge with a drawn-on smiley face.

That face was irritating. So was Martin's smile.

Speaking at an astronomical speed, Martin told me that he was my physiotherapist who would be teaching me to walk again.

'Pardon?' I couldn't have heard correctly. *Help me walk again?*

'Yes! Walk! You need to learn again 'cos you've been lying down for six days!' He grinned at me. 'Lazy bones!' he dared to say, through a nervous smile. There was a tense silence. I stared at him, feeling like I could explode. He read my expression and didn't say another thing.

I had totally underestimated this process. I thought it would take half of the time it had taken to do the operation, a quarter of the time for aftercare, and an eighth of the pain.

It was seven days post operation now. While my bandages were being cleaned and replaced, someone suggested that we do the big reveal. I jumped at the opportunity. I walked into my cubicle and was presented with a full-length mirror. *This will be it,* I thought. *I'm going to have beautiful, perfect breasts.* My nurse opened my gown and asked me to lift my arms up.

I breathed in, closed my eyes, breathed out and then opened them. I looked at myself. I took in the sight of my skinny legs and my flat stomach with a huge wound from one side to the other.

And then I saw my chest.

I regretted my reconstruction surgery as soon as I saw it. God, it was hideous. All I could see were two massive lumps on my chest wall. God knows how the other one had swollen up at this point, but I guess it just felt left out and decided to follow suit! There was red, yellow, and purple bruising all over from the alkaline strips and other treatments they'd given the skin to hold it together.

The reconstructed breast was made of white skin from my stomach. There was no nipple. That, if I wanted, would be a whole other operation, or possibly even a tattoo. They had to concentrate on the "fat mass" first, to let that be built, developed, and healed, and then we would turn our attentions to the nipple. It was not an attractive sight.

Every day the angels checked my wounds. The consultants, Dr Chinwabee, and Martin would all check it too. Every day someone would fondle my old and new breast, examining every inch of it. Never did I think that other people handling my breasts would feel so normal. A hoover-type contraction had to be shoved right up my nightie. It would blow hot air up there. I looked like a blow-up doll. It was to keep the new breast constantly warm. If there was any risk of the area becoming cold, then the reconstruction could fail and collapse.

Admittedly it felt incredible, because I was always cold. But Sammy always complained that the ward was too hot. Clearly he was knackered, and just wanted me home. But I took his complaints to mean that he didn't want to be with me, and I sent him home that night. I didn't feel too bad about it, because he needed the rest.

I had suggested that he didn't come to see me at all the next night, and he'd accepted the offer. But sure as anything, 5.00pm the night after that approached and he hopped, skipped, and jumped into the ward. 'Hello, gorgeous!' he would say each time. Then, after returning home, he would ring the ward and say to the nurses, 'Tell Annie I love her.'

I loved this man to death. Literally to death, because I knew how it felt to love someone so much you felt like you would die without them. I wasn't worried about revealing my chest to him either. This man had accepted me at my worst, and now he would just have to do that all over again.

Yes, he had irritating habits – like his whole teapot thing. Real teapots required real tea, according to him, in pure leaf form.

But once the tea's been drunk, you leave the teapot where it is. Because it doesn't need to be emptied and washed up, apparently! The fairies do it, I guess.

But when a fairy doesn't do it and he has to do it himself, the tea goes *everywhere.* How annoying!

And there were other things that annoyed me too. I'd made a whole list of them in my head.

But. He was a loyal, hard-working, and extremely passionate man. He loved his family and his work. He would always ring his granny every Sunday, come rain or shine, just to check in with her. He would always buy me flowers on a Friday and I would joke about, guessing where they were from. On a good day, the flowers would be from Tesco. And on a bad day, they might have come from a petrol garage. But most of all, he stuck to his word and never, ever, ever let me down.

I knew that I had to get better for Sammy and our relationship. He was too young to be a carer. But I felt so dreary. My mental health was worse than it had ever been before. This operation was my biggest regret so far. It was a huge problem, and it was holding up our lives together.

I told myself that things weren't as bad as I made them out to be. My tummy tuck had worked really well, and my new stomach did look good. It had healed perfectly. I had been advised by a surgeon to count my lucky stars after the surgery, a term which had never sat well with me. But what he was actually referring to was my tattoo, which was made up of little stars. I'd got it as a rebellious teenager on my stomach and hips. The surgeon who pointed this out had told me he'd put his "neck on the line" to save my stars. Nice of him, really.

I started to count them, and before I even got to the end, I was asleep.

*

'One, two, one, two, one, two ...' Martin chanted at me.

'I can't, I can't ...' I was trying to walk. Martin had forced me out of my nest and onto the freezing corridor floor. I'd been moved to the ward after spending 10 days in the HDU. I was now surrounded by recovering patients. Some were old, some were young, and all of them were women.

'YOU CAN, ANNIE! HOW WILL YOU WALK DOWN THE AISLE IF YOU CAN'T WALK OUT OF THIS HOSPITAL?' Martin would shout at me, his enthusiasm and passion too much for me to handle.

'I NEED PAIN KILLERS, NOW!' I shouted back at him. I'd grown to really like Martin, despite his stupid drawn-on smiley face. He was fun, professional. He was definitely a bully, but in a good way. He got me up and made me work on rebuilding my strength, which was exactly what I needed.

I could always hear him before I saw him. He would always embarrass me, and he wouldn't think twice about throwing me under the bus if he discovered I hadn't been doing my exercises. He could be savage.

'What have you had for breakfast?'

'Mainly co-codamol.'

'Have you done your arm exercises?' he would ask, knowing the answer.

'Yep,' I lied.

He wouldn't hesitate to shout across to the other 50 patients in the room, 'ANYONE SEEN ANNIE DOING HER EXERCISES?' No one would back me up.

But after everything, his "you-will-do-this" attitude made me walk again. The woman in the bed opposite me was called Opal. She was frail, very old, and confused. The angels were so kind to her and tried to build her spirits each day. The tea lady plonked a grey sandwich in front of her at every mealtime, which she always ignored. She probably couldn't even see it. And she asked me every day, five times a day, if I was her daughter, Diana. I was desperate to say yes. She reminded me of Bernice whom I had met at my chemotherapy sessions.

'What if her daughter is dead, Mum?' I said.

'That's even more of a reason not to tell her you're Diana.'

I didn't tell Opal that I was Diana. I said my name was Annie. She didn't care. She'd had plastic surgery on a severe burn on her leg and it was being reconstructed. Poor thing. Her little, hairless, chicken-bone-like leg often stuck out of the bed, held up by a crutch. Her weak, frail arms and tiny body in the bed made her look like a little doll. She couldn't be arsed with life any more. And Diana never visited her. Where was she? She made me miss my granny and grandpa so much.

She loved dogs. I got Sammy to bring in photos of Dorothy and I would sit by her and show them to her over and over again. She would always smile. They had a pet therapy ward in this hospital, for people who felt like shit all the time. I started to convince myself that I would bring Dorothy to the hospital after my recovery. But even with all the time I spent with Opal, I was still intensely bored and wanted to leave.

'When can I go?' I asked one of the angels.

'We think soon, but Dr Chinwabee is coming around to check your breast, so we'll have more of an idea by then,' she replied.

I was never given a time or a definite date. I just had to wait. I would sit on my bed and just watch patients go by. I felt so claustrophobic there. I hated watching the world pass me by without being able to get involved.

And I couldn't even just get up and walk to the shower. God, I needed a shower. My skin reeked, my body was dirty, and my hair – well, what was left of it – was a mess. I desperately wanted fresh air, the wind on my skin, the sun on my face. I would even take sitting by a window, watching the world go by, with a cup of tea and a biscuit. Just like when I first met Sammy.

*

It had been 12 days since my reconstruction and living in the hospital was killing me. While I waited for Dr Chinwabee and his angels, a routine developed. Mum and Sammy would visit, I'd get a phone call from Karen, and my dad would come to see me.

One day, finally, Dr Chinwabee arrived. He didn't speak; he just opened my gown intrusively. He was like a teenager sticking his nose in a stranger's fridge. 'You have some bruising. We need to keep the area hot, please,' he said to a nurse.

I learnt very quickly that, with Dr Chinwabee, if you had something to say, you needed to spit it out very quickly. The less you said and the louder you spoke, the more likely you'd be heard.

'Can I go home?' I asked, almost screeching the words.

'Yes … in due course. But you are not out of the woods yet.'

CHAPTER 31

RETURNING HOME

I was depressed. *I'm confused, tired, and anxious,* I said to Karen over text message. I was wincing at the phone screen as Sammy drove me back to our home in Acorn town.

It was so nice to be with him, in his silver Golf, stuck in London traffic on our way home – and not in the hospital. It was perfect. We drove up the long, winding roads, lost signal on the satnav, and drove to our cottage. It locked out the rest of the world and I felt safer inside its walls.

Keep an eye on your feelings, I have been there. I know how you feel and you don't want to be alone with it, Karen replied.

> Robert De Niro,
> Dad

I turned my phone off. I was starting to do that a lot. I didn't want contact with the outside world. I felt like people were stealing my time. Talking of time, I didn't like that either. I knew what I felt but couldn't describe it. I didn't want to know what time it was, or how long was left until the next activity.

I did own a watch. It was a rose gold Folli Follie watch that Sammy had bought me for my birthday. But this was used for decorative purposes only, nothing more. Sometimes it wasn't even set at the right time. And we didn't have a wall clock in our cottage.

I just wanted time to stand still.

What I did keep an eye on was the date. The days, the weeks, the month, and the year. But that just made me obsess about the wedding, about how little time I had left to sort everything out. There wasn't enough time in the world.

Dr Chinwabee's words had struck a blow. 'You're not out of the words yet.' I couldn't deal with this on top of everything else that had happened. Just as soon as I thought I'd got myself into a good place, recovering from you-know-what, meeting the man of my dreams, and planning my wedding, I'd been knocked down again.

You're not out of the woods yet.

I kept picturing Chinwabee's words flying on a banner, following me, wherever I was. I was tanked up on my trustworthy co-codamol pills. Sammy looked after me and nursed me. He cleaned the flat, helped me wash myself, cooked for me every night. He also became my communication bridge for my family, friends, and work. He was my own personal angel for the next three weeks. He had a week off work that was classed as compassionate leave, which was great, but the title annoyed me.

'Compassionate leave? So what, like someone's dead? Like your fiancée's died?' I asked.

'No, Annie. It's a period of absence from work, granted to someone as the result of particular personal circumstances …'

'Especially someone's death!' Sammy had had enough and stormed out. The door slammed behind him. God, I could be such a bitch.

I didn't mean it. I picked up my phone, ignoring the five missed calls from whoever they were and started to call him. At first it rang and rang and rang, then inevitably, the phone cut to voicemail. I sent a WhatsApp message. Only one tick showed up. JUST ONE. He had turned his phone off. The bastard. How could he?!

We were over, I decided. When he came home, he could get his stuff and go. How can he leave me when I'd just had a major operation? Actually, he could meet a far better woman. Someone with two big boobs for a start, someone who could walk, run, hop, skip, and jump. Someone beautiful inside and out. He wasn't a bastard. He was the love of my life.

'Pleeeeeeeeease donnnn't leeeeavvvve meee! I lovvvve you!' Sobbing, I left a voicemail on his phone to add to the 38 missed calls and eight angry text messages. If he wasn't already convinced, then this would confirm to him that his fiancée was well and truly crazy.

My phone cut out as another plane flew above us. I pictured the banner again, this time on the side of the plane. *You're not out of the woods yet.*

'I AM!' I shouted at myself in the mirror, looking down at my bandaged and swollen body. I couldn't have these dark thoughts.

I wanted to make an immediate appointment with Dr Dickinson. I knew that she would reassure me. But it would only be temporary. And then what? Back to hitting co-codamol again? Defeated, I sat on the sofa with a can of Diet Coke, remembering the warnings: 'No caffeine for a month after surgery.' *That advice can fuck right off,* I thought as I turned my laptop on, ready to distract myself. But instead I started to daydream, to try to calm myself down.

I pictured myself gazing into the beautiful meadow. I visualised that picture postcard Sammy had given me after our major bust-up months ago, the one with the meadow and the horse. It meant peace, and serenity. Us, happy. I pictured the lake in the distance, shining in the light, the boat tied up. It was so therapeutic. I opened my eyes and looked at my laptop. Who could I email?

I know. I'll email Clare.

Clare, Sammy's sister, was in Australia. She didn't know I had turned into a psychopathic bitch from hell and had a chest the size of a turkey.

To: Clare

Subject: wedding plans

How are you? All's going well with our white wedding …

*

I woke up with my chin hurting. I had fallen asleep on the sofa and my laptop was face down on the wooden floor.

I heard a banging on the door. Who in God's name was this? I looked out the window and saw Mum, her best friend Marie, and my sister, peering through the front door, looking concerned. Oh no! Maybe I had arranged for them to visit me following my reconstruction surgery and hadn't remembered. I felt a strong feeling of annoyance. I felt angry that they had come to see me. I didn't want to answer any of their questions, and I didn't want to show them my awful body. I knew they'd want to see it. I hated it, and I deeply hated my decision. I didn't have any tea in the house, and I certainly wasn't opening my last packet of biscuits. They would need to dump their stuff and go. Preferably to Tesco, to stock up for me.

They wanted to visit me? Fine. But they'd have to listen to me about how I was feeling. Which, at this moment in time, was extremely negative. *I hope they've brought some Ferrero Rocher.*

'He's not going to leave you. He loves you!' Polly shouted a short while later, as I sobbed and shoved Ferrero Rochers into my gob. I could see that Mum and Marie thought this situation was ridiculous and not realistic at all. They'd unpacked bags and bags of food, and produced cards, chocolates, and presents from everyone. Sammy's parents had sent me a huge bouquet of flowers, as had my work colleagues (in their blue and white logo theme). Our tiny little cottage was filled with well wishes from our friends and family, colleagues, even people we hardly knew.

I wasn't just crying about Sammy. I was crying about my entire life. I felt awful, inside and out. I wasn't physically ill any more, but my head felt so alone and so unhappy and I couldn't make it any better. My body felt well and my head felt *ill*. Really ill.

I needed to see my new wonderful GP. But what if I bloody frightened her off because of my mental problems? What if I got barred from the surgery? Where would I get my confidential support, a professional opinion, and endless co-codamol prescriptions from?

'Dr Dickinson will not get fed up of you, Annie. She's a professional and an expert in her field. Just continue with your normal routine appointments,' Mum said.

'You have your new breasts and a new life now. There won't be any more bad news. Start researching, looking into wedding dresses, and buy the bloody dress of your dreams,' Polly added. This was such brilliant advice. I was inspired.

I looked at the reflection in my dusty window. My face was thin and my hair was patchy. It looked terrible. I needed to start taking some pride in my appearance. I needed to get my hair cut and have my nails done again. I needed my life back. They all seemed relieved when I told them this, and nodded encouragingly.

'I really want to see Poppy and Lily soon,' I said to Polly as I waved her goodbye. She'd made such a long journey, and all I had done was whinge and cry. It must have reminded her of growing up with me!

'So ...' I could see Marie had been prepped to ask. 'When are you going back to work?' 'Monday,' I said.

'Brilliant! That's great news. Back to work and mind on the job! Just as long as you're ready. There's absolutely no rush.'

I was so grateful that everyone cared. But the paranoia and frustration was overwhelming. Sitting here in this beautiful house, I had time. I had a lot of time to think and reflect.

Why was everyone sending me flowers – for sorrow? For luck? What did I need luck for? Did they think it was bad news? I wasn't ill, I was recovering! Why were people sending me chocolates when I had just spent two months in hospital and was now recovering from my operation at home? Surely that was just out of spite? I imagined them watching me at my wedding ceremony, thinking *there's nothing worse than a fat bride.*

Marie and Mum left after a few more hours. We had agreed a date, all of us, to go and look at wedding dresses. Once they left, I realised just how lonely and alone I'd been feeling.

I looked around at my wedding file, my time plan, my schedule, the seating plan, and the flip chart. I tried to remind myself how lucky I was. I switched my laptop on, lit a fire in my belly and found my dream dress within the hour. It was an embellished, bodice-tulle dress with a huge train and skirt in diamond white. It was perfect. This was me. I had to have this dress.

At some point in the evening Sammy had texted me, and we'd continued our argument. We went from anger, to passive aggression, to feeling sad, to remembering that we were good together and that we loved each other. We told each other that a silly little row wouldn't be the end of us.

The next day, Sammy returned in high spirits. I was absolutely destroying a beef bourguignon in the cottage kitchen. His little face beamed at me. He was such an angel, always pleased to see me, no matter how bloody miserable I was.

I waved and sprayed some Chanel over my neck and wrists. I was trying to distract him from the appearance of my unwashed hair and Primark tracksuit. I hadn't made a hair appointment yet, but it would happen. He didn't even notice, and if he did, he certainly didn't care.

A few weeks later, the day of our shopping trip arrived. I planned to visit a boutique wedding dress shop with Mum, Marie, Polly, and Gudrun, who was going to be my bridesmaid.

The bridal gallery was in a little town called Thame in Oxfordshire. It was by appointment only, so I kept telling everyone. Our appointment was at 11.00am.

Sitting in the coffee shop opposite, my eyes were glued to the wall clock.

It got to 10.30am. We had loads of time.

At 10.45am, I started panicking. *We need to set off,* I thought.

10.51am. *Oh my god, we're going to be late.*

10.52am. I was so anxious at this point.

'We're going,' I said. We took the two steps next door to the bridal gallery. We were 10 minutes early, but they didn't mind.

We were taken into a mint green and white room, laid out like a glamourous dressing room. It was just fantastic, absolutely stunning.

'Help yourselves,' the owner said, gesturing to the rest of the shop.

Mum and Marie headed straight to the back of the shop, looking at the gorgeous and sophisticated lace, the fitted and long, flowy dresses. Gudrun headed to the middle section, looking at the vintage embellished dresses. And Polly walked around with me, asking what I liked and what I didn't.

I wanted this to last forever.

We picked out six dresses, one of each style. There was a "no" list. There was also a "try it and see" list. I thought about my chest and about my dodgy cleavage. But I also thought about my flat stomach. So I had to give everything a go to see what would fit me best.

We had so much fun drinking champagne and enjoying the big build-ups while I tried on my different dresses. I tried on every style and every shape. I loved being in a changing room full of hearts and flowers. There were no needles and scans. There was no slipping into a hospital gown, but a wedding dress instead. Every dress was nice, but nothing quite fitted the bill.

And then we saw it.

It was the last one we tried: a full-skirt tulle dress with an embellished bodice by Justin Alexander. 'It's the red-carpet dress,' the owner said. I knew I wanted it before it was even done up. I kept my eyes closed. As the bodice was laced up with white ribbon, I got a wave of nerves. I had not worn anything revealing since my operation. Would it look okay? Would it be obvious? 'You can look now.'

I breathed in and open my eyes. I breathed a sigh of relief.

I had a cleavage, and I looked good. I wasn't even wearing a bra, but it didn't matter because the real breast held up, and so did the fake one. They both looked so good.

This dress had to be mine. I came out of the dressing room and Mum's eyes welled up. We all agreed that it was the one.

'Is it white, like proper white?' I asked, my head to the side. 'Yes, it's so white it's almost blue!' Polly said. I chose a matching tiara and a floor-length veil. Perfect. There was a snag; I was still a large size 16. But I still had months to lose the weight. We left elated and excited.

I told Karen about my dress. She jumped on my positive mood and suggested that we had a day out. And so she planned to come the next day to do a cheap shop with me. Occasionally, for fun, we would spend an hour in Primark, picking up things to try on and buying them. It was a novelty, our thing we liked doing together. Walking around the shoe department, armed with white bags, white coats, white shorts, and white boob tubes, I was starting to feel good again. I picked up only the most revealing and white garments and flung them over my arm. Karen did the same, but she opted for some colour.

My phone rang. The fear of being hooked in came over me. But as soon as I heard my soldier's voice, I relaxed again. Sammy said, 'I've just sent you a picture of the groom's suits and also a full-length selfie.' At last!

'Hang on a minute, I'll check.'

I opened the picture. There was Sammy, in a white shirt and grey suit jacket (the perfect colour to match our white theme). But Sammy's tie was *gold*. It was *gold* and it had to be *white* and it was *gold*.

'Your tie is the wrong colour!' I wailed.

'Well, it's too late now. The shop had to close,' Sammy said.

'But it's the wrong colour! It's the wrong colour. IT'S THE WRONG COLOUR. WHAT THE FUCK ARE YOU TRYING TO DO TO ME?' I screamed, dropping my basket onto the floor, almost hitting a pushchair in front of me. 'IT'S FIVE MONTHS BEFORE THE WEDDING AND IT'S THE WRONG COLOUR!' I was close to crying.

The phone went dead.

I didn't understand myself. I couldn't grasp how 50 shades of white could send me over the edge. It was worrying. And it kept happening. It wasn't just my wedding obsession; everything was turning into an obsession and everything was becoming an issue. It wasn't just in my head, the anxiety. I was starting to see it, hear it, and now feel it. It was *everywhere.*

Over the next month, my mood became difficult, spiky, and unbearable for others to be around. It was a product of my fear laced with anger. A frightening combination.

I exploded at a cashier one day because the car wash was out of order. I shouted at him for wasting my time. 'I'm writing to your head office!' I threatened the poor waitress when the wrong food turned up at our favourite restaurant in Windsor.

The last straw for Sammy was me ringing him up, weeping down the phone that the internet was "fucking fucked" and that he needed to come and sort it out. I was off the rails and angry. And my obsession with my painkillers was now so obvious to everyone that I didn't even try to hide it any more.

One evening, I got back home and looked at the flipchart that I was using as the wedding planner. I looked at the table plan, the colour charts, the appointment cards, the business cards, the venue brochure. I just ripped it all up. I threw all the paperwork, samples, and previews at the wall.

Sammy came home to me sitting in complete darkness in the corner of the sitting room. I had tried to take a shower by myself. I still wasn't mobile enough to move around and Sammy had to shower me every evening. Now the bathroom had cotton buds covered with blood all over the windowsill.

'How was your day?' Sammy whispered.

'It was a disaster.' Sammy folded me into his arms, and I cried into his chest. We followed our normal nightly routine but in total stone-cold silence. Sammy cooked me my favourite pasta, we watched *EastEnders,* and he showered me and washed my hair. He wrapped me up and put me to bed on his side, the side closest to the door so that I didn't lean on my breast. He covered my chest in two blankets at a time to keep it heated. Sammy was the best man for the job. He was regimental, he followed instruction with military precision, and he handled me with care.

*

I was not ready to attend work on Monday, the following Monday or the Monday after that. Dr Dickinson was aware of my moods and advised me to get some help. She advised that I get some talking therapy. I told her that I would think about it. I didn't want the invasion.

The following day, we drove back down to the hospital in Essex. It was one month after I was discharged. I had a check-up with Dr Chinwabee and it couldn't have come sooner. My chest was still swollen. My tummy tuck was fine, but the scar was like a big smile and stretched from one side of my body to the other. It was a good 10 inches long. I was fed up, disappointed, and, above all, I was angry.

'I CAN'T BELIVE WE HAVE BEEN WAITING OVER AN HOUR,' I shouted. 'THE PARKING'S GOING TO RUN OUT TOO.'

Sammy tried to shush me.

'I BET HE WON'T EVEN KNOW WHO I AM!'

Sammy offered me some water, maybe thinking that it would calm me down.

'WHY WOULD I WANT A DRINK?' I screamed.

Sammy left the waiting room before, I imagine, he chucked the water over my head. It must have taken everything in Sammy's military training not to attack me. I'd become the enemy: a frustrated, angry, and ungrateful fiancée. Finally, we were called in.

We walked into the room where Gurpreet the nurse was standing with her usual vacant stare. This was definitely Gurpreet; there was no other stare like it.

We waited, waited, and waited. Sammy got up and started pacing the room.

'SIT DOWN!' I yelled.

His phone went off loudly.

'WHO THE HELL IS THAT? TURN IT OFF. WHO WAS IT? WHAT DID THEY WANT?'

Sammy apologised.

It was impossible. I was impossible.

Dr Chinwabee entered the room, getting my name wrong. He asked me to remove my bandages, to see my stomach and chest.

He didn't say anything. He just stared.

I could tell that there was going to be a problem. Not because of the insane mood I was in, but because of his face, his energy, and the mood in the room.

He sat down, took off his glasses, and announced my worst fear.

'Okay, we have a big problem. You have a large and suspicious lump in your reconstruction.'

CHAPTER 32

SUSPICIOUS LUMP

The room went black. Words turned into bullets, and they shot right through to my heart. I closed my eyes. I just wanted to die. Everything from then on was a blur, and I could barely hear the words over my crying. 'Scan ... ultrasound ... appointment ... two weeks ...'

I couldn't handle it. I lost control. I had a live meltdown, a tantrum. That behaviour could have got me sectioned.

Sammy lost it too. 'We need answers now. We need results now. Please just do it now!' My mind was closed in. All I could picture was being back in that room again in East London, being told I had a life-threatening illness.

This was it. It was all just too good to be true. I'd gone through treatment and it was still going to come back and kill me. My mind flew back to all the health warnings about operations and treatments, the risks that had come with every single one of them.

My mind was violent with rage, anger, and upset. It was overwhelming. I started shaking, which added to the theatre production going on in the tiny room. And then an angel appeared, whisking Sammy and me off down the corridor. She held my arm, talking the entire way through. I didn't know what she was saying. I tried to read Sammy's face, which went from purple, to red, to yellow and back to pale pink again as he calmed down.

'We're able to do an ultrasound for you now, Annabel.'

'Thank Christ. I thought she was going to be sectioned,' Sammy muttered to the angel. Not helpful, but in hindsight he was probably very close to the truth.

The ultrasound was performed. There was no communication, no eye contact, no words. Just staring and scanning, staring and scanning, staring and scanning.

'Is it okay?' I asked and asked and asked. I felt like they were fucking with my mind. Someone hated me, and they wouldn't let me escape this illness, ever. If it wasn't one thing, it was another. When was I going to be done with this?

Eventually, the light went on. The radiographer took off her glasses and smiled. 'The lump is fat tissue. You have fat necrosis.'

There was a pause. Silence.

Sammy exploded. 'Well, what the hell does that mean?'

The radiographer went on to explain. 'It's a build-up of fatty tissue that feels like a lump form, which could remind us of those similar to cancer.' I hated her for using that term here. 'While it's not harmful, it is a common reaction after major surgery.' She was calm, polite, and reassuring.

Why, oh fucking why, had we not been warned? Why had no one said, 'You're going to have an amazing pair of breasts again and be able to wear your dream wedding dress – but oh, FOUR MONTHS BEFORE THE WEDDING, YOU WILL DEVELOP SIMILAR SYMPTOMS OF THOSE THAT REPRESENT BREAST CANCER. YOU WILL HAVE A PANIC ATTACK, AND YOU WILL WANT TO KILL YOURSELF AND EVERYONE AROUND YOU'?

'What if Dr Chinwabee and the radiographer are wrong?' I asked Sammy. I could see frustration in his eyes at this point. He would never give up on me, he had always said. But this was surely pushing him. What person needed to go through all of this? Could he love me so much that he would be my future husband, my friend, my doctor, my oncologist, and my psychotherapist? I doubted it. I wanted to be better for him. I wanted him to have a life.

'He won't be wrong, not with that Rolex on his wrist,' Sammy replied. He stared at me for a moment, his eyes staring right into mine. 'Are you okay, Annie?'

'No, Sammy. My mind feels crazy and this feeling needs to go.'

Sammy was not my psychotherapist. I needed help. I needed actual therapy.

CHAPTER 33

WHERE THERE IS HOPE

'It's not the treatment. It's the people. It's getting through life battling all of them. Nosy neighbours and doctors with bad news. Test results arriving on the doorstep or through my phone. The you-know-what charities parading around me. The passengers on the train who won't give their seats up for me. Nightclubs being too hot for my wig. Fast food flyers through my door for 50 per cent off, while I'm on the most powerful steroids known to bodybuilders. Every online magazine in the UK showing me "killer curves" while I sit in a pile of Kit Kat wrappers, hating my body for what it is. The money that you-know-what has cost me and my family in hospital car park fees. The dragons on reception, not letting me see Dr Dickinson whenever I like, so I can ask her to make it all better. It's the people I've only just met, within seconds, having access to all my body parts – sometimes without even speaking to me. People around me don't like me. They just want to know what my tits look like, and if I'm having any more work done. I can't deal with them any more.'

I was breaking down to Harriet Hope, my dedicated psychotherapist. She was pleasant, petite, well-dressed, and, I guessed, in her 40s. She spent weeks listening to me, trying to work through my fucked-up head. I learnt very quickly why I had been feeling so angry. I had delayed trauma.

'You've spent two years dealing with the physical aspects of treatment, and you've left your mind behind. It's still catching up. That's all,' Harriet said. I liked that. She summed up my anger instantly. The diagnosis was simple, and it made sense. It doused my fire. I liked my therapy appointments. I liked Harriet, and I loved her surname. Hope. That was what she gave me.

At this point, I had returned completely to work, but had made an agreement that I would attend my appointments on a Friday afternoon. They were in Essex, but I liked this. I enjoyed getting in my car and turning my work and personal phone off. I liked being able to do nothing but think about all the things I was going to speak to Harriet about, all the things she was going to fix for me.

'I don't want the entire office knowing, Carl,' I had said to my boss, who completely understood.

So we decided to keep it very vague. Fridays from 2pm, Annie wasn't available. Not ever. But this didn't keep clients away. I would go to my appointments and come back to urgent messages, messages saying "call me back immediately", missed calls, emails, and repeat missed calls. I used to dread returning to work. It probably explained why I simply shouted at Harriet for the first few weeks. I felt like everyone was constantly inside my mind. I needed to shut them all out, reclaim my space. I realised how dramatic this sounded.

But it was dramatic. Everything was made huge in my own mind, no matter how small it appeared to be to other people. As the weeks went on, my rants got longer.

I told Harriet about my top 10 hit list for that week, and she exclaimed, 'That's a long list you've got.' That week the list included mobile phones, people that don't ask any questions when they meet you, and people that name drop you-know-what survivors.

'So, your anger,' Harriet said, daring to broach the subject, employing direct eye contact. She was right to address it. I felt pure, red, in-your-face anger towards anyone and everyone. It wasn't that fire-in-the-belly feeling Sammy and I had over which colour table lamp to buy. It was hate, anger, spite, and jealousy all rolled into one big, fat, massive infectious lump that was consuming me. And it wasn't subtle. People close to me would tread on eggshells when they were around me. I didn't recognise the person I had become. What sort of life was I creating for Sammy? Why should he have had to work a 13-hour day and then come home to a maniac? *This anger had to go.*

Harriet often didn't respond to my angry outbursts. She would sit there and wait for me to be done. God, she was good at dealing with me. *I probably should have started my treatment a very long time ago.* 'I just get so angry with everyone, all of the time, for wanting a bloody piece of me. And I can't calm down. I don't want to tell people how I am. Because it never changes. I'm angry, all the time. I don't want to say how my poor, beaten-up, ugly body is, because it's always sore. I don't want to meet up for drinks because I can't do whisky and co-codamol ...' *Shit.* I instantly regretted the co-codamol comment. Harriet silently scrutinised me, waiting for more admissions. I needed to change the subject, quickly. Not being able to think of a single thing to say, I kept my mouth shut.

Why did she always do this? It was so awkward whenever she went silent. I was presenting her with the problem – she needed to answer it and quickly! We only had 50 minutes in our sessions, after all. If this wasn't bad enough, the chair I was sitting in was (deliberately) in front of the wall clock. So I had no idea at all of the time.

'You feel like your time's running out?' Harriet asked.

Yes, that was it. 'I *know* my time is running out.'

That was a relief and a massive realisation. We'd worked out that I had a fear of time. Maybe this was because I had been faced with my own mortality at such a young age. I'd become seriously ill at 25, when it didn't matter if you were 20 minutes late for work, an hour late for lunch or days late with replies to emails.

Time did matter to me, hence the frantic search for love, the frantic wedding plans and control I needed to have over it all. I needed to do everything quickly, just in case the you-know-what came back, stared me in the face and told me ...

'Annie, your time's up.'

CHAPTER 34

WHAT'S THE TIME?

I got back on the treadmill to release some tension. As soon as I started walking, I was irritated. As I jogged I became angry, and as I began to run I was fuming. This wasn't fair. I had just started getting somewhere with my thoughts and emotions, and then I'd had to leave. I hated Harriet. No, I loved her. I needed her. She was the only one in the world who could support me, help me see what was going on. It was as though she'd had a peek inside my brain and found it full of horror and anxiety.

Okay, I thought, *I'll save all this for next week.* Work was getting busier, half the team had left, and the workload was increasing. The wedding plans had slowed down, but we were getting there. I couldn't do my usual email checking and contacting wedding people because my inbox was flooded and my voicemail box was full.

'Annabel, can you call me?' I woke up to a missed call and a voicemail from my boss Carl.

Oh, Jesus wept. Messages like this made me wobble. They tipped my mood in the wrong direction, leaving me with frightening and dark thoughts. What did he want from me?

I felt invaded and burgled of my rights. I panicked, and it was only 6am. What did he want? Why was he calling me so late last night? What had I done? What was going to happen? Why couldn't he have left a message? I watched the clock angrily, furious that it wasn't moving quickly enough.

6.02am

6.05am

6.20am

I was on the edge of the bed. Sammy was snoring, the chickens were clucking in the background, and my reception was dipping in and out.

6.30am

Oh, fuck it. It's halfway to go until 7am, which is a reasonable hour. I'm calling him back.

His phone didn't connect, and I felt like I was having a meltdown.

Carl rang me back and told me that he just needed some administration sent through. His text hadn't been sent through to me which was why he had rung me, to make sure that I had got the message. The dread passed, and the relief sunk in. I had literally been pulling my hair out with anxiety.

Did he realise what he was doing to me? Did any of them? I started to hate these people intruding into my peaceful life in my cottage.

This also happened with my family and my friends. I would receive missed calls at work, with no voicemail or text message attached to explain why. What did they want? Why didn't they just text me? *Oh, god,* I wondered, *do they have you-know-what?*

The wedding plans were also calamitous. Why had Angelina, my wedding planner, just called me back when I had emailed her? Why couldn't she just email me back? *I've got a job!* I thought. *I'm in a meeting, and I can't answer for the next two hours!*

OH GOD, WHAT IF SHE CANCELS THE WEDDING?!

And with this, I learnt that I had developed a new fear. My phone. I couldn't use it, not as a phone anyway. I could just about text and email from it. But I wouldn't answer calls. I spoke, in detail, with Harriet about why this was.

'You have telephonobia,' she explained.

'But I like speaking on the phone and people calling me,' I said.

No, actually, I didn't, at all. Whenever people called me it was always on their terms. It was always people having conversations with me when I didn't want to, sometimes about things I didn't want to talk about. I felt like my phone was constantly ringing. It was stressing me out. I didn't mind texting, but I couldn't handle all the calls. I always expected bad news. It had developed into a real problem.

I hated hearing phrases like the following:

'Please call me.'

'Can I call you?'

'Ring me when you have a minute.'

'You have two missed calls from ...'

Reading messages like these felt like I was facing my own mortality again. The idea of using my phone to do something so simple as ordering a pizza became such a big deal for me that it could cause me to have a panic attack. It became a serious social phobia. My friends didn't understand why I had suddenly stopped using the phone. I hadn't rung anyone, apart from Sammy and Mum, for months.

I used to love talking on the phone, so much so that Vodafone would cut me off each month for going over my £100 limit just on calls. And now I was barely able to pick the phone up, even if I knew it was something important and urgent.

'It's probably because she thinks it will give her you-know-what in the head!' I imagined my friends saying. I knew they wouldn't say that, really. They cared for me and wanted me to be okay. But I couldn't stop myself from thinking the worst anyway.

The solution? I had to be selfish with my phone. I wouldn't answer if I didn't want to. I would only ever call Sammy and Mum. But to compensate, everyone else who dared to try communicating with me via a phone call would just get a text message back. That way, everyone was happy. It would just take some time to train myself to do it.

It also took time to train others. If they rang me after I had sent them an email, that didn't mean I would answer them. Instead I would repeat the message in an email to them, asking them to bloody well email me back. I mean, who replies to an email with a phone call anyway?

I wouldn't have anyone steal my time. Especially when I didn't know how much was left.

CHAPTER 35

WHAT DOESN'T KILL YOU MAKES YOU WEAKER

One of the things I had wanted to work on as part of getting my head back and my mental health back on track was my personal appearance. I had sorted my body out and couldn't possibly have any more surgery. But I wanted to feel pretty again. And I needed some self-care and self-pride. As a child I'd always had dark brown / black hair. The hair on my head was fully growing back now, as on my legs, and definitely everywhere else. Let's just say, as much as a bastard it had been to lose my hair, I had secretly appreciated not having to use so much shaving cream.

There was one part of my body where the hair had come back with a vengeance. God, I could have named it Kate, it was so bushy. It was black and curly with bits of grey in it. During the tummy tuck that I'd had – the DIEP flap option – doctors had taken the fat tissue from my stomach and used that to bulk out and fill my fake breast. Because this was from my nether regions, pubic hair had grown into a truly repulsive sight on my chest.

It had to go.

I went into the local beauty parlour and asked about waxing. It sounded brutal. I could just imagine the pain, and I knew I wouldn't want to put myself through that again. So I requested information about laser treatment instead, one that I had seen on the QVC channel that morning while I was working from home.

'The popularity of hair removal has grown significantly,' the pretty-much-perfect beauty therapist told me while I was querying it. 'You can go for the bikini line, the Brazilian, or the Hollywood.'

'I want all my hair gone, so the Hollywood,' I said as I signed over £399 and filled in the paperwork.

'Medical history?'

Oh, here we go.

Twenty minutes later, I was still struggling to remember the order, the dates, and especially the names of treatments. I quickly scribbled down my diagnosis. I just needed to write about my treatment and give a little a summary of what was left to go. Big, big mistake.

The wait was agonising. The assistant was out the back, and I could hear them discussing something. Their hushed whispering told me that it was all about me. I knew I was going to be rejected before she said it.

'Unfortunately, because of your medical history on your form, we're not going to be able to perform the treatment on you today.' The first thing I thought was, *what did today mean? Did she actually mean just today, or did she mean next Thursday, next month or next year, when my five-year sentence was up?* Or perhaps it was for all time, and I'd never be able to do anything again because of this thing hanging over my head.

My heart dropped and I felt like a child again, being excluded from playtime and not being picked for the netball team. This was a horrible, left-out feeling. It was just awful.

Looking at her straight in the eye, I accepted the decision. I hid the tears under my fake hair and left the salon. And then I swiftly turned back around, because I needed to do the whole refund thingy with the £399. She felt awkward, I felt humiliated. I got my money and left. *FUCK THEM!* – Karen texted to me later. *I could deal with not having my bush cut off, but I can't bear the prospect of being 25 and incredibly hairy when I'm walking down the aisle!* I complained to her.

You are not 25. You're 29, and it's okay. They're just doing what they think is right because they don't understand it. Karen was always on my side.

But even so, I couldn't help but think. These people were cosmetic and medical professionals. They should have known better. They obviously didn't understand the medical implications, because if they did, they'd have known that laser treatment had nothing to do with you-know-what.

'This is all POINTLESS!' I shouted at Harriet in our third session. 'I've spent four years looking like an overweight, bald, ill person and now I'll spend a long time trying to make myself look half-decent again!' I hadn't written a letter of complaint, like I thought I would. Instead, I'd got side-tracked by adverts for another service: teeth whitening.

Lo and behold, the same thing happened.

'This kind of incident recurred how many times?' I liked it when Harriet asked questions. It felt like she was getting involved, like she was on my side and fighting my battle for me.

I winced. I didn't like the words recur, reoccurrence or reoccurring. It reminded me of my second-worst nightmare scenario – getting ill again.

So I gave her a long and angry description of my beauty diary.

Waxing: not possible.

Teeth whitening: not possible.

Tattooing of the eyebrows: definitely not possible.

I just wanted to get myself back.

Over time – and it took a very long time, with huge resistance – I realised that my mindset needed to change first. Once this shifted, and I was secure in who I was, then I could focus on my appearance. *The beauty stuff has to go.*

I didn't need to look like me at 25 any more. I was hitting 30 this year, for god's sake. I needed to accept that these five years had happened.

Harriet and I spent weeks discussing my background, my parents' divorce, my dad leaving, and my fear of men doing the same to me. We talked about my job, my relationships, my anger, my sorrow. For the first three sessions, I just cried throughout the whole 50 minutes.

I made an event of waiting in the waiting room with other patients. It was such a long drive from Windsor to Essex and I always tried to be early. I would sit in there and go over my new diet, planning meals as I waited. I had rejoined my weight loss group and it was going really well.

I would try to guess which patients were mentally ill. It was much harder to identify those than the patients who were physically ill. With mental illness, you couldn't see it or touch it. It's all inside you. 'I'm addicted to co-codamol,' I said to Harriet one morning, the words falling out of my mouth without a second's thought.

For some reason, I felt like I was sitting in a church and confessing to the priest in the tell-all booth. I felt guilty, ashamed, and humiliated, but I wanted to share the problem.

Everyone had known for over a year that I had a problem. And yes, there were hints of a junkie mentality running through my mind. I'd have panic attacks if I left the house without my white pill bottle. I would quiz everyone on what painkillers they took. Sometimes I'd just look into people's bathrooms cabinets. It was shameful behaviour, and I was ashamed of myself.

I confessed this all to Harriet, and she didn't say much. We worked out that I didn't need the co-codamol and that it was a last resort for me, a comfort blanket. The pain was in my head now, not in my body. My lymphedema was still there, but I didn't need such extreme measures to eradicate it. I could do this. I would come off co-codamol. I didn't make a big thing out of this to my friends and family. This was the last thing they needed on their plates. But gradually, over the next few weeks, I reduced my dosage to one a day. I was not going to be defeated by something so small as a painkiller.

I'd also had some wonderful news about laser treatment. Through an NHS referral I had been given, I would be treated for the hideous hair on my new breast. It would be a good use of my time – one of the only good things.

I would still ask 'How long do we have left?' at each session with Harriet.

'Long enough!' Harriet would say.

Time was still a big issue for me. I never wanted to be late. I always wanted to check the clock at regular intervals throughout my therapy. I realised that I could only feel secure once I knew what the time was and how long I had left. I would only feel happy about moving on to a new subject if I knew what time it was.

One day Harriet said, 'We can move the room around if you like?' This tested me, big time. *Move the entire room around. Hmm.* I almost wanted to do it, to see if the time it took to move the two chairs and dim lighting in the room would be deducted from my 50-minute time slot or if it would be added on to the end.

But no! I wouldn't let a £9.99 Argos wall clock defeat me. I would sit with my back to it and pretend it didn't exist, giving it only the occasional acknowledgement. And maybe with the odd question to Harriet about it.

*

It was summer 2012 and it was coming up to my hen do, which the girls had organised. One of my friends, Nicola, who I described to Harriet Hope as a ray of sunshine, had joined our gang. She was Matt's girlfriend and a lovely person, someone who had turned into a very good friend of mine in a short amount of time. Her mother had had you-know-what in the past, and she understood some of the fears I was going through.

Within my psychotherapy sessions, I often wondered who Harriet was and what was going on in her life. This was the only person in my life I had never really interviewed, who I had never really asked anything substantial. The only question I could ask her, which she would answer, was 'Which room are we in next week?'

I wanted to know her age. Did she have children? Husband? Work problems? Had she had you-know-what? I didn't think so – her breasts looked too good. But I couldn't ask anything. And if I did, she'd change the subject. She was a pure professional, much to my annoyance.

As the weeks went past, my anxiety calmed down. I started to feel calmer, but this didn't last long.

Mum called me and I didn't answer. When I finally saw her a few days later, I wished I had picked up my phone. My grandpa was seriously ill in hospital. I felt a huge wave of guilt. Why had I not taken the time to spend more time with my grandpa and granny? They were my heroes, after all, the ones I had decided to base my marriage on. As I drove up to see Grandpa, he looked so thin, ill, and tired. He looked up at me with his big eyes and kind face. 'Annabel, my dear, I'm so pleased to see you,' he said.

I loved this man so much. He was my hero and had always been in my life. He was the man of the family. Over Sunday lunch only weeks earlier, I had asked my grandpa to give me away, to walk me down the aisle with me on his arm.

'Of course. I'd be honoured,' he said firmly, with pride. Every time I saw him afterwards, he told me that he needed to start writing his speech. It was so exciting to think that he'd be by my side for something so important. And now, he needed me. Now it was him in hospital, ill and vulnerable.

The angel who was looking after him introduced herself and smiled. My grandpa was clutching on to a bit of paper and a pen, and waved it at her. 'I am lucky enough to be walking my granddaughter down the aisle in October,' he said. 'She will be very honoured to have you.'

Grandpa was writing his speech on his deathbed. I wondered what was on that bit of paper – how he had started the speech, what he was writing about. I didn't get to hear the speech, but I know he would have written about lovely childhood memories, about happy times fishing in rock pools in Lyme Regis and playing Swingball in their garden. I imagine he would have talked about our holidays, our love of baking with Granny, dog walks, and games. My granny and grandpa taught me how to play Gin Rummy, the card game. I used to love coming downstairs and seeing Granny busy in the kitchen, with Grandpa at the head of the table, doing the crossword and eating his muesli. The routine was always the same. It was safe and comforting.

But though I wanted to, I didn't talk to him about the wedding. It wasn't my time; it was his, and I let him guide me through it.

We talked – or I talked – about Dorothy, about my lovely granny, and about him. I told him I loved him. And he held my hand and said goodbye.

I questioned the angel, but she couldn't tell me much. She gave me medical facts that meant nothing to me. All I knew was that my grandpa wasn't his usual self. When I thought of Grandpa, I pictured him eating his breakfast while listening to Radio 4. I didn't think of him like he was today, sitting up in bed in the hospital ward, enthusiastically talking me through the menu choices for that evening like he was in a fine restaurant. Was he going to have shepherd's pie, casserole or lasagne?

The nurse continued to be vague when I persisted. And slowly, I began to understand why. Grandpa was really ill.

As I said goodbye to him, he held my hand and didn't let it go. As I looked at his lovely, happy face and his big brown eyes, my own green eyes filled with tears. I felt so much love for him and hated seeing him in pain. It was horrible seeing him thin and weak, and not in his comfy armchair.

A few days later, Mum rang me. I already knew what she was going to say before I answered the phone. Sure enough, she had rung to tell me that Grandpa had died. I had felt, when sitting with him, that maybe he knew he was going to die, and that was why he had held my hand for so long. That just filled me with grief.

My family were heartbroken. This wasn't a curable illness or disease, this was the death of someone we all truly loved, someone we'd all desperately miss. My granny, Mum, and her brother arranged the funeral. Everything felt black as we made our way, on a very dark day, to the church.

Standing around in the car park, Sammy paced back and forth. Mum just looked worried and upset. She didn't speak much, other than to say, 'I'm scared of saying goodbye to my dad.' She had been upset all the way to the funeral, her eyes constantly filling with tears. Sammy, Marie, and I looked after her. We put our arms around her, suggested where she should have a fag, and brought her copious amounts of coffee. Then we saw Granny and my uncle walking towards us.

'There's Mum,' Mum said like a little girl, as she hurried towards her. Mum started crying, but Granny was smiling. And she wasn't wearing black. I liked that. She was hard, harder than all of us.

She could handle this, just like she'd handled her own illness 40 years ago.

All of Grandpa's family, friends, neighbours, and relatives were there, respectfully suited up and all as sad as one another. There were tributes about him being a wonderful man, messages about him being the perfect host, and heartfelt words about everlasting love for him. This man never wanted for anything other than for his family to be safe and well. He had that. He always had that. I had spent the last six years searching for love, but now I realised I already had it. I had Mum, Dad, my sister, my grandparents, Karen, Theresa, even Dorothy. I shouldn't have been so desperate. It just always felt like there was something missing. And now there would be something missing in my poor granny's life.

But I knew that we would always be there for her, whether she liked it or not. As the service came to an end, the congregation stood up and 'What a Wonderful World' by Luther Vandross played out. We all remembered my lovely grandpa, sitting next to the window in his chair with the crossword, watching *Countdown* and never staying awake until the end. We remembered his love of cooking, self-taught as he became older, and his love of wine and beer. We remembered so many happy memories.

At the end of it all, I was overwhelmed with sadness. Sadness that we wouldn't get any more years together, sadness that he had gone, sadness that he wasn't going to take me down the aisle.

CHAPTER 36

HEN-IDORM

Benidorm was booked for August 2012. Six days, five girls, four outfits each, three suitcases, two single girls, and one easyJet flight. (And no co-codamol. Just Nurofen for when I needed it.) It was my hen do, and it was going to be amazing.

'And this is for Sammy,' we squealed as we toasted each other with a bottle of cheap, imitation prosecco on our apartment balcony. The music was loud. The girls were on a high. The booze was flowing and we hadn't even left the apartment yet.

Our apartment was on the 18th floor and oh, what a coincidence, the lift was out of order. We'd checked into the hotel, Karen eyeing up the receptionist while he handed us a bunch of keys to our apartment. After realising the lift was definitely not working – we'd pushed the button repeatedly – we'd climbed the many flights of stairs to our new temporary home. We said hello to fellow tourists on the way and made a lot of loud, obscene observations about the "wall-to-wall cock".

Kylie Minogue,
Dad

There were constant arguments when we were getting ready to go out. Who was wearing what? Who had fake eyelashes? And why on earth didn't she have any more make-up on?

Our daily routine was to get up late-ish and then spend the whole day by the pool. With me in the shade, of course. We ended up making new friends while we were there. There were a group of girls from Liverpool who were always still drunk when they woke up. One of them had already ended up in A&E when she'd slipped into a drain. And then there were the unwashed fellas having a stag do, who dressed up as Cinderella characters for the entire holiday and absolutely stank the entire time.

I loved it.

This was how my nightmare had started: a selfish and indulgent holiday. I'd fried my poor breasts to the point of you-know-what underneath the UV rays in the sunbeds. I'd then laid my poor, ruined body underneath the violent sunshine during the hottest times of the day in Spain. And I'd soaked my liver in pure, dirty, poisonous alcohol.

Oh, what fun abusing my body had been, and how it had ruined my life! I would never behave like this ever again. I didn't sunbathe the entire time we were in Benidorm this time around. We spent the days asleep or in bars or restaurants, and at night I kept my alcohol consumption within some level of moderation.

'Why would I risk my life again by sitting in the sun?' I remarked to anyone that would question why I wasn't sunbathing. The holiday was perfect, and fake tan was always so much better. Plus, it was safer. Rather that than the dangerous beams coming out of the sky, I thought, as a huge aeroplane flew by. This plane had no banner displaying dark thoughts or anxiety on it. It was just a plane. I felt at peace there. The weight of sadness and dark thoughts was no longer on my back. I just felt safe.

The girls had prepared lots of fun, clichéd hen-do stuff to do before going out on the town. There was the Sammy quiz, the L plates, the penis straws, and the cheap netty veils. I had said months earlier that I wanted everyone in attendance to wear a veil. I remembered all those times that I'd been the single one on a night out, and how it felt when you stood out like a sore thumb. This wasn't going to be the case on my hen do. And all the girls loved it.

Day two came around, and time just slipped away as we made our way out into the town like arrogant cats on the prowl for mice. The attention we got was welcomed and provocatively encouraged. There was a lot of dirty dancing and being groped by all sorts of creatures. I was surrounded by my best friends and a load of drunken Brits, none of whom knew about what I had been through over the last four years. Not a single one knew about my fake chest, and there was absolutely no chance that any of them knew about the hair on it. I was thin, beautiful, engaged, and healthy. 'Bend over!' the girls screamed as they handed me a pair of bride-to-be knickers.

We laughed like naughty little girls at school. We bar-hopped, promising to go into every club on the strip, accepting the free shots and leaving swiftly. Chatting to all the men there – then letting them down at the last possible moment – was thrilling. I loved being the one to reject. I felt in control and fabulous.

'WHERE IS SHEEEEEE?' Karen screamed down the street. It was 5am. The clubs were getting quieter, the queues in the kebab shop horrendous, and Ciera was missing. The mood was quickly deteriorating, and Theresa didn't help by being sick in the street. An audience started circling us, like magpies around shiny things.

'Maybe she ended up in Ibiza! Or brought two men back to your apartment!' someone screamed.

I called Sammy in a panic. He shouted down the phone, 'Is that what this holiday was about for you?!' Oops.

I felt guilty. Were we doing the wrong thing by acting this way?

By day four of our holiday, only two of us were still up and standing (me and Karen, obviously). We spent the whole day reminiscing and the whole evening drinking. *This whole thing was seriously stupid and unhealthy,* I thought, as I ate my way through two McDonald's burgers at Alicante airport. I could feel my arteries clogging up.

But looking back through our bruised and battered camera, we laughed at how amazing it had all been. I was so lucky that they wanted to do this with me. But now we had to go home.

I had a wedding to organise.

CHAPTER 37

THE C-WORD
(CO-CODAMOL)

'So, celebrating and having fun is deemed to be unacceptable?' Harriet questioned me at my session after I had returned from my hen do.

Sammy had not exactly told me off about this, but he had made me doubt my antics on the hen do. He'd made me doubt myself.

We'd had an amazing time, but the truth was, I just wasn't used to letting my hair down, in both senses. I didn't know what was right or wrong any more. I just knew that this wedding was a celebration, the end of you-know-what and the beginning of our married life. The beginning of my *life*.

'Are you fully off the co-codamol now?' Harriet asked in one of our sessions.

'Yes,' I said immediately.

No, I most certainly was not. It was still in my bag, in the car, and in both parents' houses. I even knew which 24-hour chemist would have it, in case of an emergency. But I had not taken one of the pills for a month now. I was caring for myself. Or at least trying to.

Sammy and I needed something else to care for too. Recently I had caught myself staring longingly at newborn babies in Tesco and looking at children with their parents. I felt like I could potentially be a mum. I knew Sammy would be a fantastic father too. We'd spent a day with Poppy, my eldest niece, when we first started going out. We took her to the London aquarium and then on to meet the horses at the barracks. She was even allowed to ride around in a horse-led carriage. And it had been amazing, a proper day out for the perfect family.

The problem was that I was broody, but he was not. We did have time on our hands though, for something else in our lives. So, of course, we decided to get a dog. He wanted a big, oversized Dalmatian. 'They used to run along the sides of coaches,' he said, as though that might make the dog more appealing to me.

I wanted another Shih Tzu, so we compromised and ended up with a silly little dog – a teacup Yorkshire terrier called Frankel, named after Sammy's first true love, the racehorse. Frankel had a lot of energy. He didn't sleep in the day and slept very little at night, a bit like Sammy. And just like Sammy, he was very loyal. He would go ape every time the postman rung the bell (okay, so Sammy didn't do that last one).

He was the perfect cherry on the top of what we already had. We had lots of long walks in Windsor Great Park and made lots of apologies to local dog walkers, as our hyperactive little nightmare had a habit of bounding up to them and refusing to come back when we called him. This was wonderful, but things started building up again as work got more stressful. I couldn't go a single minute without having to take a phone call or respond to an email, and even interviewing was losing its appeal for me. Everything had become so boring for me, and my mind would constantly drift off to other things.

I'd been "advertising" for a husband since I was 18. That was nearly eight years of searching for a man, and it had cost me my health and sanity. I had done my pre-screening in the form of numerous dates, meeting up with people at every single underground station in London, meeting 6'5 men who were really 5'2. I had sent all my rejection letters: not texting people back, giving negative feedback, using the brutal "block" on my emails. I had gotten through all that, and I had found my prince.

So why didn't this feel the way I thought it would?

*

It was three months into my therapy and just one month before the wedding. It was a cold and rainy and grey September day and I was trying to listen to the wedding playlist Sammy and I had put together with the help of friends and family. So far we were up to:

'Anywhere Is' by Enya – for me to walk down the aisle.

'Dance With Me' by Ollie Murs – for my guests at the reception.

And the first dance was definitely, 1000 per cent, going to be ...

My voicemail box rang me from the Bluetooth system in my car. Several messages came through all at once.

'Hi, it's Gemma from Dextrod IT solutions, calling about the role!'

'Hi, this is Dawn from Merthwait IT, ringing about the feedback!'

'Hi, this is Darren from Clainwet IT, could I please contest your regret letter?'

Delete, delete, delete. I didn't need this!

And when that stopped, my personal phone went off.

'Hi, Annie, please could you call me?'

'Hi! Ring me back, got something to tell you!'

DELETE THEM ALL.

I didn't just have one phone. I had two of the irritants. And my god, I hated them both. They were a constant source of interference, stopping me from getting on with my new job: a wedding organiser.

A healthy fiancée on wedding countdown. How could I be a blushing bride if I was too busy to be able to concentrate on my bloody wedding? This was a nightmare.

The phone, and my job, have to go.

I began writing my resignation letter.

Further to our conversation, I am writing with regret ... [delete] ... pleasure ... [delete] ... regret ... that I will be handing in my notice from Dants IT Recruitment Solutions, effective from 8th October 2012.

Three weeks before my wedding. It couldn't have been more perfect timing.

I sent the letter. The deed was done. And I definitely wasn't calling Carl to talk about it. I really, really didn't have the energy to talk to him, and neither did he. He would have known I'd find this difficult. He had been so incredibly supportive throughout all of this, but overall I guessed he was probably relieved. Who wanted an employee that didn't answer their phone? I wasn't right for them any more. Things had changed. I had changed.

'How did it go?' Harriet asked me.

'Fine. I know now that I shouldn't feel like anyone or anything has a hold over me. So I had to leave.' I smiled as I spoke, and I felt genuinely pleased with my decision. 'It's the perfect time too!'

'So, what else is there to think about?' Harriet asked. I paused for a long time. I burst into tears.

'Sammy. I feel so guilty about the way I was through my whole reconstruction. I was a living nightmare to be around. He nearly killed himself coming to be by my bedside every day, and all I did was complain to him. *At* him. I wouldn't blame him for not wanting to marry me. He says I'm beautiful and he didn't even mind when I only had one breast.

'Karen. I feel guilty and sorry for Karen. She came to half my chemotherapy sessions with me and I couldn't even be arsed to go and see her in Brighton unless it revolved around my wedding. I didn't ask her to be a bridesmaid and I was so defensive when she was disappointed about it!

'And Dorothy! I abandoned Dorothy. I bought her, brought her up badly and dumped her on Mum. And now she shits in my room because she's so angry!' (For a slight, minuscule second, I thought that actually Dorothy could do with some psychotherapy. I was a second away from saying this to Harriet, but I quickly stopped myself.)

'I feel terrible about it all and I wish I could go back and make it all alright.'

I wiped my tears away, checking the clock behind me for the fourth time. And then I suddenly had an urge to ask Harriet about her. I needed to stop talking about myself. I needed to hear about other people. It was like a defence mechanism. Why would people be interested in hearing about me, about what I was doing, about where I needed to be? Why would they care, for even a second ...

'OH FUCK!' I said, jumping up. Harriet jumped back in shock.

'My laser treatment. I've missed it!'

CHAPTER 38

HAIRLESS CAT

Thankfully the laser hair removal rooms were only two doors down from my psychotherapy room. I was about to have the pubic hair – the hair that had started growing out of my reconstructed breast – removed. 'You're just a little bit late ...' the consultant said to me. 'Now calm down. Can you just sign this declaration form?' *Medical history.* I sighed and resigned myself to the fact that it probably wouldn't go ahead. I filled it out, and then she took a long time reading it through. *HURRY UP AND SAY IT. REJECT ME.*

'Okay, so lie back with the glasses on your eyes ...' My medical history had been approved. She knew why I was there, why I needed the treatment. She accepted me as I was! Her name was Michelle. I interviewed her as I lay there. She was from Manchester, had been in the job 15 years, lived in Essex but wanted to live in the Lake District, and was having steak for dinner. And then she spoke to me about some of her previous patients.

'I've seen hundreds of women just like you. No one your age though. I did have one young boy in last week. Patrick. It was horrid.'

She continued to buzz away at the stubborn stems of pubic hair coming out of my chest. 'Patrick's an estate agent. He loved going out. He was 6'8, talented, and gorgeous!' *Sammy's gorgeous*, I thought. *Actually, I wonder if I've met Patrick in my past, with all the men I've been out with.* She went on. 'Patrick went out to one of those Irish Bars, O'Neil's. He hardly had anything to drink, 'cos he had work the next day, but all his friends were plastered. Patrick's friend owned a tattoo studio, and after one too many Guinnesses they all ended up back there.'

The machine seemed to get stuck. It sparked off my chest.

She continued, regardless. 'Where was I? So Patrick woke up, looked in the mirror. They had only tattooed TWAT across his forehead! Can you believe it?'

I could believe it. But though I might have said something before, joined in with her laughter, I just stayed quiet. Suddenly, I felt sad again, and I didn't know why.

I always felt like I was on a seesaw of emotions, and I hated it.

It has to go.

*

I loved Dr Dickinson. She was the epitome of a traditional doctor; local, friendly, kind, with a good bed manner. She was funny, empathetic, and definitely not patronising or negative. I wished I knew what her name was and what her hobbies were, just so I could profile her, so I could begin to see her as more than just my doctor.

One of the things I had started to do was write compliments about services and lovely members of staff whenever I'd had a good experience. I had written so many negative write-ups on people, companies, and experiences before when I was in the worst mood, and I wanted to change this, to reverse it. So I needed to know what Dr Dickinson's name was, so I could give her the biggest compliment I could think of.

As I sat in the waiting room for one of my appointments, I noticed a baby screaming. There was a couple arguing somewhere behind me. And there was an elderly man pacing back and forth. None of it bothered me like it might have done before, when the pacing and the shouting and the screaming would have given me anxiety. I was changing, and for the better.

I suddenly saw a profile sheet of all the staff on the wall, of doctors, nurses, and receptionists. *And their names. Bingo.* 'I'll give you just a little bit of Sertraline. It'll help. There's a general stigma associated with antidepressants,' Dr Dickinson explained. Lovely, lovely Dr Dickinson. So young, fresh, and warm. I loved her.

'Oh no, Laura. I'm not depressed!' *Fuck! I've just called her Laura.* Shit. It was only two and a half minutes into the appointment and I'd completely ruined it. *She's going to think I'm even more psychotic than I already feel.*

'Annabel. You have anxiety, admittedly, all or most of the time,' she replied calmly, completely ignoring my slip-up. 'I would also like to prescribe you some Diazepam. Just as an insurance policy.'

I had been given Diazepam before, when I'd had my initial nervous breakdown. It had sorted my panicking out but left me in a conscious coma. I didn't like it. I didn't cry or laugh, and I had a flat expression all the time. It had numbed my feelings, taking them away from me. But I had to accept that her comments were true.

Anxiety felt like a wave of control that had taken over my mind. Things would trigger it out of nowhere, and they'd never be consistent. Some things would make my anxiety kick in on one day, whereas on other days, they wouldn't affect me at all. But even so, I wasn't comfortable with these extra drugs.

CHAPTER 39

ALL CHANGE

'I've got to move back to London.'

Sammy had been promoted again. He was now a department head within the army, and we would be permanently based in London.

'I am so proud of you!' I said at a celebratory meal where he made his announcement. I hadn't been panicked by his news. Nothing with us was going to change and we were even given a house in Windsor to move into, an army quarter. I was secretly impressed with how I'd handled this one. Just weeks ago, this might have tipped me over the edge. I could feel the therapy helping. I felt stronger inside my mind. When Sammy and I got engaged, we had been put onto an army accommodation waiting list. As a married couple – with at least one of us serving in the army – we were entitled to army housing with subsidised rent. But they waited to give us this until we were literally about to marry. So the timing was tight.

It was two weeks before the wedding, I was two and a half stone lighter and filled with excitement. It was 7am and we were waiting on our brand new, shiny doorstep planning what room we would sleep in, what room Frankel would live in, and, of course, what room our future children would live in. I finally felt like we had made it! We were getting married, we had our own house (kind of) with a fence around it, and a dog to cement our love. I could now be one of those army wives. I could be a wag. Oh my god, they would accept me on their wags only Facebook page! This was so exciting! I could start moaning about leaky taps and lack of parking. I could talk about missing my husband and where the best schools were in the area. This would be my new role in life.

Where we lived was an army community through and through. It wasn't far from the barracks and it was very, very secure. The community, made up of army marriages, existed in the town, between neighbours, and on social media. I had half-dipped my toe back on Facebook just for this reason. I became friends with all my neighbours so that they knew everything – to a point – about me. But I knew absolutely everything about them – their children's first words, all the houses they lived in, the exes they'd left behind, problems with their homes, issues with other people.

And that was when I completely switched off again. I knew that absorbing other people's word-diarrhoea would create anxiety in me and leave my stomach churning with nerves. Just like when I was physically addicted to co-codamol, I wanted this but the after-effects were definitely not good for me. So it stopped right there. Whenever negativity started, I would run away.

Moving into our new home and training a very spoilt puppy was a lot to cram in, especially with only two weeks to go before our wedding. I also had a breast appointment at the local hospital department, but I put that right to the back of my mind. It wasn't worth thinking about. The anxiety wasn't worth it. 'When you move into an army house, do you actually march in?' I had asked Sammy. He laughed first, before he realised I was being serious.

'No, it doesn't mean saluting, marching, or any use of a horse!' he said.

Now, at the entrance to our new home, we put the key in the lock and were shown around by one of the members of the housing staff. I absolutely loved our house. Everything was cream and white, just like our wedding was going to be.

'SAMMY, LOOK, WE HAVE A TOILET INSIDE!' I shrieked when I saw it, something that we'd been sorely missing in the Cow Shed.

After we'd been through the chaos of moving in, I started to settle into my new life. Because I wasn't working, it wasn't uncommon for me to spend most days going back and forth to the garden centre and to Tescos. I'd spy neighbours in the biscuit aisles and choose my moment to bump into them.

'Have you had your kitchen tap repaired yet?' I asked one neighbour.

'No! Not until next Monday!' replied another neighbour whose husband had been away for five months.

'Oh, you must come over!' I said to another, not even bothering to mention our door number, making the correct assumption they would just know it. I loved it. I felt part of the gang, part of the team, and a proper army wag.

Sammy was making the trip back and forth to London every day, getting up at 4.30am and arriving home at 6pm completely exhausted. I would spend all day fixing the house, changing, rearranging, and inviting everyone and their dog around for cups of tea and Diet Coke. It felt nice and calm. I never allowed myself to be invaded by questions that I didn't want to answer by people I didn't want to be around. I didn't talk about you-know-what and I certainly didn't go into real detail about my life. Killing weeds and making babies were popular and safe subjects for me.

I developed my own routine of putting on my apron and busying myself in the kitchen, while Sammy ate his muesli in the kitchen and read the paper. The buzz of an interesting but placid Radio 4 programme often played in the background. Mum had started a new chapter in her life too. She was moving house. She'd had enough of busy, noisy East London and wanted out. She'd had years of maintaining a beautiful terraced, Victorian house that was very high maintenance. She was tired. She now needed change to make her life easier for herself now that she was retired.

'It has to be a new build,' she informed me, as I used my resourcing skills to find a place within her price range that looked safe and happy. It was a bloody hard task, with all the things that Mum needed to have in her house.

But finally, we found one. A four-bedroom new build, with a garden, a 10-minute drive from her existing house in London. Within a matter of months, she had sold her old house.

Mum, Dorothy, and I were standing in her new corridor a few weeks before she made the exchange. As she walked around the house, she took out her list and started questioning the estate agent. After 20 minutes of this, Dorothy and I both felt quite worried. What about the patio? The electricity box? Or lack of electricity box? I don't know what was worse – the dodged answers, the contradicting replies, the obvious lies, or the silences.

Mum's house was sold and she was moving to this place. But she wasn't happy. She didn't feel secure and I hated it.

'I can't, I can't do it! I keep thinking what my dad would say. "Don't do it." That's what he'd say. But my house is sold. What the hell am I going to do?'

I didn't know and Sammy didn't know. Dorothy could be made homeless! But Mum was right, she couldn't go back either. That house was filled with too many bad memories.

I had to make this my mission. Mum had held me by the hand and walked me through everything. I owed her big time and I was not going to let this excuse for an estate agent rip her off. We found another house – Mum's dream home – a couple of weeks later, on a little private road 20 miles from Windsor. It had three bedrooms, a big living room, and a garden. It was perfect.

After weighing up the pros and cons, considering all the reasons why it would work and the minor reasons why it wouldn't, Mum fell in love and bought the house.

She was so happy. She could spend her weekends in London and really enjoy herself with her friends. And during the week, she would have me and Sammy close by.

It also meant that Polly, Tim, Poppy, and Lily could visit all of us in one big hit too, so it worked for everyone.

Mum spent the next few weeks beautifying her perfect house. Sammy spent evenings building, putting up picture frames, and making furniture for her. She was happy at last, and so was I.

*

October 2012. Three whole days before our wedding.

I was back in Windsor and unfortunately it was the morning of my annual breast check-up. 'We really could have done without this,' I said to Sammy, while bubble-wrapping the crystal hearts which would be our wedding favours. Sammy came with me and we went through the usual wait. But it was different this time. The waiting room was calm, but the doctors were running behind. And yet, I didn't find it stressful.

The receptionists smiled at the nervously waiting patients and their plus ones in the corridors. An elderly angel called out my name and we walked down the corridor. I was not fearful like I had been before. I felt happy because I knew that I was fine. I hadn't even told anyone about my appointment. I was convinced that nothing could go wrong. Three minutes later, it did.

'It's definitely fat necrosis,' I said, slowly and calmly.

The consultant looked at me, and then at the nurse, as he pointed at my new "suspicious lump". I looked at him. Sammy looked at him.

I looked at the nurse. The consultant said something to the nurse in a muffled whisper, his tone one of concern. He started muttering, spinning his pen around in his hand.

'IT'S DEFINETLY FAT NECROSIS.' I was getting louder and louder and my eyes were filling with tears. 'We've been here before. Before my mental breakdown, we had it scanned. It's fat necrosis.' Maybe if I said it enough times, it would become true.

'If you just go down to the radiography room and hop on the bed, we will do a teeny, tiny scan. Just to make sure,' the nurse said to me. Lying on the bed while I was being scanned, I could feel my stomach fluttering with nerves. They scanned me over and over again like a bar code. They scanned and stared, scanned and stared, scanned and stared. My heart fell again and I could feel myself being pulled back into that tunnel of doom, back into depression and self-hatred. Sertraline and therapy were good, but nothing was ever going to stop the constant fear of you-know-what coming back to haunt me.

'So, we inspected the area ...'

Yes, tell me, I thought.

'And as we thought ...' *TELL ME!*

'It's fat necrosis.' *Thank god.*

This place needs to go.

CHAPTER 40

I'm Getting Married in the Morning!

I spent the next three days beautifying myself.

As I waited to have my chin hair waxed off, I filled in the declaration form. Medical history? N/A, I deliberately wrote. *Fuck it,* I thought. *If I can get through chemo, I can get through a facial wax.*

Waxing, teeth whitening, laser hair removal, and having my eyebrows tattooed – I planned all of these. They were small goals, but I wanted them to happen. I was a normal human being with no health problems now, and my image was my prerogative and my right! The night before my wedding came and my car was filled to the brim with dresses, decorations, and outfits for the family.

'Dorothy would have loved to have been a bridesmaid,' Mum said, bursting into laughter, as we dropped the moody looking dog off at the house she'd be staying at for the next three nights. This lucky person had the privilege of tending to her every whim.

We were so excited. We checked into our beautiful hotel rooms, and slowly people started to arrive – my sister, brother-in-law and their girls, Sammy's entire family, and the best man.

I didn't feel anxious or afraid. I felt excited and completely up for it. We stayed up until midnight hanging the dress, checking the to-do lists over and over again, and setting up the place cards. There was a slight mishap in that one of my nieces had been left off the seating plan.

'IT'S EASILY FIXED!' Angelina hurried behind us, moving chairs, ribbons, and vases to get to us and solve the problem.

I fell asleep and woke up feeling like I'd had a fizzy double shot of brandy, like Sammy had had the night before.

> Sharon Osbourne, Dad

The hotel where we were getting married ('Victorian with a modern twist,' Angelina had robotically described it) was just beautiful. And we had the whole of the top house, which was the best bit. Everyone else had the guest rooms. The bridal suite was utterly stunning, like a studio flat in London, but with six stars. Mum, Polly, and Gudrun sat in the living area of the bridal suite, watching me.

I was the princess and this was my tower, I decided. We peered out of the window to see Sammy arrive with his brother. He looked incredibly handsome in his country Barbour coat, smart jeans, and shoes so polished that I could see my face in them. He looked up and I ducked down. 'FOR FUCK'S SAKE, HE'S SEEN ME!' I screamed.

'Annie, language! Not on your wedding day,' Mum said, clearly embarrassed at my performance in front of the make-up artist.

Soon Polly, Gudrun, my nieces, and Mum were all ready and smiling. Polly calmly suggested that I put my wedding dress on, as it was nearing 2pm.

As I stood having my dress laced up at the back while eating a family-sized bag of Maltesers (nervous energy, making up for a year of dieting), I got a tiny bit nervous. And then it was time. Slowly, we started to walk down the corridors. This time they were nothing like the corridors of a hospital. They were beautiful corridors of a hotel fit for us to be married in.

I walked down the stairs to be greeted by the photographer and my uncle, who was giving me away in the place of my dear grandpa. I started getting very emotional. Panicking that my eyelashes would fall off, I managed to hold back the tears and speak with the registrar.

The conversation swiftly came to an end and the doors to the wedding ceremony opened. My bay trees were on either side of the aisles. They were covered with pretty white fairy lights and had big white bows on either side. Matt, my old friend, stood smiling with his finger on the CD player. The music started playing.

And my moment began. There was white everywhere. Everything felt like slow motion. 'Anywhere Is' by Enya was playing. I could practically see white petals and flowers falling from the sky.

The girls and the bridesmaids walked in. There was a deliberate pause before my big entrance. This moment had been rehearsed more times than the queen's speech, and it was my time, my moment. I walked in, holding on to my uncle Chris's arm. He was so nervous, but that didn't faze me.

I wasn't anxious. There were no phones ringing, no papers being signed, no bad news being thrown at me. Everything I'd ever dreamt of had finally happened. All the guests smiled with genuine happiness as the music continued to play. Everyone was there. No seat had been left empty. I walked slowly up the aisle, followed by my bridesmaids who were dressed in white. The lighting was perfect. And then I looked up to see my soldier in his uniform.

Sammy was in tears.

My future mother-in-law looked at me and started crying gently. She whispered, 'Annie, you look beautiful,' as I walked past. Mum was beaming. I could see my dear granny, standing right at the front, beaming over her glasses, looking so smart and so proud. I felt so tall and so proud of everything. I got to the front of the aisle and it all went quiet. It felt like I was in heaven. The room was decorated in diamante, and it felt like we were among the clouds.

Everyone in that room was an angel. They'd all known about the badness in my life. And now they were witnessing the best thing that could ever have happened to me. Karen got up and did a reading. She was nervous, and I could tell that she had been drinking to calm herself. I didn't blame her. Sammy's sister was next, reciting the poem I had written for Sammy. Everyone applauded at the end of the ceremony. I had never felt so happy. I was high on the fumes of perfection.

CHAPTER 41

MARRIED!

And with that, I had my *X-Factor* moment. I had the man of my dreams, in uniform. 'Happy Ending' by Mica boomed out of the stereo. Angelina sat in the corner, wincing. Sammy and I walked down the aisle hand-in-hand. I walked just a few seconds ahead of him, so everyone knew who to pay attention to.

'Please will you welcome, Mr and Mrs ...' Angelina announced. She struggled to pronounce our surname. 'BELACA ... BELACO ...'

'BELASCO!' the entire congregation shouted at poor, timid Angelina. She had got everything so right so far and she had just ballsed up our name. I felt embarrassed for her, but one small mistake was fine. I could handle that.

We walked in as the string quartet fired up their violins. Glasses chinked together and polite conversation filled the room. 'So, it wouldn't be a party if I didn't have something to say,' I said, as everyone laughed with me. I had to be a voice, and this wedding was about us. I spoke and thanked my husband for rescuing me, my friend Theresa for creating the invitations with me when Sammy got too pissed to come home, and Marie for being as close to family as a friend could be. There was no mention of anything else, especially you-know-what. It didn't need to be spoken about.

The speeches ended, the chocolates were served with coffee, and it was time to get drunk.

'Woo!' Karen shouted, catching the bouquet as I threw it into the air.

We had rehearsed this in a café in London one morning. She had to catch it – I owed it to her. And my best friend needed something back from me after all the things she had done for me. As much as it might have seemed that way beforehand, what followed that night wasn't at all a scene out of Disney. I very much doubt Sleeping Beauty would have fallen off her bar stool at the after party at her own wedding, or downed two Nurofen with a whisky and then been told to go to bed. She probably didn't lose her veil either, fall asleep in her wedding dress, or lose one of her borrowed items which happened to be her mother's very precious pearl earrings. 'I'm just so sorry!' I said to Mum.

'It's okay,' Mum said that following morning.

Sammy and I went back to our home and spent the next week absorbing the fantastic and magical moments of our wedding. We were so happy.

CHAPTER 42

PLANTING THE SEED

Sex. We had to have a lot of sex. All of the time. Especially on my fertile days. Sammy looked at me with concern. He was worried that the inner control freak – the one that had made wedding planning a nightmare – was coming back again.

'It's not, Sammy. I just want this to happen, and we know that I've had my eggs taken out.'

'Hmm.' 'You know, fertile eggs!'

He got it. He was just increasingly concerned about me. We didn't tell anyone we were planning a baby. I had been told over and over that the chemotherapy could knacker my ovaries and womb. I didn't go for testing; I didn't know what state they were in. But I was definitely having regular periods.

'Which is really good,' Dr Dickinson said to me at one of my monthly appointments. I was back in front of my poor doctor, one of my many loves of my life. She was like a friend, but I could never tell her that. An eight-minute appointment with her was enough to make me feel great and youthful again. It was a crazy crush. And I still wanted to know more about her.

'Fine,' I replied pessimistically.

'We may need to see though, if you are ovulating,' Dr Dickinson had said. If. I nodded in acceptance. I wasn't in denial about anything. I had always known that this was a possibility. It was the subject that I'd refused to talk about five years ago – or even acknowledge – but now there was nothing on our minds more important than having a baby.

We talked about it every evening. We went out for dinner a lot and cooed over the babies we saw. We planned what the baby would look like and what his or her first words would be. It would be "Mama", of course. I had already decided. This was a new focus for me, a new full-time job. I didn't want to go out on a Friday night, panic-buying dresses. I wanted to walk around John Lewis choosing prams and understanding the "terrible twos" that everyone spoke about.

However, we needed to get through conception first. And I was fearful that there was a huge possibility this just wouldn't happen.

'I'm so worried we won't be able to conceive. It's been a month now and nothing. I'm due my period in a few days,' I had complained to Dr Dickinson.

'You can't expect us to refer you for testing when you've only been trying for three weeks. What you need to do is have constant and furious sex!' Dr Dickinson informed me.

Furious sex. I repeated that to myself over and over in my mind when leaving the surgery. I took her on her word. I always took her word, because she was always right.

But I couldn't help but ponder over the ovulation dilemma. I didn't want to go through yet more tests, more injections, and more anxiety. So, I bought myself a conception monitor.

'ONE HUNDRED POUNDS?' Sammy roared when I showed him. We had a huge row.

My period had arrived. 'I'm trooping the colour all over our Cath Kidston bedsheets!'

'ANNIE! I don't need or want to know this!' By this point, it was Easter. I was stuffing myself full of Cadbury's Creme Eggs and I had convinced myself that I was infertile. But then I changed my mind back again. This machine was going to get me pregnant. I decided that we had to follow Dr Dickinson's advice and have furious sex on my fertile days. I became militant about it. There was scheduling, routine, precision, and, most importantly, commitment from both of us.

'WHAT DO YOU MEAN YOU'RE AWAY WITH WORK TOMORROW? THAT'S A GREEN DAY!' I screamed at him one day.

I was starting to get back into wedding-planner, absolute-psycho mentality, waking Sammy up at 2am demanding to have furious sex. We would have a girl and she would be called Matilda and look like a mini me. It had to happen.

*

January 2013. A new year.

I had continued my psychotherapy and was keen to meet with Harriet again. And to show her all my wedding photos.

'And that's my friend Craig and his sister Faith. No, sorry, that's Beth, Sammy's pretty cousin. Did I tell you about Sammy's dad dancing to Chris Brown?'

She spent a long time looking at the photos, but didn't make any comments other than 'You looked beautiful'.

I had decided, a year and a half on after I'd started psychotherapy with Harriet Hope, I was going to stop. I couldn't do these appointments any more. We discussed it and decided that it was the right time anyway, that I had come to a point where I could live by myself again.

I had always looked forward to my appointments with her. She was like another mother, sister, and friend. I had found love in an odd way with her. I was so worried about ending it all, but I knew that

I had to. It was necessary. 'I understand,' she replied, and that was all she needed to say. We said goodbye and I quickly snapped back into reality, steeling myself for the M25 rush-hour traffic I was about to face.

Little did I know, one door had closed that day and another had opened. I was pregnant.

CHAPTER 43

SICKNESS

'So that "waste" of £100 was well worth it then?' I said to Sammy as we waited for our scan. We had to wait and wait and wait, just like before. But this time, everything was far more positive. Sammy never spoke in waiting rooms and I always did the talking. *Why doesn't he have anything to say, ever?* I thought. He always grabbed the nearest magazine and just peered into it, as though he was trying to find the secret to life.

'Oh look, Jordan's pregnant again,' he said loudly. I cringed and sunk down into my seat, looking at the huge flat screen TV that was playing the news.

Comedian and actress Jennifer Saunders, aged 52, has been diagnosed with breast cancer. She is believed to be having surgery next week.

'So, do you think it's a girl or a boy?' I asked Sammy, trying to distract myself from the news.

'A boy,' he said in a mundane, uninterested way.

We went in for the ultrasound. The sonographer scanned and stared, scanned and stared. This was unbearable! It wasn't a mammogram, it wasn't an MRI, it was the well-being of my baby. And Sammy wasn't saying anything. How could I prepare myself for what was to come without his support?

'It looks like a boy,' the sonographer announced with a giant smile. 'Boys always love their mums the best,' he said with a wink. I had a thing about winking. I didn't trust people who winked, but this wink felt good. I felt like he was telling me that I was going to be the perfect mother.

We were ecstatic! I shouted the news down the phone, in the hospital car park, to everyone we knew.

We were totally in love with our creation already. And I was also in love with being pregnant. Feeling a baby grow, knowing that there was a life developing inside me, next to my heart – it was an incredible feeling. The body that was once half-dead was now creating life. I knew that I had a responsibility for this child, so I ate healthily and tried to sleep the recommended hours, which was hard. But I rested and had the luxury of not working, which really helped. I was lucky.

I developed a condition called hyperemesis, which meant that it wasn't uncommon for me to be admitted to hospital weekly for dehydration and exhaustion. But that was all part of the deal for me. Hyperemesis was a pregnancy-provoked, constant sickness type of thing. Being sick up to 15 times a day became normal.

I didn't dread it, although at times it did remind me of being under the spell of chemotherapy. But this was different. It was Mother Nature's present from our baby. And nothing would spoil it. I was, however, convinced that there was a link to my past treatment. Chemotherapy must have destroyed something inside me, I told myself, and I needed to be extra careful.

*

'I think Basil Belasco is a brilliant and also unique name,' I argued, feeling exceptionally nauseous and struggling with a sore back, on the way down to see Sammy's parents. I was eight months pregnant and we couldn't agree on a name. This was such a fun row to have. Everyone was involved – our parents, our friends, and their friends. It was a boy, we knew that much. Now what was he going to be called?

Noah, Jordan, and Basil were all names I liked. Whereas Sammy preferred names such as Liam, Kevin, and Phil. Ugh no, not Unwanted Phil again! *Horrendous!* Mum had said in a supportive message.

As the weeks went on, I did actually start to feel quite ill. Sometimes I felt so bad it hurt even to move my eyes. But I loved every second of it. I was not dying. No, I was doing the exact opposite. I was creating life.

Of course, paranoia set in, which I was told was natural. Apparently I had the same, normal concerns everyone had, but they didn't feel that way to me. What if he was born with a disease, I wondered. We would cope if he did. And what if he was born without limbs? We would cope. What if he died during birth? We … we wouldn't cope with that.

'It's not, repeat, not going to happen. Look at the bloody size of you. Whoever said the term "elephant in the room" was definitely referring to you!' Sammy joked at me, not looking up from his *Horse and Hounds* magazine.

Antenatal classes were interesting. The first one was informative. The second and third, appealing. The eighth was tiresome, the ninth definitely hard work. Sammy couldn't make the tenth, and by the eleventh session we had both given up. The classes were hard work. But they were fascinating, and the couples were all interesting too. Some of them were older and some were younger. I had a duty to my unborn child to make friends for life, I felt. I wanted him to make friends in the womb, to be accepted, not rejected by a sometimes hard and isolating society. But £450 was a lot of money and the 14-week course was becoming unbearable, for both of us. And I knew that the breastfeeding subject was quickly going to rear its head.

I spoke to our leader, Jane.

I explained about my circumstances, that I only had one nipple.

Will I, or won't I, be able to breastfeed?

Jane gave me the sideways look, something I definitely had not missed. And she gave me the "I have no idea what to say" panicked look too. I just knew I wasn't going to get an answer from her.

The breastfeeding session loomed and we had the usual chit-chat among ourselves as a group.

'Not long now!'

'Sore back! Sore boobs!' (You have no idea, I felt like saying, but I stopped myself.)

'We don't know what we're having.'

And then it began.

'So, what I want you to do is practise squeezing your breasts, one by one. Your partner can help you. Left to right, left to right,' Jane instructed.

Sammy and I looked around the room as couples awkwardly pretended to comply. Two breasts or not, this was just not acceptable teaching. Who was this nightmare of a woman? I ran into the toilets, crying loudly. Later, I was comforted by one of the other girls in the group. We spent the remainder of this ghastly class on the toilet-room floor, slagging off the teacher and the appallingly old-fashioned approach. *We have to go.* We didn't go back after that. It was a negative and horrible situation. And I couldn't believe how little had been prepared for me and Sammy. As much as I felt like complaining, I didn't need to write any letter to make it official. Our absence spoke louder than words.

My mind was empowered. I would not be ostracised because I used to have a nasty disease that tried to ruin my life. God help any other woman who walked into Jane's class without proper breasts.

'Very wise, good decision,' Mum agreed.

CHAPTER 44

GRANDPA AGAIN

Two huge blue eyes stared up at me. He was an angel. A beautiful, handsome baby boy.

'I really need to see Mum,' I told one of the midwives around me.

The doors opened and Mum, Sammy, and his parents walked in. Mum had tears in her eyes already.

'Congratulations, Annie,' she said as she hugged me. It was such a special moment that I had imagined, fantasised, and dreamt about for so long, it was hard to believe it was actually here.

Sammy's mum held the baby in her arms. I just looked around at everyone, knowing that everyone there wanted the best for us. Mum hugged and kissed me, and I couldn't help but feel like the happiest person ever. *I've become a mum!*

Our beautiful little boy was sleeping soundly in his knitted blanket. This was heaven, but we were still alive. ...

I'd walked away from late-night drinking and said hello to furiously sewing homemade Christmas stockings and ballsing up fairy cakes for birthday parties. Being a stay-at-home mum involves a lot of faffing about on other people's terms, I realised. The coffee mornings weren't too bad. In fact, for someone like me, who's obsessed with analysing people and things in life, I quite liked playing this game. I enjoyed the meet-ups, wondering where we'd go. I even liked the worrying, the over-reactions, the endless analysis of a sleeping baby's behaviour, the constant baby competition with other mums.

I took on this new job of Mum with seriousness and professionalism. Before he'd even left the womb, Joseph had been booked into every baby group in Berkshire. I had bought every book possible and continued relationships that I had created at antenatal classes, meeting them for coffee and cake. We talked about babies, poo, and milk, about sleep and black-out blinds, purée and buggies.

I felt like Kate Middleton. Joseph was like Prince George, and Frankel, our dog, the royal corgi. My home was like their castle, and Sammy was my Prince William. This was definitely the life. My baby friends and I spent a lot of time in each other's houses. Ultimately, we wanted to fill our time. We would only really talk about our babies, each other's babies, and others' babies. Who was getting it wrong and who was getting it right? It was all so fascinating to me.

Because Sammy worked so hard, and we were lucky enough to live on an army estate where the rent was subsidised, I didn't have to work. And I would spend all my days looking after our beautiful son. I wasn't going to give him up for the sake of my career. I wasn't going to wake him up and take him to an overfilled and overpriced nursery while I worked. If someone was going to look after him, I needed to be the one to do it, not some woman he didn't know. I wanted him to have a strict routine. I wanted to protect him from negativity, from people, from things. I wanted him to be with family and friends as much as possible, to feel safe. I always wanted Joseph to feel secure, so that – god forbid – if he ever had bad news, he knew he would be looked after and supported. Just like I had been.

CHAPTER 45

BREAST IS NOT BEST

It was 2014, and we were five years on from my original diagnosis. My worries about myself were gone, taken over by worries of my baby.

'You will spend the rest of your life worrying about your children,' Sammy's dad had told me. And I knew it was completely true. I had breastfed for four days, which turned out to be just utter hell. I couldn't do it. I tried and tried. He latched on, sucking anything he could get hold of. But I knew I had to stop when my nipple started bleeding. It was a pitiful, ugly sight. My body felt and looked hideous, and Joseph was bloody starving.

Once I had permission from the midwife to stop, I bloody well did. Joseph went straight on to formula and I never looked back.

But that didn't stop any of our worries about him.

'He hasn't done a poo in three days!' Sammy panicked over the phone to a poor nurse.

'Do not, repeat, do *not*, give him any more food. He's got terrible wind,' she advised, shouting to compete with the screams of our baby who was clearly in pain.

It was 4am on a Saturday morning, and we were both hovering over our baby. We were completely naked, a result of spending an evening being covered in poo, wee, and a lot of milk. But it didn't matter. Joseph came first, always. ...

I still had unfinished business, though, with my mental and physical health. I was back on the Sertraline and it was coming up to my five years' sentencing review. It was a general election the following year and I felt like Miliband on his campaign, desperate for the right answers. Desperate to win this battle, this war.

We were back in the breast unit, waiting for our appointment. Sammy held my hand. I was smiling nervously at patients all around me. I thought back to the time of my diagnosis, swanning into my appointment, hungover and arrogant as anything. I remembered being on my own, hoping for a dismissal and instead receiving a life sentence. I remembered ringing Mum, seeing her face, hearing the news, repeated over and over again. I thought of the wigs, the chemo, the scans, the breast surgery. I remembered the upset, the pain, the trauma, the mental illness, the devastation, the fear of dying. I thought about how I'd wanted to die and wanted to be alive. I'd hated my life, loved my life, wished for a life. There'd been appointment after appointment. Good news and bad. That's what had started it all. And I genuinely felt pain for every single person walking through that door, for whatever reason. I couldn't stop myself from looking at them, examining them for rings on fingers, and guessing their ages. I studied their facial expressions. I even found myself staring at their chests, looking for something.

'Annie Belasco?'

That was me. The new me, five years on from when this horror had started.

I walked into the room, holding my husband's hand. I was greeted by a consultant and her assistant who was holding a bundle of notes. Sunshine streamed in through the windows.

Annabel Belasco

Date of Birth 20/12/1983

July 2014

I saw Annie Belasco along with her husband today, and am delighted to say that she has given birth recently to a healthy little boy, weighing 9 pounds and 2 and a half ounces. Annie Belasco was diagnosed in 2009 with breast cancer. A tumour 45mms, grade 3, stage 3. She followed intensive treatment and has shown no signs of any reoccurrence. Annie Belasco was very tearful today and we discussed some of her concerns that have been causing her a lot of psychological disruption since 2009. I am pleased to say that we are approaching her five-year period and at this point, I would like to advise that we will now be discharging her from our unit.

Annie Belasco was concerned and questioned the reoccurrence of her breast cancer. I would point out that because of the type of cancer she had, it is unlikely to return and the chances are very slim.

I have discussed with Annie Belasco that she will have annual mammograms, until the age of 50 which is the national screening age. She will then go on to have regular mammograms at a breast screening unit.

*

I'm not scared any more.

I can say it. I can hear it, and I can read it. Cancer.

I now know, six years on, what type and size tumour I had. I now know how serious it was, what it did to my body, and what we stopped it from doing, with medicines, advice, the incredible support of the NHS, and, most importantly, my family and friends. I now know how dangerous and incredibly aggressive it was. I know how lucky I am to be alive. Having the physical illness nearly killed me. But the mental illness was worse. A lot worse. Doctors told me I would get better after my operations, but my mind was scarred permanently. I just had to deal with it in the way I knew best.

I'm not 25 years old any more. I'm a grown woman at 34. It takes me two days to recover from a hangover and my car insurance has gone down. I don't need three pairs of eyelashes to go out (just two). I can live like a healthy 34-year-old married woman, with a beautiful child and wonderful family and friends.

And you know what? I'm not scared of talking about breast cancer or any cancer any more. I can even say the word now. I respect and admire every person, man, woman, teenager, or child that has been or is going through it. Cancer is not a generic disease. It's individual, and there is no blanket advice to be given to anyone.

The same is true for mental health. I will always have an anxiety disorder, and be prone to depression and worryingly low moods. But at this moment in time, it's under control.

I don't avoid charities that fundraise for breast cancer now. Instead, I join them. I volunteer for charities such as Breast Cancer Now, who are doing everything they can to fund research into eradicating this disease. With charities like this, there is hope for a cure for breast cancer.

I am also part of the patient participant group at my local GP surgery, and I am also part of a group that talks about depression and anxiety twice a month. I write a lot, and I have found that it works for me. I'm writing this book to empower people, to show that love will always go on through the bad times. And you can get better – if not with your body, then with your mind.

My advice to anyone dealing with this horrible illness would be: do what you want. Don't answer your phone if you don't want to. Don't speak to the people you don't want to; don't talk about the things you don't want to. Eat what you want. Live your life the way you want.

But never use sunbeds. Fake tan is far better, and will probably not try to kill you.

I have found love and remission. Me, Sammy, Joseph, and Frankel are riding off into the sunset and never looking back. Oh, and Benidorm is booked again. Just one last time. We had to go.

Annie Belasco,
Dad

ACKNOWLEDGEMENTS

Mum, thank you for holding my hand through the good, the bad, and the catastrophic. You've always been there to pick me up. You are a truly wonderful mother and I am so lucky to have you.

Polly, thank you for encouraging me to keep going, for hiding your own successes to make me feel better. You are a kind, loving, and wonderful sister.

Karen, my beautiful best friend, I dread to think what I would have done without you. You sat with me through nightclubs, chemotherapy, and the horrendous me as a bride.

Samantha Brick, I wouldn't be here without you and I feel honoured to even know you. You've taught me so much, through the endless emails, mentoring, and never-ending faith. You believed in me from the second we met and taught me to never give up. You are my role model and I hope to always be your friend.

Kasim Mohammed, my super-talented editor, and the rest of the team at Trigger. I wouldn't be here without you, my Midlands family. Thank you for taking a chance on me.

Fiona Cotter-Craig, thank you so much for your kindness and for introducing me to Samantha.

Glenda, you taught me to write and now you've just read my book! You're part of my family, and we are all so lucky to have you in our lives.

Matt and Nicola, the most loyal, generous, and kindest friends I could have.

Theresa, my dear friend. Thank you for keeping my IT and sanity in order. I will never forget how you shaved my head.

Mr P, thank you for keeping me alive.

And finally, but most importantly, my Sammy. This is for you. You keep me going. I will never stop loving you.

the *Shaw* mind
FOUNDATION

Creating hope for children,
adults and families

Sign up to our charity, The Shaw Mind Foundation
www.shawmindfoundation.org
and keep in touch with us; we would love to hear from you.

*We aim to bring to an end the suffering and despair caused
by mental health issues. Our goal is to make help and support
available for every single person in society, from all walks of life.
We will never stop offering hope. These are our promises.*

TRIGGER™

The voice of mental health

www.triggerpublishing.com

Trigger is a publishing house devoted to opening conversations about mental health. We tell the stories of people who have suffered from mental illnesses and recovered, so that others may learn from them.

Adam Shaw is a worldwide mental health advocate and philanthropist. Now in recovery from mental health issues, he is committed to helping others suffering from debilitating mental health issues through the global charity he co-founded, The Shaw Mind Foundation. www.shawmindfoundation.org

Lauren Callaghan (CPsychol, PGDipClinPsych, PgCert, MA (hons), LLB (hons), BA), born and educated in New Zealand, is an innovative industry-leading psychologist based in London, United Kingdom. Lauren has worked with children and young people, and their families, in a number of clinical settings providing evidence based treatments for a range of illnesses, including anxiety and obsessional problems. She was a psychologist at the specialist national treatment centres for severe obsessional problems in the UK and is renowned as an expert in the field of mental health, recognised for diagnosing and successfully treating OCD and anxiety related illnesses in particular. In addition to appearing as a treating clinician in the critically acclaimed and BAFTA award-winning documentary *Bedlam*, Lauren is a frequent guest speaker on mental health conditions in the media and at academic conferences. Lauren also acts as a guest lecturer and honorary researcher at the Institute of Psychiatry Kings College, UCL.

Please visit the link below:

www.triggerpublishing.com

Join us and follow us...

@triggerpub

Search for us on Facebook